THE CULTURE
OF THE
UNIVERSITY

THE MAJORITY REPORT OF
THE STUDY COMMISSION ON
UNIVERSITY GOVERNANCE
UNIVERSITY OF CALIFORNIA, BERKELEY

by *Caleb Foote and Henry Mayer*, CO-CHAIRMEN,
and Richard Beahrs, John Meyers,
Jill Morton, Lewis Perl, Beryl J. Roberts,
Martin Roysher, Sheldon S. Wolin,
Reginald E. Zelnik

THE DISSENTING REPORT
by *Albert Fishlow and David Freedman*

THE CULTURE
OF THE
UNIVERSITY

~~~~~~~~~~~~~~~~~~~~~~~~~~~~~~~~~~~~~~

GOVERNANCE
AND
EDUCATION

LD
732.9
.A55

Jossey-Bass Inc., Publishers

615 Montgomery Street · San Francisco · 1968

THE CULTURE OF THE UNIVERSITY
Governance and Education
by Caleb Foote, Henry Mayer, and Associates

Jossey-Bass, Inc., Publishers
615 Montgomery Street
San Francisco, California 94111

Library of Congress Catalog Card Number: 68-54947

Printed in the United States of America
by York Composition Company, Inc.
York, Pennsylvania

FIRST EDITION

681015

THE JOSSEY-BASS SERIES IN HIGHER EDUCATION

General Editors

JOSEPH AXELROD and MERVIN B. FREEDMAN
San Francisco State College

Preface

⪫⪫⪫⪪⪪⪪

Like so much else in American life, study commissions are at once
promising, confining, serviceable, hackneyed, and something of a joke.
Sometimes they are used to explore issues that genuinely need study,
and sometimes their purpose is to postpone taking action on matters
that desperately need acting upon. By the time a study commission
issues its report, the intensity of the crisis that spawned it has usually
subsided. Commission members, having closeted themselves at the
height of the hurricane, now emerge to find the community basking
smugly in warm sunlight with little thought for an umbrella or even
a commission report. A subsequent crisis, although it may confirm the

commission's predictions, is no guarantee that its report will at last be taken up and seriously considered. More likely, a new commission will be appointed, perpetuating a cycle that can be endless.

One may fairly inquire, therefore, why *The Culture of the University* should be republished. Naturally we are pleased that continuing demand makes it advisable to produce the report in a format more attractive and serviceable than its original eye-straining newsprint. It is appropriate, moreover, that most of this demand has come from outside Berkeley, for the Commission's rationale for university governance is developed in a framework of general argument that extends the relevance of the report beyond the boundaries of a particular campus.

The Culture of the University argues that the special character of a university infuses its ordering of affairs and sharing of power with a unique educational purpose. The conduct of university governance is an important determinant of the culture in which education takes place, for the way the university seeks to understand and control itself greatly influences the way its members seek to know themselves. Thus, instead of drawing upon analogies with traditional political structures, corporate models of private government, or the rhetoric of democracy, this report considers alternative modes of governance primarily in light of their inevitable impact upon the culture that defines the university.

The stress laid upon the convergence of education and governance leads to an equal emphasis upon the necessity for broadening the bases of participation in both enterprises, through such measures as enhanced campus autonomy, considerable decentralization of campus decision-making power, profound commitment to the spirit of open public deliberation, and a greatly expanded role for students in the entire range of university affairs.

The Culture of the University takes on particular importance because of the burgeoning popularity, both on and beyond the campus, of "law and order" as a political issue. At a time when this slogan threatens to lead us to a narrow equation of governance with the means of repression, this report reminds us that governance can be liberating and creative. In the Commission's view, a system of university governance is not preeminently an arrangement for securing order, but is rather both the necessary occasion and the instrument for a fundamental intellectual reordering of academic values.

This approach, most explicit in the first part of the book, also pervades the second half, in which the general principles of analysis and reconstruction are given concrete application. Although some proposals apply specifically to the Berkeley campus, *The Culture of the University* retains its detailed discussion of all of the Commission's recommendations for two reasons: (1) the specific application of a principle clarifies and extends its meaning; and (2) applying general prescriptions to the highly complex problems of a University of California campus provides a case study that is suggestive for those in other—and hopefully less grave—situations.

The Commission began its meetings in mid-February 1967, and the drafting of the report did not begin in earnest until mid-summer. During the summer two members of the Commission, Albert Fishlow and David Freedman, left Berkeley to go abroad on leave for a year. Their disagreement with many of the emerging views of the rest of the Commission was fully expressed in a memorandum they distributed before leaving the campus. The ten remaining members of the Commission continued to draft, debate, and redraft the report until it was completed early in January, 1968. The two absent members elected to submit an expanded version of their earlier memorandum as the dissenting statement published here.

Essential expenses for the Commission's work were provided by the Senate of the Associated Students, University of California, Berkeley; the Berkeley Division of the Academic Senate; and the Office of the Chancellor. The cooperation of *The Daily Californian* made possible the rapid printing and distribution of the original published version to all faculty and students. The Commission was also immeasurably aided in its work by generous gifts of time and energy from a great number of volunteers—students, faculty members, researchers, and staff—who graciously performed a variety of research, editorial, administrative, and secretarial tasks with skill and enthusiasm.

We express our profound appreciation to the Center for the Study of Law and Society and its staff for providing so hospitable a home for the Commission, countless services, and a spirit of fellowship far more generous than that usually accorded guests who stay so much longer than expected.

No encomium can fully express the extent of our admiration and appreciation for Marge Frantz, editor and administrative assistant to the Commission, whose remarkable talents and boundless faith contributed so much to the fruition of this report.

CALEB FOOTE

HENRY MAYER

Co-chairmen, The Study Commission on University Governance

September 1968

Contents

░░░░░░

xiii

Contributors

The University of California, Berkeley, Academic Senate Committee on Committees appointed the faculty members to the Study Commission. The Senate of the Associated Students of the University of California (ASUC) appointed the graduate and undergraduate student members to the commission.

RICHARD BEAHRS is an undergraduate student

ALBERT FISHLOW is professor of economics

CALEB FOOTE, co-chairman of the commission, is professor of law and criminology

DAVID FREEDMAN is professor of statistics

HENRY MAYER, co-chairman of the commission, is a Ph.D. candidate in history

JOHN MEYERS is an undergraduate student

JILL MORTON is an undergraduate student

LEWIS PERL is a Ph.D. candidate in economics

BERYL J. ROBERTS is professor of public health

MARTIN ROYSHER is an undergraduate student

SHELDON S. WOLIN is professor of political science

REGINALD E. ZELNIK is assistant professor of history

THE CULTURE
OF THE
UNIVERSITY

Introduction

In January 1967, the student-faculty Study Commission on University Governance was established by the votes of the Berkeley Division of the Academic Senate and the Senate of the Associated Students of the University of California. The mandate was unique in the history of this campus. For the first time, a commission composed equally of students and faculty was delegated the task of preparing recommendations on matters of the utmost importance.

The assignment to the Commission was unusually broad in scope.[1] The Senates charged the Commission with defining the "areas"

---

[1] See Appendix A for the text of the resolution and the methods of appointment of the Commission's membership.

in which policy-making and administration "should be delegated wholly to students or wholly to faculty or administrative officers"; and the "areas" in which either students or "faculty members and administrative officers" should have "primary responsibility" with "appropriate participation" by the other segments. The Commission was specifically invited to consider possible measures for increasing the participation of students "in the formulation of educational policies." It was further instructed to examine ways of strengthening student government; of creating institutions that would facilitate "appropriate student participation in the consideration of campus-wide questions"; of reevaluating the fairness of disciplinary procedures and judicial review; and of reviewing policies concerning the campus activities of nonstudents. Recognizing that this list fell somewhat short of the twelve labors assigned Hercules, the drafters of the Senate resolution reassured the Commission that it need not consider itself limited to the subjects specified. The Commission was then instructed to report to the two senates early in the fall of 1967—a period somewhat shorter than Hercules' twelve years.

A few brief remarks are appropriate to explain the nature of the report, to establish the spirit in which we hope that it will be read, and to comment on the mood and state of the campus to which it is addressed.

In the charge to the Commission, as well as in the legislative history behind it, a certain temper was suggested by the recurrence of words such as "study," "exploration," and "definition." The connotations of tentativeness this language expresses proved to be highly appropriate because our area of investigation is largely unmapped terrain. Admittedly, there are numerous studies on the administration of universities and colleges, the problems of education, the history of higher education in America, and, more recently, a spate of articles and books on the contemporary student. Nevertheless, we discovered repeatedly that many familiar problems had changed so rapidly that the analyses and solutions of a few years ago had only limited utility for the conditions of this campus. Moreover, university governance proved to be interrelated with many other problems, particularly those concerned with education in the customary, narrow sense of that term.

As the title of this report suggests, we are convinced that modes of governance and of education are shaped by a broader campus culture and that, in turn, the campus culture is affected by what occurs in committee room as well as in the classroom. By "campus culture" we mean not only the concrete arrangements and institutions that order the educational and governmental processes of the university, but the intangible values, such as a sense of common fellowship, a commitment to free inquiry and rational discussion, and pride in belonging to an institution that refuses to judge itself and the behavior of its members by any but the most demanding standards. More briefly, by a campus culture we mean that complex of tacit assumptions about what is important that leads the members to ask not what is the letter of the law or the prerogative of status and authority, but what is appropriate to an institution concerned with the cultivation of the mind and spirit.

Concerning the points of convergence between governance and education, the existing literature was mostly silent. We received little guidance, for example, in making sense of one of the fundamental facts of life on the Berkeley campus, namely, that as a result of the experience of the past three years Berkeley students, faculty, and administration have acquired a greater political awareness than probably exists on any other comparable campus. To relate to existing institutions the expectations aroused by such awareness was sufficiently troublesome by itself, but we also had to devise some new arrangements that would be more responsive to student pressures for participation. Add to this the ultimate question of how governance and participation affect and are affected by the basic university purpose of education, and one becomes uncomfortably aware of how dated and incomplete are most discussions concerning the contemporary university. Although the Commission cannot pretend to have dealt with all the issues posed by its charge, much less with all the problems related to the state of the campus as a whole, it has some confidence that it has made a start toward identifying many of the major questions and showing how solutions to them may be fruitfully approached.

Our report is organized to give first a lengthy analysis, in Part I, of what we consider to be the fundamental problems of the university and our understanding of how changes in the structure of governance can help relieve them. This analysis is an essential prerequisite for understanding the remainder of the report. In Part II we then discuss three concepts—the process of open discussion, a decentralized structure of decision-making, and an increased role for students in policy-making—which we propose as the guiding principles of the basic redirection we believe necessary. In Part III, we outline the essential first steps that should be taken toward our goals. A variety of approaches are suggested in the frank recognition that all specific solutions are but beginnings and must be regarded as experiments subject to evaluation. Our fundamental insistence is not that the proposals form the only sound approach, but rather that some attempts along these lines must begin *now* if our problems are ever to be resolved. Our analysis and recommendations are primarily addressed to reforms in the system of governance that would establish the preconditions necessary for the revitalization of the educational program.

The process of reform will be a lengthy one. Although we believe our basic direction will lead ultimately to radically different settings and processes for both education and governance, we must caution that the immediate adoption of the first steps we have called essential will not effect a miraculous transformation of our troubled community. A few institutional changes, no matter how significant, cannot alone accomplish much unless they are accompanied by equally pronounced changes in the atmosphere that now is so inhospitable to mutual trust, to institutional loyalties, and to an affirmative belief in the value of the educational enterprise. We must shed some old habits and acquire some new ones.

A basic transformation will involve large measures of conflict and disappointment. We anticipate that no one on this campus will be equally enthusiastic about all of our proposals or analyses and that some will be enthusiastic about none of them. This report was itself discussed and written in an atmosphere of spirited and often frustrating controversy (which, it should be noted, rarely pitted the students against the faculty). There are still differences of opinion among us. No member of the Commission agrees fully with every proposition contained in the report. Some of us would have made additions to both the diagnosis and the proposals; others would have preferred to leave some things unsaid or, at least, to have had them stated differently. Despite a range of disagreement, we are all pleased to sign the report because we are committed to the fundamental principles it proposes for our redirection and the urgency with which the case is stated.

The Commission is conscious that this report may seem one-sided in neglecting to enumerate the many instances of excellence that occur daily in our classrooms and laboratories or the many episodes of quiet devotion on the part of administrators, faculty members, and students. It would be wrong to infer from the generally critical tone of this report that there is any intention on the part of the Commission to depreciate the many and considerable achievements of this university. We frankly acknowledge, however, that much that is good at Berkeley is achieved despite, and not because of, our present institutional arrangements. More importantly, we hope to deflate complacency by the reminder that this campus has been living for three years under the threat of actual or impending emergencies. The Commission itself was conceived in crisis and born in forebodings. Some of its sponsors warned at the time that "continuing on our present course will be disastrous" and that the campus "may be nearing the last moment" when its fateful course "can be halted and reversed."[2] Very little has happened since January 1967 to lessen the urgency or lift the despair. It is perhaps symbolic of our worsening difficulties that one of the institutions to which this Commission was obligated to report appears to have been transmogrified by an administrative ruling.

In the course of its investigations the Commission often found itself at a loss to explain why many members of the university could deplore recent events and criticize the actions of all parties to the disputes, yet be quite unwilling to believe that these might be rooted in some fundamental deficiencies in university structure. We became progressively persuaded, therefore, that the starting point for our inquiries should not be an inventory of our assets, but some hard questions: How many confrontations are needed before an institution of learning learns to recognize that its genuine achievements have somehow become tied to certain values and arrangements that no longer command automatic respect, but rather appear to breed crises that the arrangements seem helpless to resolve? Why is the campus so ready to view each interlude from crisis as a harbinger of eternal peace when no steps are taken to cope with the fundamental problems that lie beneath each emergency? Why have our institutions become so unresponsive that threat and intimidation appear to be the most effective means of causing us to examine our otherwise unexamined collective life?

These are troubling questions that take on added significance because Berkeley was the first major campus to witness a new age of aspiration and discontent and has thus become a test case of more than local interest. Since 1964 there has been a growing awareness

[2] Open Letter from seven members of the Academic Senate's Policy Committee, January 6, 1967, reprinted in *Daily Californian*, January 6, 1967.

that each response of the campus has been inadequate to the profundity of our problems. These problems include not only highly complicated matters of governance and education, which are formidable enough in their own right, but also an external political environment that has become increasingly suspicious and threatening. The inroads on civil liberties and academic freedom made in the past year are warnings that for the first time in many years we are faced with a consistently unfriendly state administration whose theories of educational financing are a logical accompaniment to its suspicions of this campus. This combination of internal complexities and external dangers provides a measure of the task before us.

We offer this report to the campus community in the hope that we shall all be equal to that task.

PART ONE

DIAGNOSIS

Chapter I

⚞⚞⚞⚞⚞⚞

Education and Society:
The Need for Reconsideration

This Commission is the direct product of the crisis of November 1966, when a student sit-in and strike took place. Confronted with the second major breakdown of its governing process in two years, members of the campus community believed it urgent to reassess the political structure of the university and to devise "modes of governance appropriate to a modern American University." We believe, however, that the rigidity and vulnerability of our university's governing institutions is a condition that cannot be treated in isolation. Rather, it should be seen as a reflection of certain basic weaknesses in prevailing assumptions about the university's direction and the nature of the education it provides. Before an assessment of these institutions can fruitfully be made, it is necessary to appreciate that the fundamental problem of the campus is rooted in education. The campus suffers from more than political ills, and more than political prescriptions are required to cure its malaise.

For the past few decades the definition and treatment of our problems have come largely through administrative and organizational means. For the past few years this community has defined its problems in political terms, or at least protested against their existence by political means. Both approaches are inadequate, the first because it has neglected the human dimension of education, the second because it jeopardizes the innocence and candor necessary to educational settings. Although considerable attention of late has been directed toward educational reform and some valuable changes have been made, the existing inertia defies all but the most resolute of reformers. Inertia and discouragement have combined to produce a situation in which fundamental educational problems are discussed only sporadically, and then in so prosaic a fashion as to make education seem a dreary affair when compared to the melodrama of campus politics. What is worse, the attempts to call attention to severe problems through massive student demonstrations have nourished the delusion that a brief period in which students are not massed in Sproul Plaza or milling in Sproul Hall is a sign of institutional health and success.

The inertia of our institutions and our lack of a rooted tradition of educational innovation have had a paradoxical result: they have led to a brave and unwarranted complacency, as though the campus truly believed its official rhetoric that this is a "great university," the peer of any institution of higher learning in the world. We are skeptical, however, that a count of Nobel prize winners, the high national rating of graduate departments, or the presence of a distinguished faculty provide conclusive measures of a university's greatness. These attributes do not in themselves represent a university's ultimate goals, but rather means toward achieving them. In our view, the most important single goal of a university, and therefore the best measure of its excellence, is the intellectual growth of its students: their initiation into the life of the mind, their commitment to the use of reason in the resolution of problems, their development of both technical competence and intellectual integrity.

When viewed in this manner, neither Berkeley nor any other university is adequately fulfilling its primary mission. It is true that many students and faculty are engaged in exciting and important intellectual endeavors; it is true that here and there on the campus, scattered among certain departments and sometimes outside of departments, true communities of learning do exist. Despite these moments of intellectual excitement and pockets of engagement, however, we find an appallingly high rate of disaffection and disinterest. The activist students who have made their dissatisfactions known in an epidemic of protests from coast to coast are but the most visible manifestations of this malaise. High dropout rates[1] and our assessment of what is *not* happening to many of those who complete their degrees add to our concern.[2] Recently, for example, one of Berkeley's largest departments conducted a series of two-and-one-half-hour interviews with sixty upper division majors selected at random. These conversations revealed that less than 20 per cent of the interviewees could be described as intellectually engaged with their major, while the rest were discouragingly indifferent. The lack of involvement, it should be emphasized, was not confined to average or poor students, but prevailed even among students with grade point averages above 3.0.

[1] While the dropout problem can never be accurately reflected by a single figure, it is worthwhile to note that only about 50 per cent of those who enter Berkeley as freshmen receive baccalaureate degrees from the University. More important than number is the fact that this group includes so many of our most promising students. Less than one-half of the men and less than one-third of the women who left were in academic difficulties at the time they dropped out. Moreover, academic achievement aside, to the extent that the dropouts can be described by personality tests, they seem to have characteristics that would make Berkeley a more exciting place to attend and at which to teach. Robert Suczek and Elizabeth Alfert, *Personality Characteristics of College Dropouts,* Cooperative Research Project No. 5-8232, Office of Education, U.S. Department of Health, Education, and Welfare, 1966 (mimeographed). See also *Education at Berkeley,* Report of the Select Committee on Education, Academic Senate, p. 13.

[2] Professor Martin Trow describes students of this kind: "Still others [at Berkeley] and there are many of these on every large campus, have no great passion for education, little interest in or conception of what higher education might be, and exhibit something like the 'wantlessness of the poor,' a passive and even cheerful acceptance of conditions as they are, almost whatever they are." Martin Trow, "The Large Campus as a Context for Learning" (mimeographed paper), p. 3. And compare comments of Professor Michel Loeve, one of the three newly appointed "Professors of Arts and Sciences" at Berkeley. "What happens to the student when he enters the University world? We build some 80 types of cages and we fit the adolescent into one of them—tightly, so he won't take too much initiative . . . without realizing it, we kill their possible selves. . . ." *Campus Report,* November 22, 1967, p. 2.

We recognize that a university cannot *give* an education to its students, let alone impose it upon them. We believe, however, that it should awaken the complacent and provide a liberating but demanding milieu in which the uncertain and aimless have a fair chance to develop intellectual autonomy. A faculty critic of the Free Speech Movement called attention to this untapped intellectual potential when, noting the "prodigies of work . . . in organization, in research, in writing" that were evoked by FSM, he observed that "many professors have been given quite a start to discover what stores of energy are locked in our students and untouched by the normal routine."[3]

One major source of our troubles is found in the uncertainty and skepticism concerning the proper relationship between the university and society.[4] In the past, a reciprocity existed between them in which society was willing to extend economic support to higher education in exchange for useful knowledge and trained personnel. That relationship was based on the assumption that the existing organization of society not only would allow university graduates to contribute their skills in ways that would be socially useful and personally satisfying, but that the broad goals of society were such as to command general approval. As long as that situation prevailed, it was possible for students to view with equanimity an education aimed at preparation for specified careers. Now, however, they are increasingly critical of the world and of the institutions that shape it. Some of the most thoughtful and serious students have come to repudiate many of the social goals and values they are asked to serve in the university and upon graduation. That repudiation is directed, in part, at the conditions of technological society that seem to threaten human dignity. The new world emerging seems to exact greater conformity, more routinized lives, more formalized relationships among individuals, and a deeper sense of helplessness amid an increasingly abstract world devoid of humane values.

This repudiation could be interpreted as the esthetic posture of traditional collegiate disillusion were it not for the growing belief,

---

[3] Nathan Glazer, "Reply to Philip Selznick," *Commentary,* March, 1965. Reprinted in S. M. Lipset and S. Wolin, *The Berkeley Student Revolt,* Anchor Books, Garden City, New York, 1965, p. 315.

[4] For an analysis of this relationship and its consequences, see Henry D. Aiken, "The American University: Part I," *New York Review of Books,* October 20, 1966, p. 12.

by no means confined to students, that contemporary society is afflicted with grave problems that it cannot solve and can only worsen. Racial conflicts have become so intense that conventional solutions seem superficial; the ugliness and squalor of cities seem beyond repair and fit only for the violence that erupts in their streets; the skies are fouled and the land and forests ravaged; above all, the republic seems hopelessly entangled in a nightmare of a war with ever-widening circles of suffering, destruction, and cynicism. Faced with this crisis, many students express intense dissatisfaction with the university, since it provides much of the knowledge and most of the trained personnel required by the technological and scientific society. The university is, as one economist put it, a vital part of the "knowledge industry" and thus it contributes in important ways to shaping society in forms that evoke neither respect nor affection. It is little wonder, then, that many students are no longer content to spend their college years preparing to "take their places" in such a society. Nor is it surprising that many students regard as irrelevant the miscellany of superficial, uncertain choices and professional training that often passes as the curriculum.

Such discontent with the university is deepened by the degree to which the university's atmosphere reproduces the characteristics of the society. The university is large, impersonal, and bureaucratic. The acquisition of specalized skills has often been substituted for the education of persons instead of supplementing it. Some of the most marvelous expressions of human dignity—the activities of learning, inquiring, and sharing that are brought together in education—are being dehumanized. "Instruction" tends to usurp the place of inquiry; specialized "training" gradually commences at ever earlier stages of education; and the tempo of education is stepped up to meet the pressure of enrollment, the resentment of taxpayers, and the competition with other technological societies for national supremacy in the space age. The result is that instead of the warmth and cordiality that are the natural accompaniments of learning, relationships tend to be remote, fugitive, and vaguely sullen.

The lack of intellectual fellowship within the university, the relentless pressures placed upon it as a vital national resource, the resulting premium attached to the production and application of specialized knowledge, and the growing tendency to reinforce and even mirror the society have all contributed to the crisis in American higher education for which "Berkeley" has become "a convenient shorthand name."[5] This crisis goes far beyond the recent upsurge of political challenges to university ruling authorities and sharply illuminates the university's two crucial failures: its failure to develop a student body that respects the value of the intellect itself, and its failure to order its activities according to a conscious conception of its unique purpose of nurturing that intellect.

The failure to generate respect for intellectual activity may be seen in several ways. Many students move routinely and unthinkingly through the system. Many others, while reacting passionately to the failures of American society, have not linked their emotional reaction to an appreciation of the need for disciplined analysis of these urgent problems and a search for reasoned solutions. The reaction against the narrow, instrumental uses of intellect and of the university has led to a growing tendency to reject all uses of reason, a rejection that leads either to an enervating quietism or to a form of nihilism that admires only the passionate assertion of humanity through direct, physical protest.

The second crucial failure relates to the university's function of providing useful knowledge and expert consultants to assist society in its efforts to satisfy human needs. Somehow this function of "service" has gotten out of hand so that it has come to dominate the direction, form, and tone of the university. These tendencies have encountered very little critical scrutiny from this campus, primarily because the issues have not been clarified and squarely posed. The campus does not possess institutions capable of such critical appraisal, the establishment of general agreement on the nature and value of various kinds of services, and the process for determining the priority to be assigned such services among university activities. These issues deserve the kind of discussion and publicity that can best be provided by institutions that permit wide participation by the campus community as a whole. Because such institutions have been lacking, we have imperceptibly slumped into a posture in which the demands of external interests—strongly reinforced by economic lures, rewards of prestige and status, and other powerful resources which only those with power can marshal and wield—have increasingly dominated the ethos of the university and shaped the direction of its educational activities.

Revision of the university's governing structures and processes

[5] John William Ward, "The Trouble with Higher Education," *The Public Interest,* Summer 1966, p. 76.

cannot in itself revitalize the university's intellectual life. Such goals require great changes in spirit and conviction as well as changes in institutions. We can look to the governing process, however, for the most appropriate means of recognizing genuine conflicts of values and functions, and for establishing a framework of priorities and relationships for discriminating among the growing tasks and demands placed upon the university either by society or by the institution's own sense of intellectual obligation. Changes in governance also provide means for building communities of a size that human beings can manage and in which they can live creatively. Such community settings provide the minimum conditions through which a large university can enlist the greater involvement of its members in its educational venture.

Chapter II

⋩⋩⋩⋞⋞⋞

The Need
for Radical Redirection

The phrase "university governance" conjures up a kaleidoscope of images of Regents, a president, a chancellor, vice-chancellors, special assistants, deans, chairmen, a faculty senate, and a student government; it also suggests a congeries of intricate relationships dotted by crucial points of authority and decision-making. This complexity offers a salutary warning against the common assumption that a system of university governance is a simple instrumentality or tool designed to serve the institution's goal of education. It is more enlightening to think of governance as a complex set of relations, powers, and influences embedded in a broader, more general campus "culture." The context in which governance operates helps to shape the actions and style of the participants; at the same time, the manner in which governance operates, the procedures it follows, and the spirit in which it treats problems and people will, in turn, help to shape that broader context. Campus governance, then, is not simply a method for arriving at decisions about educational policies; it is itself a method of educating those who participate in it or who are affected by it. How well such a system operates is not to be determined solely or even primarily by criteria of efficiency, but must be evaluated by reference to the quality of life appropriate to an educational community.

☙ SHORTCOMINGS OF INTEREST GROUP CONFRONTATION ❧

Our system of campus governance and the broader context surrounding it have been shaped by a form of interest group politics that has set the style and tone of campus politics, determined the mode of decision-making, and defined the possibilities of educational achievement. The identity of these groups and the ways in which they are supposed to interact are suggested by the charge given to this Commission. That charge is worth quoting at length because it reveals how deeply imbued we have all become with the pressure group mentality. The Commission was asked to define

> those areas in which, and the institution through which, the making and administering of policies should be delegated wholly to students or wholly to faculty or administrative officers; those in which students should have primary responsibility, with participation by faculty members and administrative officers; and those in which faculty and administrative officers should have primary responsibility, with appropriate participation by students.

We are thus asked to assume that the campus consists of three components, the "students," "faculty members," and "administrative officers," each having an area of primary concern. Clearly the campus "society" is here viewed as a collection of status-bound interest groups, each having a special preserve and each possessing claims to participation in varying degrees—subject to negotiation—in the activities assigned to the other components. The political problem set by this approach is one of devising institutions and procedures that will enable each group to pursue its particular concerns as efficiently and harmoniously as possible in areas that overlap with those of the other groups. Politics, in this view, consists of finding techniques for promoting particular interests and conciliating conflicting ones.

Although this view may be an accurate description of our present situation, we do not regard it as an adequate, much less ideal, process for creating an educational setting fit for the cultivation of the mind and the strengthening of the human spirit. Most issues of university policy are questions requiring qualitative judgments rooted in values and principles. Such questions cannot readily be broken down into component units over which highly politicized interest groups can bargain and for which some mutually agreeable form of distributive justice can be arranged. Moreover, an issue of university principle should not be decided on the basis of which group has the most bargaining power. To pursue university policy as a task of trading off the interests of competing groups is especially damaging because the interests themselves often remain unexamined and no process exists by which the community as a whole can openly assess the cumulative effect of many isolated exchanges on the value and direction of the institution. Hence, a major weakness of the interest group conception of university policymaking has been that it has imposed narrow and artificial limits on the process of discussion and decision in the university. Moreover, it has obscured the special character of a university by regarding it much as one does any other pluralistic society populated by diverse interest groups and lacking a common commitment to anything more than the bargaining process itself.

Much of the thinking on this campus, like the thinking reflected in our charge, continues to be dominated by past crises and by the fact that those crises were defined by the participants in terms of political interest groups, joined by them on a political plane, and temporarily resolved by political confrontation. One manifestation of this mentality can be seen in the extent to which the public life of this campus since the fall of 1964 has been preoccupied with rules: rules governing freedom of speech and political activity; rules relating to those who are not yet students, to those who once were students, and to those who may never be students. When the campus has not been distracted by disputes over rules, it has been convulsed by the determination to defy them or obsessed by the determination to enforce them. Although the campus has quarreled over the rules governing the time, place, and manner of political activity, it has failed to consider the deeper conflicts over the concept of "law and order" appropriate to a university, nor has it addressed itself to the problem of devising institutional arrangements for recognizing areas of fundamental conflict and agreeing upon means of resolving them without recourse to physical confrontations between students and outside policemen. Severe confrontations over procedural rules for political activity have not yet led to reform of the "rules" pertaining to the conduct of all decision-making.

The severe conflict over political rules has followed a sterile circle in which the separate interest groups of "the" students and "the" administration exchange threats, resort to escalated demands and tactics, and create situations that inevitably drive the two "parties" toward a confrontation. The general result is a dangerous form of politics, which can easily become violently disruptive. The most tragic aspect of this kind of politics is that it is an endless process in which both sides lose; it is a true minus-minus game in which the game itself becomes the focus while the main purpose of the community, namely education, suffers.

Very few look back upon the political crises of the past few years with anything but mixed feelings. There have been some real gains, many of them shamefully overdue. The liberalization of the rules governing political activity on the campus; the increased sensitivity of the campus to due process in disciplinary proceedings; the slowly growing receptivity to educational experimentation; the beginning of a serious interest in restoring the importance of teaching; the appearance of grave doubts about the value of a centralized system of statewide control over education—all of these gains have been due, entirely or in part, to the politics of conflict.

The significance of these gains and the striking contrast between the years before and after 1964 are easily forgotten, largely because a heavy price has been paid for these changes. At times the main educational purpose of the university has been obscured by political controversies; an adverse public reaction has led to political reprisals against higher education in California; and an atmosphere of distrust and suspicion exists on the campus.

It would be comforting to prophesy that a simple operation that eliminated, depending on one's preferences, a small band of student agitators, a clique of bureaucrats, or some members of the faculty would put an end to our troubles and restore harmony to the campus.

We believe this to be a false prophecy and a superficial diagnosis. The sources of our conflicts are very deep. They lie in the heterogeneity of values and concerns of a complex campus; in the numerous functions, over and beyond teaching and scholarly research, that the university has acquired or has had thrust upon it; in the failure of the State of California to give adequate support to education, which has weighted the university in the direction of an impersonal educational environment of large classes and anonymous relationships among and between students and faculty; in the extreme vulnerability of the campus to outside political pressures; and in a concept of education which —tailored as it is to the demands of a society devoted to economic growth, technological advance, and increased international influence and dominion—has ceased to nourish the best aspirations of the contemporary student.

Given these fundamental conditions, there will continue to be conflicts concerning the objectives and values of the university, the distribution of resources among some of its major activities (such as governmental research and assistance to private economic groups), and the proper ways of making decisions in a community dedicated to nurturing the intellectual and moral qualities of its members. If one is to understand the problems of Berkeley, he must begin by recognizing that the dominant form of the university is being challenged politically and educationally. To meet these challenges, major campus decisions in the future will have to be aired and justified more openly and frankly than they have been in the past: decisions, for example, that allocate resources to undergraduate teaching; that establish the architectural environment and assign space to teaching, research, cultural activities, and student housing; that define the scope and nature of student participation and organization; or that determine the shape and content of educational programs.

⊰ TOWARD RATIONAL MEANS OF GOVERNANCE ⊱

The Commission is convinced that a radical redirection of our institutions is required so that these decisions may be reached in different settings, in a different temper, and with different roles and relationships for administrators, faculty, and students from those assumed in the past. If conflicts are to be resolved, as they should be, in accordance with our fundamental educational objectives, it is clear that we must eschew the blunt, noneducational methods of agonistic politics. Certainly, these problems cannot be solved by interest groups defined crudely on the basis of status as an administrator, a faculty member, or a student. Such interest groups are the result of our failure to develop means for promoting and sustaining effective debate among conflicting points of view and our failure to develop institutional settings of human dimensions that would provide a focus for loyalties and discussion cutting across the boundaries of status. In the absence of these institutions and other rational means of governance, what have emerged are lowest-common-denominator interest groups, groups that come to confront one another harshly and fail to recognize the stakes of their own members as well as others in the common university enterprise.

The problem, as we see it, is to find ways of converting our conflicts from destructive interest group warfare for partisan ends to constructive argument for educational ends. What is needed, in essence, are settings for productive argument and processes of reaching decisions that command the confidence and respect of the community. When substantive disagreements occur they should be resolvable without the bitter antagonism and mutual hostility that have marked the past few years. A first major step must be to settle the long-standing controversy over campus rules and the proper concept of campus "law enforcement." We make specific recommendations on this issue in Chapter Ten. But more important, new institutions and practices must be developed to enable all concerned members of the campus community to identify and formulate their views and to encourage the widest public discussion and criticism of such formulations and proposals.

Our most critical need is to create both the spirit and the settings in which genuine issues can be analyzed and problems engaged. One major cause of suspicion at present arises from the lack of focused public discussion preceding important policy decisions. In the past, important decisions, such as the adoption of the quarter system, the institution of the "Academic Plan," new environmental schemes, and changes in the requirements for conducting certain student activities, have been taken without extensive discussion. Sometimes discussion has been encouraged, as in the controversy concerning the quarter system, but with little prospect that the decision would be affected by the results. At other times it has been the practice to consult "representative" committees or to "bring in" particular individuals. The Commission believes that the campus must break with these past practices and develop new ones that will ensure that public discussion takes place well before decisions are made; it must be clear to all parties that such discussions may in fact change the policies being proposed. Further, we believe that considerable effort must be made to bring crucial matters to the attention of the campus and to press for the fullest possible airing of them. Promoting a greater degree of open discussion in a spirit of mutual trust is the first major theme of this report.

Our conclusions are based on the belief that, in its present form, the campus embodies a paradox: it is an institution devoted to inquiry and discussion, yet it is badly organized for discussing its own affairs. Except sporadically during the spectacular crises that have rocked the institution, there has rarely been intensive public discussion centered on matters constituting the fundamental sources of our conflicts. When such matters are raised, the invariable response is a sense of helplessness in the face of the staggering complexity and unwieldiness of the campus, so that even the dedicated reformer is compelled to deal in palliatives. The urge to think of fresh and dramatic possibilities has atrophied.

Developing forums of a size most likely to encourage a high level of creative discussion regarding the central matters of a university is a problem of crucial importance. Forums located among the smaller units of the university offer the most favorable opportunity for well-attended, informed, and productive conversations. At the "local" levels there can be more firsthand experience, more common commitment, a greater probability that, in a setting where many of the participants will know each other, a vital element of trust and respect will exist, and hence a greater possibility for coming to grips with the sources of our conflicts, rather than with their symptoms.

In view of the unexplored promise of decentralized forums, we think it all the more necessary to avoid overemphasizing the change that the reform of central institutions, such as senates, university-wide committees, or campus councils can bring about. The dimensions of these institutions run counter to genuine and direct participation, discussion, and resolution of issues. Because issues dealt with at the center are often of a broad and general nature, they tend to appear as abstract and remote; because most of the participants lack experience at this general level of decision-making, discussion tends to be ill-informed; and because policies intended for the university as a whole are often superficial in their effects, the inevitable discrepancy between input and output leads to disappointment and eventually to apathy. In addition, the fact that most central institutions operate on a principle of representation, which may be elective or appointive, means that they provide a narrow basis for participation. Of necessity only a few can play an active role, while the many are passive spectators whose lethargy is periodically disturbed by a superficial form of participation, namely voting.

By contrast, most of the departments, schools, and colleges (including the lower division colleges outlined later in this report) potentially offer locales in which the effects of decisions are visible, the range of problems is within human grasp, and the realities of participation are more genuine. In short, they are units commensurable with human possibilities. The development of viable local institutions has the additional promise of creating a sounder base for the reform of those central institutions that will continue to be necessary.

Decentralization of decision-making constitutes a second major theme of this report; here we have only suggested ways in which decentralization might ameliorate the effects of conflict among the main groups on the campus. A small community sharing common purposes is more likely to counteract the influence of artificial, rigidly defined interest groups. In smaller units student-faculty-administration consultation and participation are natural forms of activity rather than contrived formalities.

Having examined the shortcomings of the general concept of interest group politics in the university, we must now attempt to examine some of the specific problems this way of thinking has created in the governance of the university. We therefore turn to an analysis of the roles and organization of administrators, faculty members, and students in the governing process in an effort to understand how the shortcomings of the existing concepts work out in practice. Only then can we consider how new roles and relationships among these three elements can be developed.

Chapter III

❧❧❧❧❦❦

Roles in Governance

In this chapter we examine the conception of strong central authority located in administration, the ambiguous conception of faculty self-governance, and what is essentially the nonconcept of student government. Because the function of governance is most closely identified with the administration, we consider first the main ideas that have defined its role on campus.

❧ THE ADMINISTRATION ❦

For many years governance has been equated in this university with efficient execution of statewide and campus administrative policies. The ideal of administrative efficiency has provided the context in which the educational and research activities of the university operate. Efficient administration, in turn, has been identified with a system of hierarchical authority. In the minds of those who have presided over the statewide university system during the past several decades, the notion of an effective pyramid of authority has been uppermost. According to this conception, each campus is headed by a chancellor or "chief campus officer" who is appointed by the Board of Regents and is delegated authority to direct affairs under his jurisdiction along strictly delineated lines. The notion of a centrally administered university system is more clearly embodied in the complex structure of the statewide administration. Not only are crucial decisions made at this level concerning admission standards, enrollment levels, and the allocation of resources among the separate campuses, but also the manner in which these resources will be employed in each of the campuses is specified in intricate and endless detail.

During the past two decades the rapid growth of the university system has combined with the inevitable limitation on available financial resources to present an irresistible case for statewide centralization. If limited resources are to be allocated rationally among the several units of the system, so the argument runs, there has to be a determinate locus of decision-making. In recent years, however, the logic of the statewide system has come under attack for being rigid and inflexible. Almost every major criticism of the system has urged decentralization. This is the direction of proposals considered in the state legislature; of faculty resolutions requesting greater local autonomy; and of the efforts of the chancellors to gain final authority over certain local matters. Ironically the most searching indictment of the system was produced by a research group appointed by the Regents themselves. In the spring of 1965 the Byrne Report recommended drastic devolution and greater local autonomy, but its proposals have been allowed to languish.[1]

Thus, despite criticism from many different quarters about the anachronistic state of the present statewide system of administration, this campus and the others continue to be encased within a structure designed for a state of affairs that no longer exists. During the years after World War II, the phenomenon of "growth" seemed sufficiently common to all campuses to justify a single set of standards for the

---

[1] See Appendix B for the Byrne Report's recommendations.

governance of the entire network. Differences between the campuses were posed primarily as quantitative questions of "more or less" or "rapid or slower" rates of growth. However appropriate a centralized system of administration may have been for coping with the demands of growth during the past two decades, it does not follow that those same means are still the most appropriate. Berkeley and Los Angeles, for example, are no longer "growing" campuses; even among relatively new campuses, such as Riverside and Santa Cruz, which have not yet met the target figures set by the Master Plan, differences exist in the rate of growth as well as in the purposes growth should serve.

Once we turn from physical, fiscal, and demographic criteria and begin to admit qualitative standards such as excellence, the criteria for shaping and evaluating the educational program for each of the campuses become substantially more complex and extraordinarily difficult to apply in a centralized manner. Under present circumstances, instead of being able to develop new forms of excellence and to cultivate the older forms intensively, the energies of the faculty and the administration have been preempted by the task of molding the educational system to statewide requirements that were formulated with little thought beyond the necessity of accommodating ever-increasing numbers of students.[2] Physical size and population have not changed in response to the internal needs of the campus; rather, they have been responses to the requirements imposed by the statewide system. The campus is thus thrust into a situation in which it is powerless to determine its size or the pace of its academic operations[3] by its goals and possibilities and in which, of necessity, it tends to look to the statewide authorities for clues to its own identity.

Another drawback of the present system is that it compels local units to adapt to the needs of centralized reporting and control. The

[2] Statewide procedures require that resources be appropriated to each campus and each unit according to a formula that assigns differing weights to the types of students enrolled. This ratio counts each lower division student at 1.0 for budgeting purposes; an upper division student is scored 1.5, a master's student 2.5, and an advanced graduate student 3.5. Such rigidity, of course, makes it impossible to meet the needs of lower division education, and almost as difficult to make any substantial structural innovation in the educational program.

[3] For an example of the relationship between the statewide administration and the campuses, see *University Bulletin,* March 8, 1965, a special supplement on the historical record of the decisions and actions relating to "year-round operation of the University and revision of the academic calendar."

result is a system of matching and interlocking bureaucracies extending from the statewide center to the campus and eventually to the colleges and departments. When structural innovations and experimental programs are proposed at local levels, they cannot but appear as troublesome anomalies that have to be adapted to the uniform standards of a centralized system.[4]

The existing system is, we believe, ill adapted to the needs of a contemporary university that is being challenged by changing values, a changing student population, and widespread uncertainty about the proper role of the university in a troubled society. It is a system designed to cope with the unprecedented growth of the economy and population of the state. But one dimension of change, expansion, should not be accounted the only important dimension of change. Some forms of transformation, particularly those involving qualitative judgments, should be handled differently from essentially quantitative problems such as increases in the student population.

It would be naïve to conclude, however, that because of the weakness in the present system a modern university can dispense with the skills and resources possessed by administrators and that administrative tasks can be assumed by faculty or students. Rather, the present challenge is to find new and more decentralized forms of organization

---

[4] Moreover, despite this monolithic structure, the pressures for uniformity, and the resulting rigidity of the system, the findings of the Byrne Report regarding uncertainty in the placement of authority and responsibility are of great interest:

> There is great confusion as to the actual distribution of power within the University, as to the sources of various policies, and indeed as to their substance. We found that statements regarding the responsibilities of various administrators were extremely vague, that most faculty and students had little or no idea which offices had which responsibilities, and that even administrators themselves were often unable to tell where their responsibilities began and ended. This vagueness produced many side effects. It allowed campus administrators to handle matters which legitimately lay within the purview of the statewide organization. Then again, it allowed statewide officials to preempt decisions which should have been made on the campuses. Sometimes the vagueness made lower and middle-level officials take responsibility for decisions which had actually been made at a higher level. At other times, vagueness created the impression that decisions had been made by the Regents when, in fact, they had been made by the Administration. And finally, this vagueness encouraged those administrators who were reluctant to take personal responsibility for their actions and decisions to pass them on to others within the University. (pp. 20–21)

that will break with the restrictiveness and uniformity of the present system, provide opportunities for experimentation and innovation, and encourage the creation of diverse yet integrated communities of manageable human size.

We turn now to an analysis of the role of the campus administration and an assessment of its ability to maintain the respect of the campus community, to respond to its needs, and to provide the leadership and energy required to achieve the transformation we believe necessary.

Any attempt to characterize the administration's role in campus governance is made more difficult by the intense conflicts of recent years which, to a significant extent, have centered around it. Of all the consequences of interest group politics on the campus, none has been more unfortunate than their effect on the administration. No topic approached by this Commission was more fraught with distrust and more laden with suspicion. No topic exposed so sharply the widespread contradiction, reflected in the charge to the Commission and in much of the thinking current on the campus, between lofty expressions about "community" and political rhetoric that would relegate the administration to pariah status.

It seems clear that the role of the campus administration has been badly skewed by repeated confrontations with dissident students and near-confrontations with the faculty. The administration has borne the brunt of the profound politicization of the campus and the major costs of conflict politics. It has had the unenviable task of trying to govern under conditions in which the rules of the game lacked legitimacy and, consequently, obedience to the rules was anything but automatic. It has often seemed, at least in the eyes of many members of the campus, that the major role of the office of the Chancellor is rule enforcement and representation of the "interests" of administrative efficiency and law and order. It is also clear that the office's responsibilities within the statewide system impose severe limitations upon its freedom of action, as does the political role it is expected to perform toward citizens who are voters, taxpayers, and often alumni. These demands are severe and inescapable, but they leave the Chancellor with little opportunity for the task of defining campus goals, critically analyzing its achievements, and proposing new policies for consideration by the campus community.

The office of the Chancellor has been further weakened by a phenomenon characteristic of contemporary societies. Most forms of authority—familial, religious, political, and cultural—are foundering in a crisis born of distrust, and it is not surprising that the heads of colleges and universities can no longer count on the deference and respect that, presumably, were accorded their predecessors. Add to this difficult situation the consideration that campus authority is exercised over a community that makes a way of life out of questioning accepted authorities, and certain conclusions begin to take shape.

The first conclusion is that it is quite doubtful that the authority exercised by the executive of a contemporary university can be of the kind associated with hierarchical administration. Highly centralized administrative authority has ceased to command much enthusiasm on this or any other comparable campus. The second conclusion is that if authority is to be effective in promoting voluntary compliance with campus rules and policies and in enlisting the energies and idealism of the campus in the common cause of educational excellence, it must be secured and continuously reinforced by actions that command respect by the standards appropriate to a university. Third, the legacy of suspicion must be dispelled by building new habits of cooperation between students and administrators, as well as between faculty and administrators, so that the administration does not remain politically isolated from the campus community. Such patterns of cooperation will have to be based on new institutions and processes of policy-making that would enable the office of the Chancellor to exercise the perspective of broad leadership for the campus while making it possible for the entire community to share significantly in both the definition and resolution of policy questions. Discussion of specific proposals for achieving these goals must be deferred (see Chapter Seven) until we have considered the present roles of faculty and students in governance.

⇥ THE FACULTY ⇤

The conception of "faculty self-government" assumes that the faculty exercises autonomous power, largely through the central institution of the Academic Senate. As a deliberative and policy-making body, the Senate functions through a committee system to execute Senate policies, formulate proposals for its consideration, supply periodic reports on conditions in those areas belonging to the jurisdiction of the Senate, and, finally, provide a bridge between the faculty and the administration in matters of mutual concern.

Historically, some of the authority of the Chancellor has devolved upon the faculty, particularly in the area of course instruction, curriculum, degree requirements, the conduct of research, and faculty appointments and promotions. Yet in most vital areas of campus life the key role of the administration remains intact. The resolutions of the Academic Senate, for example, are only "advisory," not binding on the Chancellor. In such matters as faculty appointments, the formal use of the Chancellor's final authority to override faculty decisions is rarely used,[5] but administrative influence in the complicated procedure of processing an appointment is considerable at many stages. In practice, the relationship between the Senate and its committees on the one hand, and the administration on the other, can be described as a relationship of dependence tempered by suspicion. Dependence has its origins in the constitutional principle that the practice of faculty self-government is a concession from the comprehensive, final authority vested in the Regents. The dependence of the faculty is accentuated by the administration's strategic role in the preparation of the budget, its access to special funds, and its control over building space for classes, offices, and research. In addition, certain administrative officers such as deans and vice-chancellors have significant powers in matters of curriculum, the appointment of departmental chairmen, the initiation of new instructional programs, and the recruitment and promotion of faculty.

The confusion created by this web of dependencies was accurately described in the Report of the Byrne Committee:

> In some areas the Senate is a legislative body making basic policy, which the administration then carries out. In other areas, the administration makes basic policy, and the responsibility for implementing it is left to faculty committees, either appointed by the administration, appointed by the administration with the advice of the Senate, or appointed by the Senate itself. In still other areas, the administration makes policy and also attends to the problems of implementing it. There appears to be some variation between campuses as to which areas fall into which category.

[5] See Report of Budget and Interdepartmental Relations Committee, Minutes of the Berkeley Division, Academic Senate (hereinafter Minutes), October 16, 1967, especially pp. 6–8.

There has been no consensus, either among administrators or faculty, about the extent to which an administrator should follow advice from faculty committees when he does not personally agree with it. Nor has there been any consensus as to the extent to which faculty opinion should be weighed by the Regents in making policy. Where consensus has not existed there has been a tendency to "play it by ear" and avoid any clear statements of policy. (pp. 25–26)

The phrase "faculty self-government" thus tends to cloud an accurate understanding of the faculty's role in the governance of the campus. The power of the faculty is considerable, but it is exercised within a milieu of confusion and uncertainty as to the precise jurisdiction of the Senate or the extent of its autonomy. Thus, the paradox: the faculty is powerful but lacks self-government.

These assertions can be supported by a brief examination of the two committee systems—both administrative and Senate—in which faculty participate. The related themes of Senate power and Senate dependence are immediately evident. There are perhaps one hundred committees[6] that contain some faculty members but that are not the creatures of the Senate. These so-called administrative committees are selected by the administration, usually from a list submitted by the Senate's Committee on Committees, and are expected to be advisory to the administration. On the whole, past experience with this device has been unhappy. The administration tends to select faculty members in whom it has confidence or to select them on the basis of the administration's conception of a "representative" faculty point of view. The faculty member is placed in the awkward position of deciding whether he is to represent the Senate's viewpoint, his own, or whether he should simply try to assist the administration.

Turning to the Senate's own standing committees, one might expect to encounter autonomous committees. In committees such as Academic Freedom or Privilege and Tenure, there is a strong tradition of independence, perhaps because they deal with matters in which the interests of the faculty are more united and the faculty is capable of

---

[6] "A recent survey counted a total of over a hundred administrative committees, nineteen of them inactive, and the great majority of them constituted mainly of Division members." Senate Policy Committee, State of the Campus Message, March 7, 1967, p. 11. Earlier Acting Chancellor Meyerson put the figure at 114, "not including committees shared with other parts of the University," and added: "Such a span of control is unmanageable." *Daily Californian*, March 19, 1965, p. 8.

mustering considerable external support. But there are other Senate committees that operate in ways indistinguishable from those of administrative committees. Faculty members on the Educational Policy and Budget Committees, for example, have labored long hours at the task of implementing directives from statewide administrators or responding to their inquiries. Often, little time and energy remain for deliberations concerning campus policies, with the further result that the power of the committees is exercised along the lines laid down by the administration, local and statewide. This situation was described in a report of a subcommittee of the Senate Policy Committee:[7]

> . . . the committees have become so intimately involved with administrative officers in policy formulation as to be virtually incorporated into the administrative machinery; and in fact many Senate committee members have moved easily and naturally into regular administrative positions. At such times the Senate committees, and therefore the administrative officers, have tended to lose touch with the Senate as a whole, and misunderstanding and conflict have resulted.

This system of dependencies is increased further by a number of other factors. One is the lack of administrative expertise among the faculty; another is inadequate staffs assigned to assist Senate committees. Inevitably the committees tend to rely on the skill and information of administrators. This is accompanied by another practice that has contributed to the style of Senate committees. In order to offset the expertise of administrators, the faculty comes to rely on those of its members who have the most experience in particular areas. Consequently, there is a marked tendency for a relatively small number of faculty members[8] to monopolize the membership of the most powerful

[7] Report, Subcommittee on Senate Government, Senate Policy Committee, November 20, 1966, p. 1. This report was never circulated generally, although some of its conclusions are summarized in the Policy Committee's State of the Campus Message, March 7, 1967, p. 9.

[8] These were described in the 1967 State of the Campus Message as "a small number of faithful 'Senate hands' . . . ," *idem,* p. 12. Of course this phenomenon is a general one; see Burton Clark, "Faculty Authority," *AAUP Bulletin,* Winter 1961, p. 293 for an analysis of the reasons for the relative conservatism of faculty oligarchs and the fact that they tend to have much closer ties to the administration than to the average faculty member. See also Ruth E. Eckert, "The Share of the Teaching Faculty in University Policy-Making," *AAUP Bulletin,* Autumn, 1959, p. 346, for a University of Minnesota study, showing that over a thirteen year period ending in 1957–58,

committees and to rotate the chairmanships among themselves. The existence of a Senate oligarchy and a Senate bureaucracy has tended to discourage the appointment to Senate committees of faculty members whose views are regarded as unorthodox. This situation has contributed significantly to the fact that over the years the Senate has been relatively ineffectual as a vehicle for promoting educational change or stimulating discussion of the fundamental purposes of the university.

The confused multiplicity of committees, the lack of coordination among them, and the inadequacy of their practices in reporting their deliberations and advice to the Senate as a whole both strengthen oligarchic tendencies and reinforce the apathy of the great majority of the faculty, all of which, in turn, vitiates the validity of faculty self-government. There are committees with the same name and the same function at departmental, college, division, and even statewide levels; committees with nothing to do or that meet formally once a year and committees that are heavily overburdened; committees performing the same function at the same time that do not know of each other's existence.[9] The "administrative" and some important Senate committees report directly to the Chancellor, and although their members act on behalf of the faculty, the committees "have rarely formulated and submitted to the Senate for action comprehensive statements of policy which could be used to govern their decisions; nor has the Senate requested such statements. Consequently there has been little Senate debate and direct vote on some extremely important matters of policy. . . ."[10] Nor is the form in which the membership is informed about important Senate affairs calculated to generate much interest in its functions. In such a context, the extent of faculty apathy about the faculty role in campus-wide governance is perhaps not surprising. The average attendance at the monthly meetings is about 10 per cent of the membership, and on only four occasions in recent years has a majority of the membership been present.[11] These occasions have been

80 per cent of faculty eligible for committee membership never held a committee position.

[9] Senate Policy Committee Report, March 7, 1967, p. 11.

[10] Senate Policy Committee, State of the Campus Message, Minutes, October 11, 1965, p. 7.

[11] Senate Policy Committee, State of the Campus Message, approved March 7, 1967, at p. 12; Minutes, p. ii (correcting report). This message was distributed in mimeographed form and was not printed in the Minutes or notice.

the "great crisis debates"; in contrast, when the agenda centers on fundamental educational questions such as those raised by the Select Committee on Education, there has been difficulty at times in mustering a quorum.[12]

The concept of faculty self-government is further weakened by the place the Berkeley Academic Senate occupies as merely one division of the University's Academic Senate, which, through its Statewide Assembly, has final power concerning all "legislation substantially affecting more than one Division or the statewide University."

To some extent, faculty organization thus mirrors the hierarchical structure upon which administrative conceptions of governance rest. Just as chancellors can only communicate with the Regents through the central organization of the Presidency, so the Berkeley Senate must go through the statewide Academic Council to communicate with the President, who in turn channels the communication to the Regents.[13] As with the administration, the controlling assumption of this system has been the efficacy of highly centralized governance of a uniform, growth-oriented multi-campus university.

Two facts stand out in an examination of this campus-statewide relationship in faculty governance. The first is the failure, noted by the Berkeley Division's Policy Committee, of the attempt to replicate the administrative structure and make it effective at the faculty level:[14]

> The Senate system . . . was originally devised to participate in the government of a single campus, and did not make (and apparently cannot make) a truly successful transition to the predominance of an over-arching state-wide administration. Since 1945 no state-wide institutions for the articulation of faculty opinion have been developed that are comparable in effectiveness to the powerful presidential administration.

Second, with more limited resources and the growing pressure for

---

[12] "Recently a meeting had to be terminated in the middle of important business because the minimal quorum of seventy-five (out of a membership of 1,657) could not be mustered." *Ibid.*

[13] Communications from the Academic Senate to the Regents can be "presented only by the President," who in turn receives them from the statewide Academic Council. *By-Laws and Standing Orders of the Regents of the University of California,* II, 4; IX, 2(e).

[14] Interim Report, Senate Policy Committee, Minutes, November 8 and 15, 1965, p. 25.

campus autonomy, diversity, and freedom for experimental innovations in education, the present statewide Senate faculty structure will become increasingly anachronistic. It is intolerable that the Berkeley Senate has no formal channel for communication with the Regents regarding the acute problems that have arisen on this campus in the last few years;[15] only with difficulty was the division's Emergency Executive Committee able to arrange a meeting during the free speech crisis, and then only with a committee of the Regents, not the full Board. Moreover, the kinds of issues over which the statewide Assembly asserts final authority have, in recent years, included such matters as the membership of students on Senate committees, rules for participation of department members in tenure decisions, pass-fail grades, and standards for undergraduate admissions. It is apparent that the problem of autonomy is as critical for the sphere of faculty governance as for the administration. To meet this problem, substantial decentralization of governing authority will be required.

≥\ *THE STUDENTS* ⩽

A third conception concerns what is euphemistically called "student government." This concept is extremely difficult to describe with any precision, and it is subject to very rapid change.

---

[15] The chairman of the Senate Policy Committee stated in his report to the Berkeley Division of May 16, 1967:

We believe that the Academic Council would be an appropriate body for communication with the Regents on matters of statewide importance, provided it is careful to ascertain the opinion of the various Divisions. But we also feel, more strongly than ever, that each Division must be able to communicate with the Regents on policy matters that concern it. . . . The crisis on the Berkeley campus at the end of the fall quarter brought the Regents into special session on December 6th. At such a time one might think that a committee of the Regents would have found it necessary to meet with last year's Policy Committee, or with the Committee on Student Affairs. Given the Regents' action at that meeting, consultation with the Berkeley or statewide Committee on Academic Freedom would also have been in order. We find it appalling, therefore, that *no* faculty committee was consulted. One source of the trouble is not difficult to find. Many of the Regents still think of the faculty essentially as employees, rather than as participants in the government of the University. . . . Either the Regents will have to agree to open channels of communication and consultation, or members of the faculty will have to search for means to protect themselves from the arbitrary acts of their employers.

The University "has long been noted," our official policy once proclaimed, "for its fine traditions of student self-government" through which students "have been given a strong (and usually decisive) voice in the determination and the administration of broad areas of University policy of the most direct concern to students in their out-of-classroom activities."[16] The passage suggests an instrument that is representative of students and that exercises governmental powers. Its premise, moreover, is that there is a separable category of functions that is both the dominant concern of students and of little or no interest to any other segments of the university community, implying that a kind of autonomous separatism is an appropriate model of governance. This conception implies that a separately constituted "government" performing specifically delegated tasks provides the principal means through which students can implement their views and interests. We believe that such an approach has serious flaws and that the time has come for a searching examination of the present model of student self-government.

As a historical phenomenon, student government had little to do with university governance; rather, students found it convenient to organize themselves for their own leisure-time activities, such as athletics, housing, eating, debating, literary, and theatrical endeavors. At Berkeley, sponsorship and control of these pursuits became centralized in a campus-wide organization known as the Associated Students of the University of California. The ASUC also assumed certain responsibilities for campus governance, especially the promotion of the "honor spirit" and attendant judicial bodies.[17] Over the past forty years, a recent study notes,[18] the university administration has taken over the operation of many activities and enterprises first established and supervised by the ASUC. Student government control over athletics, food services, cultural programs and facilities, and student disci-

[16] "Regulation on Student Government," November 30, 1959. See also *Unity and Diversity,* Office of the President, University of California, 1965, p. 31.

[17] During the first two decades of the twentieth century, the ASUC held de facto responsibility for campus disciplinary proceedings. Teresa E. Sevilla, *Student Authority: Its Development and Role in the Governance of the University of California at Berkeley,* unpublished Ph.D. dissertation, School of Education, University of California, 1967, pp. 160–165 and pp. 451–452. For the early history of ASUC, see Sevilla, pp. 131–235.

[18] *Ibid.,* pp. 458–465.

pline has greatly diminished, and many specialized services for students originally directed by ASUC have become the province of the Dean of Students and his staff. Thus while the ASUC has expanded its central jurisdiction over the range of student extracurricular activities, a parallel loss of control over student services and general campus matters has sharply decreased its influence in the overall process of university governance.[19]

The ASUC has been delegated management of the student union and student office buildings, the sponsorship of a program of extracurricular activities, the allocation of resources to particular organizations from a block budget for student organizations, and the appointment of student members of the Academic Senate's Student Affairs Committee. It does not have management authority over other buildings in the Student Center Complex, nor does it play a policy-making role for the housing, health, and placement services operated primarily for students. Moreover, within the circumscribed sphere of assigned managerial responsibility, the students' governance role is restricted by the extensive power exercised by the full-time Executive Director of the ASUC and his staff. Ostensibly the Executive Director is responsible to the ASUC Senate, but his role inevitably casts him more as its adult supervisor and as a de facto member of the Chancellor's staff.

It is obvious that to view the ASUC as a "government" stretches that concept beyond recognition, for the ASUC possesses none of the powers normally associated with the governmental function. The ASUC Senate by itself cannot impose compulsory taxes or other obligations, nor can it to any significant degree restrain anyone, confer rights, impose sanctions, or exercise independent power. The

---

[19] *Ibid.,* pp. 454 and 510. See also Mahlon H. Hellerich, "The Vital Relationship Between Student Government and Campus Community," *College and University,* Spring, 1960, pp. 261–280, which argues that this development is not a strictly local one: ". . . with the proliferation of the administrative apparatus in even the smaller colleges in recent years, not too much attention has been given by administrators to the articulation of this expanding administrative apparatus with the existing structure of student government. Indeed, there has been a tendency to assign new administrative personnel functions which previously had been carried on by student government or which might have been assigned to it. In a sense, then, the development of student government has been limited at a time when other segments of the college structure have undergone a steady growth." (p. 276)

ASUC is more realistically regarded as an "official unit" of campus administration, and the Chancellor retains the exclusive power to state the powers and responsibilities assigned to it.[20]

Frequently the practice of describing the purpose of an institution in symbolic language that connotes something quite different from its actual function is harmless enough. Indeed, for a limited class of students whose interests are not primarily academic, existing structures are quite adequate to achieve what the ASUC once defined as its goal: improvement of student welfare by promoting "a state of well-being and happy college life" by means of "the various extracurricular activities which are sponsored and regulated by the Associated Students. . . ."[21] But for most of the student body the misleading use of the concept and vocabulary of government has had consequences that we believe to be harmful and that are likely to be accentuated in the future. Those students who initially take the symbolism of "student government" literally are likely to be left either with the pathetic illusion that their carefully restricted management of expensive physical facilities constitutes self-government or with profound resentment of the discrepancy between the symbols invoked and the power actually extended to them. Relationships of mutual trust between students and administration may be impaired, for the model invites manipulation and its capacity for creating illusions is not restricted to students; as one college president has remarked in connection with student government, "the administrators and faculties find themselves pulling the puppet strings, hopefully repeating democratic phrases, often deceiving themselves into thinking that the democratic dream is being actualized through the paternalistic process."[22]

[20] On November 28, 1967, the Chancellor announced the revocation of ASUC authority to manage the facilities, personnel, and programs associated with the Student Union Complex, effective as soon as final details for a new Union Program and Facilities Board (on which students will lack a majority) can be arranged. (*Daily Californian,* November 29, 1967, p. 1.) The action, taken without prior public discussion and debate, was in response to an ASUC Senate decision to allow graduate students to vote in campus elections being held that week. See text of Chancellor's Letter to ASUC Officers, *Daily Californian,* November 30, 1967, p. 9; and Editorial, *Daily Californian,* December 8, 1967; for a review of the graduate student controversy, see Philip D. Roos, "Graduate Students In and Out of the ASUC, 1955–67," in *Daily Californian Weekly Magazine,* April 6, 1967, pp. 7–10.

[21] ASUC Executive Committee, May 21, 1947, quoted in Sevilla, p. 396.

[22] Buell G. Gallagher, *American Caste and the Negro College,* Columbia University Press, New York, 1938, p. 269.

We have been struck, moreover, by the frequency with which the symbols of government have aggravated the tendency to cast students and administration in the roles of contending interest groups. Traditional concepts of democratic government have been used as verbal arsenals, pushing debate in directions that needlessly build up mutual distrust, concealing the real issues, and rendering sensible institutional solutions politically unobtainable. Debate becomes a tiresome competition in which each protagonist seeks to find authority in alleged controlling principles drawn from governmental or administrative models quite inappropriate to the unique environment of a university. On the one hand is the repeated demand by students for governmental autonomy, which is understandable if the model of self-government is taken at face value, but which as a goal is both unobtainable within the constitutional structure of the university and undesirable in a collaborative educational enterprise. On the other hand, university policy mixes constitutional analogies with administrative rules, and this produces, as in the controversy over the enfranchisement of graduate students, a debate more appropriate to Gilbert and Sullivan than to a university community.

In pointing to the weak implementation of the concept of a separate student government, we do not wish to imply simply that improvements in the working of this model would be a satisfactory response to the problem. We question the validity of the entire conception and believe that serious consequences flow from certain premises implied in the model itself. Existing ASUC arrangements promote the centralization of student politics, symbolized by campus-wide campaigning and at-large offices; yet, as we emphasize repeatedly, substantial decentralization will be necessary to secure educational improvement and achieve genuinely effective student participation in governance. The constitutionalism that is presumed to create an exclusively student organization assumes that institutional separatism is the most viable channel for student participation in governance and implies federal, bicameral, or other political analogies. Our study has emphasized, however, the rigidity and limited utility of such political models, and it has led us instead to search for arrangements premised on the values of community interaction and continually shared responsibility.

Moreover, the incessant squabbling and the residue of traditional extracurricular concerns have obscured the efforts the ASUC has made to engage in significant academic and community projects.

These attempts have not revitalized the ASUC's prestige among students, but have tended to be overwhelmed by the structural and administrative burdens of the association. It is understandable that the most recent student election—which even had substantive issues on the ballot, but which took place in the familiar, fatiguing atmosphere of political crisis and administrative confusion—attracted only 4,500 voters out of approximately 15,000 undergraduates and 10,000 newly enfranchised graduate students. The legacy of disinterest, bungling, interference, and distrust that is fixed in the minds of much of the community poses serious obstacles to using the existing ASUC as a vehicle for introducing increased and meaningful student participation in governance and education.

Only a radical reformation of the models for student organization can do justice to the range and seriousness of this generation's concerns about their society; only this can enlist their creativity and allow the university to reap the educational benefits that student convictions and experience could contribute to the educational life of the campus. The concept of a separate student domain is entirely unworkable in such a context.

We are convinced that there are few student interests that can be successfully acted upon by a separate student organization removed from the general process of campus decision-making. A modest example will illustrate the point. The student residents of a housing unit might be delegated final authority to make and enforce their own living rules subject only to the restrictions of "campus constitutional law" which, for example, require due process in disciplinary actions and forbid racial discrimination. To have done anything to influence the style, design, location, and facilities of such housing, however, students would have to have been associated in the general process of campus planning and building design. Moreover, if living units move, as we hope they will, in the direction of becoming small educational communities (some faculty members in residence, nonresident faculty associates who are frequently available, libraries, tutorials), then a separatist student government would be inconsistent with the concept of such a community; one does not promote genuine participation by faculty members in such a residential community by excluding them from some of its most important functions. Thus, even in a residence hall, a local, separate student government will have limited utility and will become an anachronism as (hopefully) local communities of learning develop.

The inadequacy of the model of separate student government becomes clearer in the light of recent assertions of "student power" and insistence that students play a significant role in university governance. Throughout the nation, student governments have expressed great discontent with their present status and have pressed demands for the acquisition of power over more than the assigned areas of trivia. We think it is important to distinguish between the important goal of expanding the student role in governance and the erroneous assumption that a strengthened separate, central government is the most effective means to that end. There is great incongruity in calling for increased student power for an organization that inescapably keeps students separated from the total process of university governance and away from the context in which university policy is actually determined. Surely one of the more ironic aspects of the modern campus is the slogan of autonomy for student government when it is such splendid isolation that accounts for so much frustration.

Our task, then, is to overcome such segregation by devising a variety of institutional means through which students can be incorporated into the decision-making process rather than confined to haggling over the extent of peripheral powers delegated to a separate organization. Such institutions must be developed at local as well as central levels, for the student population of 27,500 cannot easily be assimilated *en bloc* into the decision-making process.

Although a representative central student organization will continue to be an important agency for securing student participation in governance, not the least of its tasks will be the creation and promotion of decentralized student constituencies and modes of participation in local units. A central senate could also be the means for expressing general student opinion and for channeling student delegates into the remaining central policy-making functions. It is hard to see how it could serve these ends, however, without strong local constituencies. Our primary responsibility in seeking to increase meaningful student participation is to distinguish the trappings of power from the reality of decision-making. This requires constant alertness against the inherent error of underrating diffused arrangements for exercising genuine influence in the same proportion as one tends to overrate ostentatious symbols of apparent power.

⇘ POSTSCRIPT ⇙

One additional comment should be made concerning the short-comings of thinking of the campus as divided into the three rigidly defined interest groups of administrators, faculty, and students. It is important to realize that, in addition to the heterogeneity of these three groups, the community also consists of many people who do not fall neatly into any one of these categories. We refer to the growing number of full-time research workers who do not have standing as faculty members, a large number of other academic and nonacademic employees who lack any effective channel of communication with policy-makers, and the corps of teaching assistants whose ambiguous standing as a mixture of teacher, student, and employee should be a cause of concern.

Two years ago, the Academic Senate's Policy Committee noted that "the Senate membership does not include many academic and research workers on the campus who have what in fact are permanent appointments" and therefore urged that the Senate should study whether "either to broaden its membership or assist in the establishment of an appropriate new additional academic organization."[23] The acute and tangled nature of this problem has been emphasized recently by Burton R. Clark in a discussion of the massive and growing faculties of large universities[24] that are

> . . . surrounded by ever-larger aggregations of educational workers who do an ever-larger share of the teaching and the research, who do not have full rights. There is a Ph.D. research non-faculty in the research centers; and there is also a B.A. to Ph.D.-level research-assistant non-faculty in these centers. Back in the departments, there is an army of teaching assistants, an aggregation whose use and abuse has become a scandal on more than one campus; and then in the new university, with its metropolitan location, one increasingly finds a fourth fringe faculty in the person of the lecturer. . . .

[23] State of the Campus Message, Minutes, October 11, 1965, p. 18.
[24] Burton R. Clark, "The New University," to be published in the *American Behavioral Scientist*, May, 1968.

Thus such simple age-old descriptive statements as "professors teach" become inaccurate; and not alone because professors do other things, but also because other people do much of the teaching and other people provide much of the informal instruction that is at the heart of the best research training.

The campus has already experienced one crisis in which the ambiguity of the status of teaching assistants almost created a major problem of academic freedom. It is clear, too, that the community of this campus has an increasing number of permanent members who are neither faculty nor students as those terms are presently defined, who are nevertheless closely tied to the educational enterprise while excluded from participation in governance. There is an urgent need to discuss with the researchers, the librarians, the teaching assistants, and persons in similar categories, ways in which they can be most appropriately classified and identified as part of the scholarly community, so that their concerns can be formulated as part of a participatory structure of governance.

PART TWO

≈≈≈≈≈≈≈≈≈≈≈≈≈≈≈≈≈≈≈≈≈≈≈≈≈≈≈≈≈≈

REDIRECTIONS

The burden of the preceding pages is that the system of governance on this campus displays faults of structure, an inability to generate a widely shared concern with the common problems of the campus, and a method of operation that excludes significant parts of the community and inhibits focused attention and discussion on current problems. It is a system that has developed sensitivities to some forms of pressures and expressions of need while remaining relatively unmoved by others. Because its processes of decision-making are basically administrative and confidential rather than deliberative and public, it has attracted relatively little positive support and, in times of crisis, little spontaneous

loyalty. The typical device it can offer to those who wish to participate is an invitation to assist in administering the campus; the fundamental political instrument of this system is the committee that enlists
faculty, and sometimes even students, in work that consists mainly
in elaborating policies primarily determined at higher administrative
levels.

Whether, in the coming years, this system will be able to function effectively is doubtful. The turbulence of the past few years has
not only been a test of university arrangements and leadership, but
of the loyalty of its members. Each of us is entitled to make his own
appraisal of how effective these arrangements, leadership, and loyalty
have been; although there would probably be wide diversity in the
appraisals, we suspect that there would be general agreement that the
system has proved disturbingly fragile and surprisingly vulnerable. If
this campus is to avoid the experience of institutional breakdown, it
must develop modes of governance that will encourage forms of civic
commitment appropriate to a university. We must experiment with
arrangements that will more surely draw out the energy and idealism
of the campus community, arrangements that honor the promise of
sharing in governing processes that may make a difference in the life
of the campus. The controlling proposition that renders governance a
supremely important question for a university is this: the way in which
a university handles its common concerns is, whether intended or not,
a vital experience in education or miseducation. There are modes of
governance that may encourage a manipulative outlook, induce apathy
and cynicism, or promote an urbane form of the ethic of "I'm all
right, Jack." There are also modes of governance that encourage the
members to test their capabilities to the utmost because of a belief that
what each does really matters, not only to the self but to the others
who are similarly implicated in a set of common involvements. At its
best, a university can aspire to a kind of civic culture of the mind in
which arrangements for decision and deliberation are designed to draw
out what is special about a university culture: its commitment to rational inquiry, tolerance, goodwill, and unabashed idealism.

In the discussion that follows we have attempted to render this
vision of university governance more specific by developing certain
basic ideas: the process of open discussion preceding policy decisions;
the substantial decentralization of the decision-making structure at
both the statewide and campus levels; the significant expansion of the

student's role in governance. Accompanying these fundamental proposals are some suggestions for institutional arrangements for translating these ideas into practice. The consideration we have tried to keep uppermost is that of developing beliefs and practices that will measure up to, while strengthening, the ideal of university governance as education in the civic culture of the mind.

Chapter IV

※※※※※

Open Discussion

One requirement for reshaping the system of university governance is the establishment of practices that evoke public discussion and deliberation on policy questions before such issues are resolved.[1] It is vital that the university conduct its own decision-making process with equal

[1] We recognize that open discussion may on occasion threaten to expose matters often held to be properly private; indeed, this issue occasioned many hours of discussion by the Commission. At the outset it is important to state that we think a spirit of openness can pervade the process of policy formulation and decision even while means are found for protecting the integrity of deliberations that might be damaged by excessive public exposure. We discuss the problem of confidentiality later in this chapter.

devotion to the principles it applies in scholarly contexts: open inquiry, reasoned justification of conclusions, and the submission of findings to public evaluation and criticism. Deviation from these norms undermines the character of life in the university by positing a double standard between the concerns of governance and the concerns of scholarship.

Furthermore, the quality of the decisions themselves can only suffer from a pattern of policy-making based on selective and private consultation and covert bargaining among interest groups. There is no group on campus—administration, faculty members, students, or any subgroup—that has a monopoly on the wisdom needed for serious deliberation on questions that affect the common welfare. Only when the entire community is able to interact in an open manner can we be relatively sure that all the implications of a proposed policy have been explored and that all alternatives have been considered. Searching dialogue is needed to enlarge the range of criteria used in formulating issues and making decisions, and to eliminate both the sense and the reality of unilateral imposition of decisions that has so often characterized this campus.

ACCESS TO INFORMATION

The general participation in campus governance that we envision cannot materialize effectively unless participation is accompanied by the fullest possible opportunity for access to pertinent information. Much information is collected by various agencies, but at present the campus is alarmingly ignorant about the details of its own operations. Seemingly straightforward questions, such as the amount of money being spent on lower division education, are complicated research problems for which it is difficult for members of the community to secure a satisfactory answer. More complex questions, such as the relation between the use of federal funds to underwrite additional FTE (full-time equivalent) positions in some fields and the resulting imbalances in faculty-student ratios between fields, are seldom formulated, much less studied or discussed.

Available information is often limited to narrow administrative data for specific and immediate needs. This reflects the fact that the search for data is not always placed in the context of continuing evaluation of the university's purposes and programs. We must develop

the practice of setting forth broad questions permitting policy evaluation, as well as questions concerning managerial and administrative
efficiency.

Extensive public discussion must be predicated upon a great
range of opportunities for institutional self-examination, particularly
the assessment of our educational policies. To this end, it would be
desirable to incorporate analysis of university policies and problems
directly into the academic program.[2] As one useful approach, courses
in a variety of departments could be developed as contributions to the
process of institutional self-study. In addition, faculty, students, and
administrators could develop special cooperative seminars (perhaps
under the aegis of the Board of Educational Development) on significant university problems, such as the nature and impact of outside
research services, an evaluation of the campus physical environment,
relationships between the university and the State Legislature, or the
philosophy of mass education.

We view such courses and seminars as a means toward involving the entire campus community in research and analysis of university
policy, since it would be possible to publish such worthwhile research
and policy papers as are prepared. These, too, could be subjects for
open discussion. A program of courses and seminars devoted to study
of university policy, and open discussion of the results of this work,
would promote a greater degree of intellectual exchange between administrators, faculty members, students, and others on campus, and it
would help develop and facilitate access to necessary information. Efforts of this sort could facilitate more adequate formulation of issues
and solutions by making visible the thinking about these matters that
is taking place in all parts of the university. Without such concern and
awareness, issues will continue to be poorly formulated, and the campus will continue to disintegrate into the clash of narrowly represented
interest groups we all wish to transcend. Legitimate and perhaps rec-
oncilable differences in points of view will be seen as illegitimate and
irreconcilable "interests" resolvable only by manipulation, pressure,
and counterpressure.

     [2] Clearly, some of this activity takes place now, but its extent is un-
clear. Knowledge about the university, generated by campus coursework, is not
made available widely or systematically; nor has anyone given thought to the
range of necessary courses and studies. Our proposal (see Chapter Nine) for
creating a special collection of material relevant to university governance in the
Eshleman Hall Library may provide a focus for coordinating such work.

≱ FORUMS FOR POLICY DISCUSSION ⩰

An appreciation of the need for more searching consideration of policy issues, including more adequate information about the operations of the university, helps temper expectations that greater public deliberation can be achieved simply by creating more channels of communication. In addition, the structure of such channels requires examination. The breadth of a channel and its rate of flow are often controlled by those who specify the kind of information wanted and, with the best of intentions, often restrict what passes through.[3] Moreover, channeling, as conventionally instituted, often means that communication takes place only when a policy-maker wants reactions to a position already formulated. What we need, clearly, are channels that develop minimum restrictions and that help ensure effective communication before positions are finally formulated.

We suggest that continuing discussion of university affairs be encouraged through the institutionalization of formal and informal forums for the exploration of problems and the formulation of policy alternatives. In such contexts, major policy questions could be subjected to thorough discussion and debate before decisions were reached. In the course of such deliberation it would be much easier to elicit and appraise the information on which policies are constructed and decisions must be based. Through the public questioning of officials, the device of public hearings, the presentation of studies and reports, and improved access to university documents, it would be possible to open up the process of policy-making, both by increasing the scope of participation and by broadening the criteria for evaluation and the range of concerns expressed on a given issue.

Extensive public discussion can make an important contribution both toward improving the quality of decisions and minimizing the degree to which decisions are imposed unilaterally. An illustration is provided by a brief examination of the recent controversy over changes in the system of pre-enrollment for classes. In August 1967,

[3] How circumscribed a channel may be is illustrated by the statement in a brochure prepared by the Office of the President, University of California, several years ago: "Student leaders will be encouraged to continue and refine their gathering of reasoned student opinion on matters which affect students in their University affiliation." *Unity and Diversity: The Academic Plan of the University of California, 1965–1975,* Office of the President, 1965, p. 31.

the Registrar announced significant changes in the academic calendar and a new system of advance registration for all classes during the last two weeks of the preceding quarter.[4] Since this was regarded as a change in administrative procedure, it did not go before the Academic Senate, nor were students and departmental administrative personnel consulted in advance of the decision. When the campus became generally aware of the new procedures and the difficulties they entailed, a strong reaction developed, several critiques of the plan were prepared, and ultimately the decision was rescinded.[5]

The lack of prior public discussion was costly. Because the issue was not presented in the context of the need to reevaluate the problem of the pace of academic activities, no fruitful exploration of this problem has yet been attempted, and no constructive suggestions for policy changes have developed. Because the decision was announced as a *fait accompli*, the resulting protest contributed to the aura of resentment at administrative imposition that so marks the campus. An important question of academic policy threatened to become a quarrel among adversary groups. It is possible that the entire controversy could have been averted had there been prior discussion of the proposal.

Whenever the administration reaches decisions without prior public discussion, the likelihood of campus misunderstanding is increased. When an actual change in policy is announced as merely an administrative adjustment, that decision may give rise to suspicion that the real reasons for change are not being stated, and *post hoc* discussion of the issue will take place in an atmosphere of distrust and hostility. In June 1967, for example, the Dean of Students announced a new policy of charging ten cents a seat for the use of campus facilities by registered student groups for events at which admission is charged

[4] Memorandum of Registrar, August 24, 1967. For other relevant information, see Memorandum of Vice-Chancellor for Student Affairs, October 6, 1967; ASUC Senate Resolution on pre-enrollment, October 31, 1967; and "Student Views on Pre-Enrollment," study prepared by ASUC Student Education and Faculty Relations Board, November 3, 1967.

[5] Such discussion exposed the discrepancy between the stated intention of the plan—to provide a one-day break between the end of classes and the beginning of final exams; and the means—to gain the time by using the last two weeks of classes to engage in a pre-enrollment process which, in the eyes of students, would have consumed at least the equivalent of the one day assumed to be saved. Students also expressed great resentment that the new plan would prevent the widespread practice of "shopping around" during the first days of classes, and considered the new policy as a step toward greater rigidity in the curriculum.

or donations solicited. The decision, according to one administrative officer, had been under discussion within the administration for months, although leaders of the groups most affected claimed they had not been consulted about the plan.[6] The policy change was justified on the grounds that increased use of campus facilities had generated additional maintenance costs that the groups should be asked to defray, but no evidence was ever presented publicly to document the additional expenditures involved nor the rationale for the size of the fee imposed. Because of the absence of such justification, the lack of prior consultation, and the fact that the regulations most immediately affected campus political groups, it is not surprising that students reacted with anger and the suspicion that more than administrative costs were involved in the decision. The object here is not to assess the validity of such accusations, but to point out that a reasonably full exploration of the problem could have been conducted, even in the inadequate forums currently available, had there been the willingness to submit all policy proposals to the test of open discussion and justification. If policies win public approbation when justified by the standards of rigorous, scholarly inquiry, then a substantial cause of suspicion and hostility is removed and the community has moved a step closer to conducting its affairs through sustained dialogue rather than intermittent negotiation.

❧ OPEN DISCUSSION AND DECENTRALIZATION ❧

The relevance of our hopes for decentralization to the problems of encouraging extensive open discussion should be evident. It is our belief that both the type of problem that invites and lends itself to a full-scale, campus-wide discussion and the type of problem that by its nature is best dealt with privately represent a fairly small minority of the issues that comprise the vital business of campus governance. The great majority of policy matters are most effectively and meaningfully discussed through an open dialogue among those segments of the campus most concerned with the matter under consideration. Hence the decentralization of the campus into smaller integrated units of students, faculty members, and administration enhances the

---

[6] See *Daily Californian,* June 22, 1967, p. 1, and June 27, 1967, p. 1, and text of letter from Dean Arleigh Williams, p. 7. Students also complained that the decision was the latest in a long line of policy changes announced during the summer months when many students are not on the campus. See *Daily Californian,* June 27, 1967, p. 1.

possibility of serious, frank discussion of important issues that are more apt to be of local rather than global scope. Such discussion will contribute to the atmosphere of intellectual give-and-take that is likely to make the decentralized units more vital and more effective. At the same time, in areas such as personnel decisions, as distinguished from policy problems, where a freewheeling public interchange is clearly undesirable and confidentiality is of prime importance, more effective communication can occur in the context of smaller integrated local communities.

✄ OPEN DISCUSSION AND CONFIDENTIALITY ✄

Commitment to the principle of maximum open discussion of policy matters does not, as we understand it, preclude in principle private discussions among colleagues, nor does it rule out confidential consultation by administrators—even were such practices preventable in reality. The point is, rather, that such discussion and consultation will no longer be the main, and sometimes the only, route to policy formulation and decision; they will be one means among many, and will take their proper place in a context of public dialogue. Except in very specific situations such as personnel decisions, the academic evaluation of individual students, medical records, and certain types of sensitive academic freedom cases, confidential discussion and consultation are never adequate substitutes for public dialogue with opportunity for debate prior to final decisions. Such dialogue must go well beyond private consultation among and with knowledgeable individuals to take account of the insights and possible reactions of larger groups.

Private consideration of decisions can never be a complete substitute for public debate—and yet, in some circumstances, due consideration for both informed decision and for the protection of individuals means that the bases of decision are not made fully public. In some circumstances, to deny decision-makers the opportunity to assure informants of confidentiality would be to deny them access to pertinent and perhaps crucial information. In other circumstances, to require that decision-makers reveal fully the information on which decisions are based is to condemn persons to unnecessary pain and indignities. These are age-old problems not readily, if ever, resolvable in advance or through neat recipes. It is not our intention, therefore, to attempt to bar or even inhibit candid confidential discussion or private communication from the process of campus governance. It is our intention to commit our institution to substantial public dialogue so that there will be a greater degree of correlation between arguments presented in private and reasons advanced publicly for a particular policy decision.

Although the apparent contradiction between these two positions can never be neatly resolved, it can best be met by finding and promoting new methods for encouraging a broad dialogue concerning the dimensions of the problem and the principles that underlie the specific proposal under consideration, not by constructing mechanical devices designed to minimize the exchange of closed communications. At the campus-wide level, improved and restructured relationships between the Chancellor's office, the Academic Senate, and the Student Senate are likely to lead to the kind of many-sided interaction that will enable the final decision-making authority to balance privately gathered information against various additional opinions that the broader campus community has expressed. In some cases, such devices as the advance publication of draft proposals, improved access to information and documents, public hearings, and the circulation of minutes and agendas will be valuable supplements to the structural changes that the Commission is proposing, particularly if we are to encourage a mood of civic mindedness and concern on the campus beyond the confines of formally representative bodies.

Certainly in those cases where public discourse leads to something approaching a general consensus, decision-makers will be in a position to act with broader vision and greater foresight than if they are trapped in a crossfire of repeated visitations and communications from individuals and groups who have only their special interests and influence, and perhaps only their self-certainty and aggressiveness, to commend them.

If our own experience on this Commission is any criterion, no controversial issue looks the same (or as simple) once it has been subjected to the fire of criticism, debate, evaluation, and reappraisal in the light of conflicting views, however strong the subjective forces that pull us in our original direction. If these processes are of value for the development of the intellect, as most members of an academic community will agree, they are equally of value for the development of intelligent formulation and solutions for the difficult issues that have and will continue to beset a campus as large and diverse as ours.

Chapter V

꙰꙰꙰꙰꙰꙰

Decentralization

During several months of deliberations, the Commission found itself returning again and again to the idea of decentralization. Whether the discussion was focused on participation, or the quality of education, or the reduction of bureaucratization, or the impersonality of the campus, we invariably were led back to questions of size and scale. Many of the objectives and values espoused over the past several years—and earlier—now appear to be impossible to realize or even approximate, given the present structure of the university. On numerous occasions university spokesmen, faculty members, and students have deplored a lack of institutional loyalty as well as a decline in civility and common decency; some voices have talked of the need for closer personal relations between faculty members, students, and administrators for the nurture of a sense of community that would enable the participants to be part of a common enterprise; others have contended that unless the university can find ways to encourage serious educational experiments, it will become stultified by its routines.

Aspiration and hope are difficult to sustain in the presence of a centralized, bureaucratized, and relatively immobile organization. Loyalty and affection seem misplaced rather than displaced when their object is a conglomerate of nearly 40,000 persons distributed among colleges, professional schools, and research installations that have in common only their geographical location. Like the French voter who prided himself on being the bearer of one fifty-millionth of the nation's sovereignty, we at Berkeley may perhaps derive a vicarious sense of power from being associated with a large and imposing organization. But as the experience of the past few years suggests, academic grandeur does not appear to promote much loyalty, and certainly little predisposition to sacrifice one's personal interests for a greater good that all too often seems only greater and not good. Size and scale are important conditions in promoting a lively sense of membership. What student or faculty member is likely to feel part of an intellectual community when his department may contain faculties of nearly 100 members, 700 undergraduate majors, and over 300 graduate students? What idea of membership is imparted to the lower division student by a structure such as the College of Letters and Science that succeeds only in conveying a sense of isolation, anonymity, and frustration to the faceless thousands within it? If the ways in which the members feel about an institution are affected by size and scale, their influence is even greater in deterring effective action. When one tries to imagine making decisions supposed to apply to all the varied and diverse parts of this complex campus, what can participation really mean? If participation culminates in deliberation, how is it possible for deliberations on these affairs to be anything more than an exercise in masking ignorance?

Decentralization recommends itself because it represents an attack on size and scale. Decentralization offers a method for transforming the structure of the university from an obstacle to a positive instrument for the realization of the values and commitments of its members. Although it would be foolish in the extreme for us to offer a blueprint that would dismantle the present complicated structure, which includes not only the arrangements on campus but also those which link this campus to the other campuses, to the network of statewide institutions, and, finally, to the Regents and certain political agencies of the state, we are convinced that the situation is not irremediable. A start was made a few years ago by the Byrne Committee, which dealt mainly with the problem of campus autonomy and proposed a far looser system with greater independence for the local campuses and far less control by the Regents and the President of the University. Despite several recent changes, notably those that transferred final power over certain decisions from the President to local chancellors, the overall centralization of the system persists and interference by Regents with internal campus affairs poses a constant threat. The Byrne Committee failed to initiate fundamental changes, not because its proposals were impractical but because they were not seriously considered. The most important reason for this failure was that the proposals themselves challenged prevailing assumptions about size and scale, as well as the structure and distribution of power involved in the existing scheme.

The basic step toward inaugurating an era in which the physical and political dimensions of education are conceived differently would be to relax the system of statewide governance and replace it by a looser association of autonomous campuses. This would be only a beginning. Just as there is an urgent need for a renewal of efforts to secure genuine campus autonomy, there is an equally pressing need for a thorough reconsideration of the centralized educational structure at the campus level. Especially is there a need for a serious reappraisal of the units appropriate to synthesize the educational and human objectives of the Berkeley campus. There is a close relationship between campus decentralization and campus autonomy because a highly centralized statewide system makes it exceedingly difficult, although perhaps not impossible, to undertake serious decentralization measures locally.

We propose two specific measures for continuing the work of decentralization and attaining its goals:

1. The Commission recommends that the Academic Senate instruct the Senate Policy Committee to prepare, or cause to be prepared, a model charter for Berkeley campus autonomy, in accordance with the Byrne Report's recommendation that the Board of Regents

"charter separately each campus as an autonomous university within a commonwealth of universities under Regental jurisdiction, according to each university maximum authority over its own affairs and maximum freedom to shape its own profile of excellence."[1]

2. The Commission also recommends that a special Commission on Campus Decentralization be established under the auspices of the Vice-Chancellor for Academic Affairs to plan means for achieving decentralization of decision-making and the creation of communities of more manageable size on the Berkeley campus. (Additional details and suggested questions for this commission are presented at the end of this chapter.)

⚔ STATEWIDE RESTRAINTS ⚔

In the space of less than two years we have witnessed actions by the Regents that have raised serious threats to the academic freedom of this campus, the effective governance of its affairs, and the personal freedom of its students. In December 1966, the Regents declared that "University personnel . . . who participate in any strike or otherwise fail to meet their assigned duties, in an effort to disrupt University administration, teaching, or research, will thereby be subject to termination of their employment . . . , denial of re-employment, or the imposition of other appropriate sanctions."[2] In July 1967, the Regents announced their concern with the "reports of rapidly increasing use of dangerous and unlawful drugs by college and university students" and translated that concern into a policy "that students shall be subjected to disciplinary action, incuding dismissal for the use, distribution or possession of unlawful dangerous drugs and narcotics. . . ."[3]

This latter action illustrates vividly how problems that are extremely complex when seen in their specific context give the illusion of being easily resolvable when viewed from a Regental distance. During the past few years, the Berkeley campus has been struggling desperately to establish a number of principles that it believed appropriate to its academic culture and environment: the private lives of its stu-

---

[1] See Recommendation 1 of the Byrne Report for detailed discussion of the concept of the charter and suggestions for principles to be contained in it (Appendix B).

[2] *University Bulletin,* December 12, 1966, p. 81.

[3] *University Bulletin,* July 24, 1967, p. 19.

dents are their own matter; students should not receive academic pun-
ishments for off-campus violations of the law; and the Administration
should not assist in the compilation of dossiers dealing with the personal affairs of its members. Despite the travail and trauma of the
achievements, which were only partially established, they were quickly
and brutally reversed by a single Regents' ruling. To mention another
example of how local self-governance is subverted by the statewide
system: during the recent campus disturbances arising out of anti-
draft demonstrations, it was an open secret that the Regents' Counsel
was seriously hampering the freedom of the Chancellor to respond to
the shifting events of that period. This is no new development; the
presence of the same Counsel was felt during the turmoil of 1964. The
point of this example is that statewide control is not always a consequence of administrative considerations but is likely to be a response
to those political pressures against which the statewide agencies are
supposed to protect the local units.

    These incidents are but the most recent examples of a long
series of abuses that make a mockery of the official theory that the
Regents serve as a buffer between the university and the political pressures emanating from a hostile environment. What may have been
intended as a buffer has become a conduit for transmitting pressures
dangerous to the continuing integrity of the campus. By concentrating
responsibility in the Board rather than diffusing it among the many
campuses, the system has been made more, rather than less, vulnerable.
A Roman emperor once declared that he wished the Roman people
had one neck so that they might all be choked at one moment. In
times of crisis, the campus-wide system comes close to realizing that
wish.

    As the above remarks suggest, the present system is at once rigid
and quixotic. The Byrne Report had the great merit of proposing a
sketch of principles that might lead to a new and more decentralized
state of affairs. In the Byrne Report, the Regents were advised to
"provide for" the existence and functioning of the several autonomous
campuses consistent with the constitution and laws of the State. Only
the most basic principles regarding the governance and educational
goals of the several campuses were to be set forth by the Regents. The
Commission strongly supports this approach. Under such a system,
the statewide administration would assign block budgets to each campus without specific instructions for their internal allocation, the only

requirement being that campus decisions be generally consistent with the basic principles referred to above. The Regents, as defenders of the interests of the various campuses, would be expected to resist any attempts by the State government or legislature to specify the uses of the budget. At the next lower level, that of the campus administration, the basic principles set forth by the Regents would be more precisely interpreted so as to provide the framework for the formulation of policies appropriate to the needs of the particular campus; the campus budget would in turn be subdivided and allocated to the various schools and colleges, again without specific instructions for their internal uses. Again the only requirement would be consistency with the basic principles of the university, as interpreted in the light of the particular needs and goals of the campus. A similar procedure would be carried out by the schools and colleges in providing for their respective departments, institutes, or whatever new formations might arise within the decentralized system. At all levels, the performance of individual units would be subject to periodic review rather than the detailed scrutiny of particular decisions as they are taken.

CAMPUS DECENTRALIZATION

If decentralization is to serve the ends of participatory education, greater responsibility and autonomy must be lodged in smaller units. This would require the abolition of most of the controls now exercised by agencies such as the College of Letters and Science, the Graduate Division, the Committee on Courses, and the Committee on Educational Policy, and the transfer of these functions to units such as colleges and departments. The principle that ought to govern these changes is that autonomy should be lodged in groups that are intimately and vitally involved in the substantive processes of teaching. If these smaller units are to be encouraged to take full responsibility for the basic tasks of education, they must be equipped with the powers and resources necessary to make that responsibility genuine.

At the most obvious and immediate level, administrative decentralization would eliminate such time-consuming and irritating problems as the department's present lack of authority to decide how best to distribute its funds among senior, junior, and visiting appointments, secretarial and administrative staffs,[4] offices, lounges, library

[4] Departments should be able to hire their own nonacademic personnel

space, and so forth. Admission to the major program, course requirements within and without that program, and similar matters should
be decided within the department itself[5] without the inhibiting need
to refer to a series of detailed regulations and limitations imposed from
without, but with just that proper degree of restraint and calculation
resulting from knowledge that the wisdom of its decisions will be subjected to periodic outside review. Increased freedom will also help to
provide more opportunities for serious, practical discussions of departmental educational policies, both among faculty and students, than
can presently take place, given the powerfully inhibiting role of legal-
istic strictures on academic innovation. Moreover, as each department
develops its own special character and approaches, students would be
provided with a more diverse range of choices in finding significant
academic "homes."

The problem of control and accountability for academic performance might be handled by numerous ad hoc devices, such as personnel review committees and "external" review committees drawn
from outside the campus. Promotions and appointments might be handled by establishing a modest central agency for groupings such as
the Humanities, which would appoint appropriate committees for personnel as well as establish external review committees, drawn from
outside the campus, to evaluate the performance of departments and
colleges. The main power of these central agencies would be to approve, rather than establish, the general principles governing the quality
of appointments and promotions. The actual translation of those principles into practice would be the responsibility of the college, school,
and other units. Specific appointments and promotions, including the
formation of ad hoc committees to approve tenure decisions, would fall
within the authority of these lower units. Provision could be made for
periodic review by intercollege committees coordinated by the Office
of the Chancellor. Unsatisfactory patterns of appointment and promotion uncovered by such review committees would be brought to the

---

and define their jobs. The Personnel Office should provide services to campus
units rather than straitjacket their personnel decisions for the sake of rigid
symmetry and standardized procedures. It should continue to provide centralized
recruiting service, grievance procedures, standards for reasonable working conditions, and prevent grossly unequal compensation for similar work.

[5] Recently, a positive step in this direction was taken by placing graduate admissions and fellowship administration within the jurisdiction of the
individual department.

attention of the Chancellor's office and the appropriate committees of the Academic Senate. Methods might then be worked out for apprising particular colleges and departments of their failure to conform to general campus standards. Under this proposal, existing Senate committees, such as the Educational Policy Committee and the Committee on Courses, would exchange their present function of prescribing policies and standards for the whole campus for a new function: cooperating with the administration in devising ways of evaluating the performance of lower units.

It would be absurd to believe that the benefits of decentralization will be realized merely by settling greater autonomy on existing departments and colleges. With some exceptions—especially certain small departments and professional schools—most of our academic departments have tended to reproduce the impersonal conditions prevalent throughout the university. Although many individual faculty members have struggled against these conditions, most departments conform to their administrative designation: they are "instructional units," narrowly conceived as organizations that offer courses. Some of our departments at Berkeley are larger than many liberal arts colleges elsewhere in the nation, yet they attempt to supply a comparable sense of intellectual affiliation for the students without enjoying any of the educational conditions necessary for the achievement of that purpose. Hemmed in by a centralized system, with inadequate resources, departments and colleges often take on the character of vested interests resistant to change and largely inspired by the false value of growth. More often than not, their complaints against the administration amount to a desire to substitute their routines for those of the administration, to reduce reporting and other central controls, not because they have real plans for educational revitalization, but simply because they wish to reduce the amount of administrative time spent responding to external agencies. They want to be masters of their own house, but ignore the correlative requirement that the house be reformed.

Thus the principle of decentralization appears as a cul-de-sac if it results in devolution toward units that are already too large. Sufficient mention has already been made of the problems that large aggregates create for students, but the threat posed for the faculty needs equal emphasis. It is not often appreciated that the environment of this campus is often as discouraging to intellectual communities among the faculty as it is among the students; it is equally true that the desire for such communities is as strong among some of the faculty as it is among the students. It is difficult to specify exactly at what point a department becomes so large that it is impossible to speak any longer of its common culture. A fair guess might be 20 to 30 faculty members, 200 undergraduates, and 75 graduate students; but more important than any particular figures is the principle that intellectual community is incompatible with conditions in some of our major departments.

Centralization, as we have already noted, also presents formidable obstacles to change and experimentation. Most departments are willing to assume new fields of study, but, except for the greater experimentalism in programming permitted among some natural science departments, most departments elsewhere in the university are reluctant to encourage new ventures that appear to rival existing ones. It is important, therefore, to realize that decentralization is an important condition for enabling groups of faculty members to form programs and departments that more nearly meet their felt intellectual needs. Decentralization offers much potential for encouraging and sanctioning intellectually meaningful groupings of faculty and students who have developed curricula and programs that draw on the techniques and concerns of several existing disciplines and units. Smaller, multidisciplinary enterprises offer one set of possibilities for dividing some of our exceedingly large departments into more manageable and responsive settings for learning.

The present structure of university decision-making militates against this form of natural evolution. Present procedures, for example, require that a proposal for a new department or other academic program run a gauntlet of possible vetoes guaranteed to weary all but a fanatical few.[6] At every stage it is possible for influence to be exerted and for the proposal to be blocked by any determined group (including an existing department that considers its interest threatened). In the immediate future, as the university enters an era of growing scarcity of resources, this path promises to be strewn with even greater pitfalls. The Chancellor indicated in his speech of December 4, 1967, before

---

[6] The proposal must be acceptable to the Dean of the College of Letters and Science and its Council. In addition, approval must be gained from the Graduate Division and from the Academic Senate's Educational Policy Committee and probably from the Committee on Courses. It then goes to the Chancellor's level where it must secure final approval before being sent to the Regents.

the Berkeley Academic Senate, that new programs and departments can be authorized only if there is a compensatory retrenchment elsewhere. Presumably, this means that to establish a new department or program, an existing department or college will have to volunteer to make a cutback in its own resources, a form of altruism that runs wholly contrary to the present ethic of self-interest.

Although existing university legislation and practices make the evolution of new groupings extremely difficult, a gesture is made in this direction by solemnly sanctifying "interdisciplinary" courses, or by establishing a "star system" whereby a handful of eminent professors are freed from university "duties" so that they may "teach."[7] The most recent example is provided by the proposal for establishing interdisciplinary courses (cross-listed by departments) and professorships under the aegis of the College of Letters and Science. Not only is the plan lacking any informing vision indicative of its substance and direction, but it has all of the deadening effects that come from its being an administrative solution rather than a response of a committed group of faculty who want to put an exciting educational idea into practice. Instead of confronting the real nature of the problem, the university has sidestepped it by expending precious resources on educational changes that appear exciting but bear no subsequent fruit beyond their initial bloom; above all, these changes are diversionary because they create the illusion—reinforced by the standard publicity releases— that something is happening.

The principle we propose must of necessity be stated in general terms, but its purpose should be clear enough: the university should make it far easier for concerned faculty members to initiate new departments and colleges as a means of breaking out of the rigid patterns presently imposed by departmental size and organization. It would be utopian to propose that larger units be dissolved immediately and reconstituted as smaller ones. A minimal first step, however, would be

---

[7] As William Arrowsmith points out, "[W]e will not transform the university milieu nor create teachers by the meretricious device of offering prizes or bribes or 'teaching sabbaticals' or building a favorable 'image.' At present the universities are as uncongenial to teaching as the Mojave Desert to a clutch of Druid priests. If you want to restore a Druid priesthood, you cannot do it by offering prizes for Druid-of-the-year. If you want Druids, you must grow forests. There is no other way of setting about it." "The Future of Teaching," *The Public Interest*, Winter 1967, pp. 54–55.

to establish procedures that eliminate many of the present levels of review and thus facilitate the consideration of proposals for the creation of new and smaller programs.

Finally, the flexibility provided by decentralization will enable departments and other small units to use their resources to encourage local milieus that enhance personal and intellectual contact among students and between students and faculty. By emphasizing the autonomous college and the semiautonomous department or institute as the primary locus of student and faculty activity, we can increase the *effective* size of the institution without reducing its absolute size, as Martin Trow points out. For such endeavors to be successful, each small unit will require the freedom to develop the intellectual characteristics and traditions that mark it as a special community, a process that can only be inhibited by overly detailed outside supervision. Of extreme importance in the creation of such communities is the establishment of a physical location (particularly in departments without studios or laboratories) for intellectual and social discourse, "lounges or spaces that are formally or informally owned by a delimited group of students and faculty who share some academic or intellectual interest."[8] For this to be achieved, there must be freedom for each community to experiment with its financial and space resources on the basis of such intangible considerations as the need to improve its spirit and intellectual atmosphere. Standardized and uniform criteria of efficiency, economy, and "maximum utilization" only retard such experiments and their potential growth.

Decentralization ought not to be viewed as a method for reproducing many smaller facsimiles of the present overcentralized and bureaucratized system. Not only is it necessary to devolve certain powers from higher units to lower ones, but devolution must be accompanied by simplification that reduces the number of administrative routines and controls, such as reporting and accountability, and makes possible flexibility, experimentation, and the cultivation of diverse methods for handling comparable problems. At the present time, a vast array of procedures works to stifle initiative and experimentation and to accumulate expertise and power in the hands of academic and administrative officials who alone are versed in the intricate procedures they have devised.

[8] Martin Trow, "The Large Campus as a Context for Learning" (mimeographed), 1966, p. 18.

Elimination of much of the unnecessary levels of review and the attendant avalanche of paper work would release central administrators from the hopeless task of securing a high degree of central coordination and enforcement, freeing their energies and ingenuity for the more important tasks of long-range planning, improving the public's understanding of university values and activities, and developing new programs and finding receptive homes for them. Rather than eliminating the need for central administration, decentralization would enable it to focus more directly on its obligation to provide vision, leadership, and patient guidance for a collection of diverse communities. Of course, there will be residual management and policy functions that must be exercised centrally if such communities are to be provided with essential services like libraries and finances and are to coexist with each other and with the other units that make up Berkeley. The design of the appropriate central structure poses complex problems. Whatever ultimate forms these central institutions may take, it seems clear—and not really paradoxical—that decentralization will require creative central direction.

Decentralized units cannot do without administrative assistance, but administrative experts are presently concentrated at levels above the department, in colleges, professional schools, divisions, and at the chancellorial level. Such personnel should be similarly decentralized. Whether this can be achieved in the near future is doubtful, for the administration of this university is notoriously understaffed and it would be highly inexpedient to spread more thinly the already limited administrative resources. The only feasible strategy is to proceed toward forms of decentralization that diminish the need for administrative staff while simultaneously utilizing untapped administrative resources. The need for staff can be eased by abandoning elaborate procedures of reporting and control, and by locating final responsibility for decision-making in the smaller units themselves.[9] In this way

[9] C. Northcote Parkinson relates a program undertaken by the firm of Marks and Spencer, Ltd., a British retail-store organization, operating through 237 branches. This company made a decision in favor of decentralized responsibility. The head office would respect the branch managers and the branch managers would trust the girls behind the counters. By so doing, Marks and Spencer found that it could eliminate the time cards, catalogue cards, complaint records, and stockroom forms. This decision abolished twenty-two million pieces of paper weighing 105 tons. Herbert Stroup, *Bureaucracy in Higher Education,* The Free Press, New York, 1966, p. 167.

the reduction of administrative costs may be made to serve the cause of flexibility and freedom to experiment.[10]

⚡ *LOWER DIVISION COLLEGES* ⚡

The potentialities of decentralization as a means for establishing manageable structures, promoting academic excellence, and encouraging a sense of common involvement can best be illustrated by presenting a concrete proposal for educational and institutional reform aimed at one of the most urgent problems on this campus, the sorry state of lower division education.

It has long been recognized that the College of Letters and Science, which theoretically accommodates the majority of undergraduates, is an unwieldy administrative device. Its jurisdiction is too wide and variegated for its present powers and personnel. As a source of identity for the student, it is too remote, impersonal, and overburdened. Its inadequacies are readily apparent at the most crucial point in undergraduate education, the first two years, when the student is, in most cases, undecided about his field of concentration. Except for the students who initially enroll in certain colleges, such as Chemistry, Environmental Design, or Engineering, the lower division students in Letters and Science (about 5,000 out of 7,000) occupy a kind of academic limbo, uncertain about their future direction, without defi-

---

[10] One possibility for seeking out new sources of administration is linked to the theme of student participation. If a genuine effort is to be launched toward greater student involvement, students might well be encouraged to contribute to the administrative work of departments, colleges, and schools, particularly in those matters that directly affect their education. Arrangements regarding registration and advising, for example, might well draw on the energies and time of students, graduate and undergraduate alike. Above all, students might take a major responsibility for initiating new students into the life of the department or college. The faculty can only devote a small amount of time to this matter and, generally speaking, the success of their efforts is necessarily limited by difference in age and outlook. Every department and college tends to acquire a set of customs, unwritten lore, and tacit assumptions that can only be conveyed by exposure to the special atmosphere of the department or college. Students could make substantial contributions to developing academic loyalties, but this would be satisfying and important to them only if they felt some stake in the enterprise. This form of identification presupposes that the enterprise is of sufficiently comprehensible scale that they could identify with it and of sufficiently intrinsic worth that they would want to.

nite intellectual affiliations, and bewildered by the problems of choice.

The diversity and range of course offerings and major fields of study, instead of enriching the act of choice, tend to confuse it for the beginning student. Most students in the lower division possess only the vaguest orientation in one direction rather than another: some incline toward the natural sciences rather than the humanities, others are drawn to the social rather than the biological sciences. Very few are convinced that they want to be political scientists rather than sociologists, and fewer still are clear about the difference. The department has had little contact with and responsibility for the student during the time prior to his choice of a major. The student may have taken one or two lower division introductory courses in the department, but in most cases will not have been exposed in any meaningful way to the experience of membership in the department's intellectual enterprise. He will probably not have encountered faculty members in anything except the impersonal setting of a large lecture class. Even if the student can find a few small classes in lower division, the value of this experience is limited because it forms an isolated moment: it begins and ends at fixed times, and does not provide adequate opportunity for the students to congregate and exchange ideas, experiences, and reactions with each other or with the instructor.

In this setting, the student is a prime candidate for either a passive, administratively defined education or an extended game in which he seeks, alternately, to exploit opportunities and cut corners or to bait the system and compel it to take notice of him as an individual.

These serious shortcomings of lower division education limit the student's ability to make the most of his last two years and adversely affect his capacity for developing the kind of personal and intellectual ties that will prepare him for membership in the campus community. The price is unrealized intellectual potential and personal isolation.

As a first step in trying to deal constructively with some of these problems, the Commission proposes a major reform in lower division education. We specifically recommend the immediate establishment of four new lower division colleges, each with autonomous control over its budget, curricula, staff, and physical resources.[11] We believe that if

[11] This proposal is sketched in further detail in Appendix C. A pioneer attempt to cope with the problem of lower division education has been the Tussman Experimental College. Although we have not adopted it as our model,

the proposal is implemented by the support of the administration and faculty, an important step will be taken toward improving education and the climate surrounding it. The relatively small size of the colleges (each will have a total of 500 students) will enable the members to evolve a form of community appropriate to an educational institution and thereby help students and faculty to realize the goal of learning as shared experience and mutual participation. Small seminars and individual and group tutorials are envisaged as major methods of teaching. Advanced graduate students are expected to play a vital role in the tutorials and seminars and to participate as junior partners in discussions with the faculty concerning curriculum, teaching, and academic planning.

It is planned that each college will differ from its sister colleges in curriculum, style of academic life, and student body. Its institutional identity will be derived from the blend of subjects embodied in the curriculum, or from the topics selected for emphasis. Among the several objectives the college curricula hope to achieve is to facilitate a more rational choice of the major by the lower division student. Assuming that the colleges will at least partially represent some of the general choices a student might make, for example, social sciences, humanities, and the natural sciences, it is hoped that each college will embody a particular cluster of subjects, such as History and Literature, Political Science and Economics, and that at the end of his two years in a college, a student will have a fairly well-formulated notion of the department with which he wishes to affiliate. At the same time, the existence of the colleges should serve to strengthen the teaching programs of the traditional departments. The latter will be relieved of what is now regarded as an unsatisfying task and freed to improve the quality of upper division instruction for students who, it is anticipated, would be more broadly prepared for their major field of concentration.

We would hope that eventually the entire lower division student population will be accommodated into a structure of colleges. Important educational benefits might be reaped from the opportunity to experiment with new blends of subjects and to create a more coherent conception of lower division education; from the closer personal relationships made possible by the college setting; and from the greater encouragement given to individual self-determination as provided by

we regard it as a hopeful sign that it is possible to make significant changes at this level.

tutorials and individual research projects. The closer association between faculty, advanced graduate students, and lower division students should promote greater responsiveness both to the intellectual needs of the students and to the demands of scholarly inquiry. It should be relatively easy for students and instructors to exchange views about the curriculum and to appraise its operation.

This proposal seeks to formulate new educational structures that would make possible a beginning toward the goals of participation and the development of a genuine intellectual community, a beginning that will retain and strengthen the fundamental educational purposes of the university. The problem is to satisfy legitimate student desires for involvement and shared experience in such a way as to strengthen and improve the quality of education, not to dilute education with sentimentality and render it subsidiary to participation and community. One goal of education is to prepare men and women with a confidence in their own intellectual and moral resources, rather than to instill a kind of insufficiency that can only be overcome by identification with a group. In short, the colleges should provide a setting for participation of the type most appropriate to education—sharing in a common enterprise.

The Commission regards the colleges as truly experimental, and for this reason it has not attempted to suggest more than a skeletal structure. It is our strong belief that each college should be as free as possible to develop its own curriculum, methods of teaching, and style of life. Within each college the final responsibility for curriculum, recruitment of faculty, and establishment of standards will lie with its faculty, but we fully expect that each college will develop its own distinctive modes of discussion and consultation with students. It would be a serious mistake to impose on every college a preconceived formula for its structure and operation. It would be something less than an act of good faith to bewail uniformity at one level of the university and to insist upon it at another.

We have presented so detailed a proposal both to meet the urgency of the problem of lower division education and to illustrate how the concept of decentralization may be given practical shape. Beyond the lower division colleges, we also urge a wide variety of experimental efforts to develop new communities of learning. A number of potentially exciting proposals exist,[12] although the scope of the Com-

---

[12] One particularly interesting idea advanced by Nevitt Sanford would

mission's assignment has prevented consideration of them in this report. We hope that the measures of decentralization we suggest will encourage the preparation and realization of new ventures of this sort.

⇘ COMMISSION ON DECENTRALIZATION ⇙

Beyond what has just been presented, the Commission has not attempted to work out a detailed plan for statewide and campus-wide decentralization. We believe that a viable approach to the former has already been outlined by the Byrne Committee; the task of our campus is to continue and intensify its efforts to press the case for campus autonomy and statewide decentralization upon the Board of Regents. There is no comparable set of proposals for immediate legislation for campus-wide decentralization. The subject is so broad and so complex that to deal with it effectively the Commission would have had to disregard all other aspects of its charge and, in fact, greatly exceed it. As an alternative we have presented a broad outline of the direction we believe desirable for the campus and offered a specific proposal for the urgent problem posed by large-scale lower division education. We believe that except for the establishment of lower division colleges, a much more thorough study will be needed before the basic approach we envision can be put into effect.

Much as we regret having to suggest the creation of new study commissions, we have reached the conclusion that a special body should be established to continue the task of developing proposals for campus decentralization. We have already noted that strong central leadership is needed to effect serious decentralizing reforms. Accordingly, we propose that the Chancellor's office, in the person of the Vice-Chancellor for Academic Affairs, be requested by the Academic and ASUC Senates to form a Special Commission on Campus Decentralization. The Vice-Chancellor should serve as Chairman of the Commission, which should include delegates from the Academic and Student Senates, and representatives of the full-time research professionals and the departmental nonacademic administrative staff.[13] Faculty and

directly link undergraduate education to research institutes. See *Where Colleges Fail*, Jossey-Bass, San Francisco, 1967, Chapter 18.

[13] There is no present method for selection of the last two representatives by the groups concerned. Nonetheless we think it important to emphasize the need for such representation, and presumably devising such methods would be part of the study suggested by the Senate Policy Committee and discussed

student members should be chosen by the Vice-Chancellor for Academic Affairs from a slate of persons nominated by the Committee on Committees and the Student Senate respectively, with special attention to their experience, commitment, and devotion to educational excellence.

We strongly believe that the task of the proposed commission should not be to "study" whether or not decentralization is desirable. We think the case for decentralization is clear, and the charge to the Special Commission should be to determine what forms of decentralization are most desirable from an educational standpoint and what are the best means for achieving them. Some of the more immediate questions the Special Commission will have to deal with are as follows:

> What are the most promising alternatives to the College of Letters and Science, given the need for a variety of new settings to provide the intellectual coherence and administrative simplicity Letters and Science presently lacks?

> What other modes of decentralization should be considered in addition to the subdivision of existing units? In particular, what approaches can be devised to counteract the drawbacks imposed by the size of some of our existing departments?

> What particular steps will require additional funding, and which are likely to be self-supporting through the reduction of the present costs of centralized administration?

> What procedures can be devised for facilitating the consideration of proposals for new units and securing financing for them on at least an experimental basis?

> How can increased educational use be made of institutes and centers, in the context of decentralization?

> How can future planning of the campus physical environment be shaped to promote the goal of creating decentralized educational communities of manageable dimensions?

> How should graduate education be linked with proposed decentralization schemes? For example, should the Graduate Division be abolished and its functions transferred to special sections of the new colleges or schools?

Several questions of concern to the Special Commission will have to be examined in conjunction with the assignment concerning

at the end of Chapter Three. See also our proposed Emergency Advisory Committee, p. 102, where similar problems would arise.

decentralization we have proposed for the Academic Senate's Policy Committee. Such questions include the following:

> To what extent does effective decentralization within the campus require changes in Regential policies, and to what extent may effective reforms be executed even in the present statewide context?

> How can the Academic Senate structure be correspondingly modified to meet the changes created by the decentralization of the educational system?

> What decisions will still have to be made on a campus-wide basis, and what are the most desirable procedures for making them?

Other questions will obviously suggest themselves. What is needed now is clear expression of opinion from the faculty and student senates on the desirability of pursuing reforms in the direction suggested here, and a commitment by the administration to lead the examination, assessment, and realization of appropriate measures, in cooperation with concerned faculty and students.

In pressing the case for decentralization of decision-making, smaller units, and greater student involvement in the main concerns of the university, our goal is not to secure a cozy haven of warmth and affection. Rather it is our belief that the conditions that overcome dehumanization are the same as those that sustain excellence.

Chapter VI

⚕⚕⚕⚕⚕⚕

Student Participation

A study of university governance prepared for the Carnegie Corporation in 1960 declared that to meet future demands upon the university, "administrators and faculty, both, must find improved ways of enlisting all members of the enterprise—trustees, academic and administrative officers, faculty members, librarians, and maintenance employees—in a dynamically improving collaborative effort."[1] Since those

---

[1] John J. Corson, *The Governance of Colleges and Universities,* McGraw-Hill, New York, 1960, p. 3. Students are mentioned on page 196 as an "external group" (along with the alumni, professional associations, and state governments) with which officials have to deal.

halcyon days, the notion of also incorporating students directly into the governing structure and intellectual life of the university has gained some forceful exponents, although there is very little experience to guide those who attempt to specify the details of the students' role.

A national report on university governance issued in 1966[2] declares, for example, that students constitute "an institutional component coordinate in importance with trustees, administrators, and faculty," yet is unable to explain what is meant by this heady assertion because "the changes now occurring in the status of American students have plainly outdistanced the analysis by the educational community." To a Berkeley audience the anticlimactic conclusion of the report exudes a quaint ante-bellum nostalgia:

> The respect of students for their college or university can be enhanced if they are given at least these opportunities: (1) to be listened to in the classroom without fear of institutional reprisal for the substance of their views, (2) freedom to discuss questions of institutional policy and operation, (3) the right to academic due process when charged with serious violations of institutional policy and operation, and (4) the same right to hear speakers of their own choice as is enjoyed by other components of the institution. (p. 14)

It is striking that such stipulations have little to do with the report's purported subject of governance and deal only with the protections afforded students rather than the nature of authority exercised over them or by them.

The experience of the most recent past shows only the urgency of discouraging the resort to tactics of direct confrontation and disruption and of creating institutions that more successfully command the respect and allegiance of students. We are agreed that bold innovations are required that significantly increase the extent of student participation in university affairs, especially in formulating and influencing educational policy. Such participation may help create a com-

---

2 "Statement on Government of Colleges and Universities," issued jointly by the American Association of University Professors, the American Council on Education, and the Association of Governing Boards of Universities and Colleges, 1966, pp. 3–4. (The full statement is reprinted in Minutes, April 10, 1967, pp. 26–33.)

munity that cherishes the intellectual growth and moral autonomy of its members, and can thus exert an honorable claim to their allegiance.

≱ BEYOND THE SLOGANS ⚱

Cries of "student power" or "student participation in decision-making" have become distinguishing features of student demonstrations on campuses throughout the nation and have engendered both intense emotional commitment and great perplexity.[3] Used as slogans, however, such terms as "participation" or "power" evade the difficulty of specifying the kind of participation that is appropriate or the concrete objectives served by extending power to students.

It is possible, for example, to contemplate formal and informal structures in which students directly share the authority for final decisions; or an advisory role for students through joint or separate committees that prepare policy recommendations; or more autonomy for a separate student government; or realization of the opportunity to be heard before decisions are made, as when a proposed decision is announced and comment and reaction are invited before that decision is made final; or mechanisms for increased consultation so that student opinion can be fed into the decision-making machinery; or the indirect influence on policy-making that is a by-product of increased interaction between students and faculty or administration in the educational process. In its application, "participation" may bring about changes that are either innocuous or radical, and the means proposed to effectuate the goal may range from general changes in the structure and process of education to highly particularized political arrangements.

In assessing these possibilities and developing both the justification and the program for increased student participation, we must also resolve such fundamental difficulties as the following:

1. Any mechanical analogy of a university with its very specialized functions to a democratic society is inapposite; yet such attributes

---

[3] Compare, for example, the assertion of the student members of a committee similar to this Commission at the University of Chicago that "many of today's students feel that a university in which they have neither voice nor power is an affront to their personal dignity," with the cartoon in *The New Yorker,* in spring, 1967, depicting a woman holding a telephone in her hand as she called to her husband across the room, "It's our Oliver, calling from Wesleyan. He wants a greater voice in something."

of the democratic spirit as freedom of speech and inquiry, respect for personal autonomy, and the preeminence of the appeal to reason are the essence of a genuine educational climate.

2. The growing pressure to make some concessions to student demands for more "power" is most likely to result in an expedient compromise that gives only token or peripheral "consultation"; yet a tokenism that offers the promise but withholds the substance of participation can only worsen our situation.

3. If students want more "power" in helping to formulate university policies, they must be prepared to engage in slow, time-consuming, laborious collaborative efforts; yet this frustrating process offers neither the excitement nor the seductive appeal and militant posture of direct confrontation that subverts a necessary partnership with administrators and faculty.

4. Significant student contributions to shaping the life of the university depend upon an intense involvement by students in their own education; yet we noted earlier that it is precisely the infrequency of such personal engagement that constitutes our major educational problem, so that the kind of participation we think the university most needs from students is that which will be hardest to elicit in the present setting.

We do not pretend that there are any easy solutions to these problems, nor are we convinced that our specific proposals will ultimately prove to be the most satisfactory answers. Change in the patterns of governance, which depends in large measure on achieving substantial campus decentralization, is inevitably a gradual process to be undertaken in an experimental spirit that expects, recognizes, and corrects mistakes. But we are convinced that major effort along the lines we advance is long overdue and urgently required.

In endorsing major extensions of student participation in university governance, we do not proceed in the naïve belief that such a move will end all campus political crises or provide a cure-all for our educational malaise. We do think, however, that a program of greatly expanded participation and shared authority is a forward step commensurate with the new maturity students have asserted and wish to have acknowledged. Such a program sharply challenges students to act on their newfound concerns and responsibilities and offers some hope of creating a more open, searching, and stable community in which intellectual inquiry and growth may flourish.

❧ RATIONALE FOR STUDENT PARTICIPATION ❦

Developing the rationale for student participation[4] is only confused or inflamed by the two theoretical positions that dominate most current discussion of the subject. The first argues that students have the democratic right to make the decisions that affect their lives. The second, superficially similar, is distinguished by its peculiarly status-bound limitation: students should be given the widest possible latitude to regulate their own affairs.

On inspection, both views prove more rhetorical than helpful. Proponents of the first seldom state either the extent of the proposed participation or the methods for realizing it. The second, or separatist, position appears different and radical but is seen to be trivial in substance as soon as its advocates proceed to specify what they regard as the "affairs" students are to regulate: for example, dormitory rules, making policy for a marching band, or determining the maximum size of political posters on the Plaza. In any case, it is difficult to see this position as anything but innocuous. It is possible to delegate only trivial issues to one segment of the campus because most issues of consequence are community matters to be resolved in the context of shared powers rather than within a system of separate domains and vetoes.

Either view becomes untenable once one realizes that the decisions that most directly affect students are such matters as the content of their courses, the academic workload expected of them, the competence of the professors who teach them, the grades they receive, and the requirements for obtaining a degree. Since not even the most ardent advocates of democratic decision-making by students would decide degree requirements, course grades, or the assignment of teachers to courses on the basis of "one man, one vote," it is apparent that the

---

[4] With the influx of GI's into American colleges after World War II, the question of student participation was raised briefly and led to programs of student participation, at, for example, the University of Minnesota and Dennison University, and to the establishment of the National Students Association. See Hellerich, *op. cit.,* pp. 273–274; Gordon Klopf, *College Student Government,* Harper, New York, 1960. Recently, student leaders at Minnesota have called for a reconsideration of the modes of participating there, charging that the policy "has stagnated at a level acceptable, twenty, fifteen, at best ten years ago." Board of Presidents Statement, *Minnesota Daily,* May 11, 1967.

degree of effect upon students and the commitment to democratic formulas are not persuasive or practicable grounds for justifying the degree or mode of power students should exercise in a given area of university affairs. Any attempt to utilize either of these theories is also complicated by the narrow sense in which they conceive the exercise of power and the process of decision-making. They assume specific jurisdictions and easy tests by which policies can be assigned to the segment of the community or the jurisdiction most affected and ignore the deeper meanings of what might be called citizenship in an educational community.

The heart of the problem of student participation is that a university is not a natural democracy composed of members each of whom is distinguished by an equal claim to power; it is a highly artificial community deliberately arranged so that the educational relationships among the members constitute the starkest kind of contrast to relationships based on power. Properly conceived, it is a fellowship that should prize persuasion based on reason and evidence; that excludes coercion and pressure because they destroy the uncoerced agreement which is at the heart of the search for knowledge; and that relies on trust and tolerance among its members, recognizing that suspicion and dogmatism can destroy the conditions for pursuing and sharing knowledge. Although a university is organized around the principle of freedom of inquiry, it is far from being committed to the belief that any idea, opinion, or theory is as worthy as any other of a place in the university. A university is a society whose life is ordered around the necessity of constantly making qualitative distinctions concerning both ideas and individual achievements, whether of faculty or students. It may perform this qualitative function well or badly, but this is only to question its performance, not the need for judgment itself.

Yet the standards for making such judgments are by no means fixed and unchanging, so that at the heart of university life lies an obligation to examine the criteria by which all judgments are made, to teach people how to seek truth, develop standards, and act upon them. This process rests upon the conviction that members of a university are autonomous men and women able to define and gradually accept a system of values for themselves. Although "participation" or "citizenship" in a university may not take the form of majoritarian democracy, its substance is democratic in the intellectual freedom such citizenship offers all its members, the continuous opportunities it affords for making uncoerced, genuine choices, and the promise it holds for creating persons fully conscious of their intellectual and moral powers and truly free to use them.

It is a mistake born of impatience to jump directly to the question of the forms of participation without considering the deeper values embedded in the concept itself. When we acknowledge the student's membership in the university by asking him to share responsibility for governing it, we express the hope that such participation will enrich the relationships and reinvigorate the intellectual fellowship that have been desiccated in the process of maintaining an efficient system of mass education and training. We hope that such participation and the new relationships it creates will help promote the growth of human communities, and thus transform an environment that has become fragmented, confining, and impersonal into one that is liberating.

In our attempt to explore the range of meanings present in these hopes, we have found it useful analytically to distinguish the educational enterprise of the university from two other quite dissimilar relationships the modern university holds with its students. The first is its role as purveyor of a growing number of welfare services whose major educational relevance is to render the student's life more pleasant or economical or efficient, for example, student housing, employment, and recreation, or placement, health, and food services. Second, as a community of persons dedicated to the achievement of specified ends within a finite geographical domain, the university regulates the conduct of its members within terms that, hopefully, allow each individual the maximum freedom consistent with that community's objectives and the freedom of its other members.

We believe that this classification of distinct areas of policy-formulation opens up useful avenues for understanding the arguments for allowing students to enter areas of decision-making from which they have been largely excluded in the past. In all cases we are most concerned with the relationship between modes of decision-making and the achievement of the university's ultimate educational goals, but it is also necessary to consider the extent to which policy decisions in each area should turn upon questions of specialized, professional expertise.

✑ EDUCATIONAL POLICY-MAKING ✐

The question of the propriety of student participation in the shaping of educational policy gave us much difficulty. We were immediately faced with the realization that in this area professional judgment is admittedly critical, and that by comparison with faculty and administrators, students are substantially disadvantaged in experience, professional judgment, and long-term responsibility to the institution. It was also argued, however, that increased participation would not retard but could improve the quality of policy decisions, especially by promoting more effective self-evaluation of the program of education and by providing systematic "feedback" of information and reaction from those affected by a decision to those with the responsibility of making it. Such a development, it was also contended, would generate an increased acceptance of the legitimacy of governing authority by promoting greater confidence in the processes and institutions through which decisions are reached.

We by no means minimize the possibility that increased student involvement will produce worthwhile innovations and better decisions. Nor do we discount the potentiality of such participation as a partial corrective for a major deficiency in American university practice: the failure to evaluate adequately and systematically its own educational performance. We do not, however, regard these considerations as the major rationale for student participation. Incorporating students into academic policy-making is essential if today's large university is to create an environment that more successfully promotes the realization of its still unfilled educational ideals. The preeminent argument for achieving greater student participation in the shaping of educational policy thus springs from our long-range educational ambitions and our apprehension about the wide gap presently separating our educational performance from the desirable goal of deeply involving students in the direction of their education.

The central educational problem for this campus stems from the alienation, intellectual somnambulance and noninvolvement, or narrowly instrumental goals which, singly or in combination, characterize far too many students.[5] Earlier we contrasted with this torpor the

---

[5] This is not a new problem for the university. The theme of the

intense involvement of many students in activities outside the normal routine of the university, which revealed a potential untouched by our teaching. In endeavors such as the Free Speech Movement, civil rights activities, or in urban ghetto tutoring, students of apparently ordinary quality have transcended their own self-interest, examined their society from entirely new perspectives, and proved capable far beyond their presumed capacity. We do not claim that such engagement of mind and spirit does not occur within university walls; there are countless instances in which individual students realize by their own growth the goal of the university. Nor do we believe that the forms of day-to-day engagement should carry the emotional intensity and heroic aura so manifest in times of crisis. But as we contemplate the relative infrequency of those instances in which personal intellectual liberation contributes to our community life, we echo the lines of T. S. Eliot: "Ridiculous the waste sad time/Stretching before and after."[6]

We cannot offer a simple prescription for drawing out more untapped creativity and latent intellectual energy and incorporating it into the exploration and persuasion that mark the exacting life of the mind and the university. We do think, however, that modifications in educational methods, expansion of the students' share of responsibility for policy-making, and the development of new institutions for governance are relevant in gaining solutions for this problem. Philip Jacob has suggested the kind of correlation we have in mind when, in talking about "growth of a student's values," he notes that this process can come about only if the college:[7]

Tenth All-University Faculty Conference in 1955 was "The University of California Student, 1945–1965," and the extremely interesting report of the Study Committee No. 2 on "Motivation of Students" discussed "ways and means of motivating all students in the direction of the zeal for knowledge and intellectual fire that a university should kindle." Its tone was disconcertingly similar to ours: "Nascent idealism and corrosive cynicism are, however, the minor extremes of a process in which little or nothing happens at all, that is, within the largest section of the undergraduate body which moves through its four years, in cheer or in apathy, as the case may be, untroubled and unmoved, often unheard and always unremembered." See Proceedings of the U.C. Tenth All-University Faculty Conference, Davis Campus, 1955.

[6] "Burnt Norton," *Four Quartets*. New York: Harcourt, Brace, 1943, p. 8.

[7] Margaret L. Habein, editor, *Spotlight on the College Student*, American Council on Education, Washington, D.C., 1959, p. 5.

. . . penetrates the core of his life and confronts him with fresh
and often disturbing implications, which are different from those
which he and his society have taken for granted. This can hardly
occur as a by-product of a curricular assembly line. It requires a
highly personal relationship between the college community and
the individual student—a relationship that is warm and consid-
erate, but at the same time mutually aggravating.

This seems to us the essence of the educational climate we require: an
environment that values the student as an individual and demonstrates
this respect by soliciting his participation in significant policy-making
for the community, that thrives on the discomforting intellectual challenges that encourage the search for answers to questions previously
unasked.

Such intellectual liberation and growth should not be equated
with life adjustment or release from doubt and uncertainty. Rather,
it rests upon unremitting hard work, the imposition of the highest
standards of excellence upon oneself, the painful questioning of values
that the unexamined life takes for granted, and the willingness to expose oneself to public criticism. From the possible loneliness, probable
frustration, and certain abrasiveness of such a regimen, an intellectual
community can offer no escape. It can, however, accept the student as
a member of that community of seekers and permit him to share fully
its challenges, discouragements, complexities, and rewards. Just as students must share with scholars the burdens and tensions of the intellectual life, so should they also share the genuinely difficult responsibility
for posing sharp questions about the success and direction of policies
and for making major decisions for their community.

Our goal is the creation of a community in which students educate themselves and attain intellectual autonomy, not an institution
that gives an education (including a certificate of completion and a
transcript that may only be viewed under glass in the presence of a
clerk)[8] to all those who put together the jigsaw puzzle of course units,
breadth requirements, grade points, and an examination in American
History and Institutions. Such a community can only be inspired and
sustained in a framework of genuine freedom that asks the student
to make choices more significant than the selection of the particular
course he takes to fulfill his natural science requirement. Students
should share the responsibility for developing innovations in the cur-

[8] At Window 4 in Sproul Hall.

riculum, for evaluating the success of the entire program, and, indeed, for devising the indices most appropriate for measuring and assessing a student's individual growth. Learning should not be regarded as an isolated classroom experience, but rather as a sustained, continuous public experience. Hopefully, so communal a venture would blur the lines of authority between dependent students and dominant professors.[9] Intellectual exploration would become a common experience of developing understanding and would include sharing all the pain and triumph of intellectual creativity, instead of concealing that process and displaying to the student only the finely distilled result.

⫸ CONDUCT AND WELFARE SERVICES ⫷

The distinction between "strictly" educational policy and the university's roles as purveyor of student welfare services and regulator of student conduct is not a rigid one. The latter activities expedite and strengthen classroom activities; but as important determinants of the environment in which formal academic work takes place, they also form part of a continuum of intellectual operations in which students should share. By asking students to join in reflection about the character and quality of life in the university, we can make an important contribution to the communal life and thereby to the resources and self-awareness students bring to the process of acquiring knowledge.

The intellectual and communal dimensions of those activities tend to be neglected in present arrangements for planning and executing them. In comparison with the work of shaping the curriculum or establishing courses and their content, the tasks of providing the students' noneducational needs or governing their nonacademic conduct arouse little interest among the faculty. Although some faculty members serve in an advisory capacity to the Chancellor on various administrative committees concerned with discipline or services, the Academic Senate at Berkeley has never much concerned itself with non-

[9] Cf. Michel Loeve: "The teacher ought to come down from the podium, shed his magisterial aloofness, and expose himself to the buffetings of the group he joins. The students must do, the teacher must help and catalyze, but never command." *Campus Report,* November 22, 1967. See also Edgar Z. Friedenberg, "A Polite Encounter Between the Generations," *New York Times Magazine,* January 16, 1966, p. 10.

educational services, and its responsibility for the enforcement of student discipline was terminated at its own option in 1921. Authority over student conduct and welfare is now exercised by a panoply of deans and administrative officers. In the professional, bureaucratized administration of "student personnel services,"[10] such officers presume to exercise authority over students in a relationship similar to the one between students and faculty. But the relationships are fundamentally different, and the unthinking transfer of authority derived from one to serve the needs of the other is the source of much misunderstanding and friction.

When students bow to the qualitative judgments of their instructors, or when untenured teachers defer to the judgment of their older colleagues, the premise that induces and justifies such submission is a scholarly one that rests on the subject-matter expertise of the evaluator. Status in the academic community is earned by the scholar's mastery of his subject and his skill and originality in the application of his knowledge. Of necessity, the scope of any particular scholar's mastery is limited and the range of his authority, which is defined by his expertise, is correspondingly narrow. Such natural authority does not extend beyond the limits of the scholar's specialty. When we admire a chemist for his common sense or his sense of responsibility or his compassion or his value judgments, the deference we pay him for such attributes has nothing to do with his mastery of chemistry; they would as likely appear in a farmer or housewife as in an academician. Although the chemist's academic prestige may be transferred to other causes and concerns, that prestige is not the basis for a claim to exercise governing authority in such matters.

We think students today distinguish, intuitively at least, between the natural authority which stems from scholarship and the misuse of that authority which stems from status. One cannot expect the academic status of administrators or the claims of academic or administrative expertise to provide legitimacy for decisions in such areas as lock-out hours for a dormitory, the penalty for stealing a book from the library, or the size of a political poster allowed to be displayed on a plaza or bulletin board.

[10] See E. C. Williamson, *Student Personnel Services in Colleges and Universities,* McGraw-Hill, New York, 1961, especially Chapters 1–4, for a discussion of the scope of this field and its "professionalization" over the past forty years.

If the authority derived from academic or intellectual relationships cannot be used to justify decisions imposed upon students in these auxiliary areas, the only other possible source of moral authority[11] stems from the fact that students are younger than faculty members and deans, and that administrators may therefore stand *in loco parentis* for these not-quite-adults whose capacity for responsible judgment is not fully developed. We believe that such paternalism is anachronistic and should be forthrightly disavowed. Almost half of our students are twenty-one or over; the university registers more students who are in their thirties than students who are eighteen or younger; almost one quarter of our students are married.[12] Had our students not gone to college, many more of them would presumably be married,[13] and the vast majority would be living apart from their parents in separate households or perhaps in Vietnam. We find it strange that college students as a class are treated as if they require a longer period of maturation in a protected environment than do nonstudents of the same age.

A Canadian commission has declared that "University students ask to be treated as adults, and it is fitting and fortunate that this should be so."[14] We agree with this statement and we believe there are compelling reasons to act upon it, reasons that far outweigh the risk that students will act improvidently or that the university will thereby alienate that minority of parents who wish it to perpetuate their own supervisory role. The university at its best challenges the student to impose upon himself the rigorous self-discipline his own self-education requires. It is incongruous to set him this challenge and

---

[11] Some might see a possible source of authority in the chain of command extending from the Board of Regents to the President to the several Chancellors to campus officials. Our arguments against resting the exercise of coercive authority in a university community on the brittle and narrow base of a legal hierarchy are made throughout this report, but see especially page 29.

[12] Figures on student age are not reported in the university's annual Statistical Summary of Students. But "A Ten-Year Survey of Certain Demographic Characteristics of the Student Population" was made in 1963 by the Office of the Registrar which showed that approximately 35 per cent of undergraduates and virtually all of the graduate students were twenty-one or over (Table 19). A more recent Registrar's Office study of undergraduate women shows a higher percentage over twenty-one. Figures on married students are compiled by the Housing Service in its quarterly Survey of Residence.

[13] The marriage age for those not attending college is significantly lower.

[14] Report of the Royal Commission of Enquiry on Education in the Province of Quebec, vol. 2, par. 360 (b).

at the same time demean him by a regulation that if a member of the opposite sex is in his room, his door shall be left open a prescribed number of inches. If we are asking the student to question, to substitute reason for habit or prejudice in the determination of how he is to use his life, then it seems unduly suspicious and aggravating to subject him to restrictions on either his private or political life more onerous than those applicable to his peers who are not in college.

It is hard to avoid the conclusion that, at present, the regulation of student conduct and the direction of welfare services take place in a vacuum in which such matters are considered as isolated questions involving administrative expertise or law enforcement and in which no one manifests concern for the quality of the entire environment or its impact on learning. The degree of deference owed by laymen to experts is a perplexing and disturbing question in most areas of modern life. In the university context, at least, we believe that one significant way of restoring the moral and intellectual concern for the quality of public life is to ask the entire community to share the responsibility for shaping standards of conduct and the character of services to be provided.

We do not believe the policy decisions that have to be made in the performance of these regulatory and service tasks should be confined to those who possess a special form of managerial expertise.[15] Both faculty members and students are likely to be deficient in such professional skills as the designing and financing of new buildings, or the maintenance of fiscal solvency in the operation of stores, restaurants, or housing services; but such management skills are not the essence of responsible policy formulation.

If there is to be a store in a Student Union building, for example, experienced managers can relate alternative methods of operation to expectations of profit or loss, or can advise how maximum profits can be obtained. They are at no advantage over laymen, however, in determining to what extent profits should be a major criterion in a university store in an urban setting, or whether items directly rele-

---

[15] Certainly there is no clear proof that those who have had responsibility for planning much of the existing architecture, for example, have possessed great expertise in educational matters. See Sim Van der Ryn and Murray Silverstein, *Dorms at Berkeley, an Environmental Analysis,* Center for Planning and Development Research, University of California, Berkeley, 1967; and Douglas Lummis, "Barrows Hall," *Steps: Journal of the Free University of Berkeley,* No. 2, 1967, p. 72.

vant to intellectual interests are to be carried even at a loss, or whether the profits derived from the promotion and sale of gadgets or department store merchandise are worth the resulting pollution of the atmosphere an intellectual community might wish to engender in its store. In such matters it will fall to the administration to provide the necessary experts, facts, and training so that policies appropriate to a university can be intelligently formulated and executed. However, policy formulation itself requires above all the reconciliation of conflicting values, a process in which students can cooperate as equals with professors or administrators.

The analogy to a democratic polity is thus more compelling (although not entirely so) in these auxiliary areas than in strictly academic ones. The university is the major community affiliation of students during the years they are here. The campus (and its immediate geographical periphery) is the center of their professional and social lives; it is where they eat, sleep, study, argue, or organize. While the living quarters of the majority are not university-owned, it is the campus, not Berkeley, Oakland, or San Francisco as municipalities, around which their lives are oriented. This geographical concentration and these campus-centered interests have less importance for faculty members and administrative personnel, who are usually rooted in the surrounding communities where they have their homes and are involved in many nonuniversity activities and social relationships.

It is therefore both natural and appropriate that when students want to have meetings, circulate petitions, raise money, or organize activities, they should turn to campus facilities, just as citizens of other communities use its public parks, sidewalks, schools, churches, or clubs for similar communal purposes. It is also natural and appropriate that students, like members of any community, should want to be actively involved in the operation of its services and the making and administration of the rules by which the institution governs itself.

This is not to say that students should acquire exclusive control over rule-making, rule enforcement, and the provision of auxiliary services. These activities are conditioned by their university context. Rules are required to preserve the integrity of an educational community in which every member has a stake. Similarly, it is not enough that health and employment services function as they might in an ordinary community setting; as a part of the university, faculty members share a concern that such activities stimulate rather than hinder the maintenance of an environment that is centered upon intellectual inquiry. Once again, a recognition of inherent democratic values does not lead to strictly majoritarian forms for realizing them. Procedures must be developed that promote shared responsibility and fully elicit the intellectual and moral concerns of both students and faculty members. Just as we seek the growth of intellectual autonomy, so do we seek to make the community life genuinely self-governing.

≥ *STUDENT TRANSIENCE AND APATHY* ≤

To round out our consideration of the rationale for student participation, it will be useful at this point to examine two of the arguments most frequently advanced against the concept. The first argues that student participation is unwise since the transient status of students renders them less likely to act responsibly. The second argues that student participation is unnecessary since most students care nothing about these matters and are likely to be apathetic about taking advantage of opportunities to participate.

Experience in the general educational functions of the university, as distinguished from expert knowledge in a particular academic field, often provides valuable direction and continuity in policy-making. It is self-evident that the permanent faculty, whose appointments are "continuous in tenure," have more advantages in this respect than students. Transient students are said to have less interest in university affairs because one who spends time in an institution knowing he is going to leave is more likely to regard problems as inconveniences and will not be concerned to change them. It is also assumed that such interests as students do have will tend to overemphasize short-term, immediate issues and that because they will not have to live with their mistakes, they will be less accountable for what they do. In short, the students' sense of responsibility is believed to be impaired because they are transients.

Obviously, there is no absolute contrast in this regard between students and faculty. Academicians are not exempt from the mobility that increasingly characterizes our society. Nor is faculty loyalty to the long-run interests of the institution undivided, for it competes with one's standing in a discipline, and relationships with professional colleagues cut across institutional lines. If a faculty member's own professional interests will be advanced by a move to another institution, such a consideration will often take precedence over any university loyalty.

However the balance may fall in comparing these respective qualifications of undivided loyalty, it seems to us unnecessary to resolve the validity of the arguments against student participation that are deduced from the student's transitory status. While this argument would have some merit if the wholesale delegation of power over educational policy to the student body were at stake, we find it much less appropriate when the matter under consideration is simply the granting of opportunities to concerned students to assume an appropriate share in policy-formulation, particularly since many of our students have indeed demonstrated a strong commitment to the future quality of this institution.

Moreover, while students may lack the experience of professors, many of them are capable of injecting a freshness of approach, based on youth and freedom from entrenched routines, that should serve as a healthy counterweight to the inevitable, and sometimes appropriate, conservatism of faculty institutions. We should not forget that the failure of the university's existing institutions to promote badly needed changes in educational policy and other areas has occurred in a context devoid of significant student participation. A proper balance between the freshness and sense of urgency of students and the experience and traditionalism of faculty members[16] may well turn out to be the formula that ventilates what is stagnant in the existing pattern.

With respect to the argument that student disinterest makes their participation unnecessary, we must grant that student apathy does present a barrier on which a number of contemplated innovations have already foundered. This lack of concern is a symptom of our most fundamental problems. The many students who feel, often with justification, that the university has treated them with indifference are likely to respond in kind. The student who views his education in instrumental terms as a series of steps to be surmounted as prerequisites to a career is more likely to perceive problems connected with that process, even those directly affecting him, as temporary obstacles that are easier to endure than to try to modify. Nor can one expect the student who has little or no interest in his own education to be concerned about general educational policy. We have already advanced

[16] See Christopher Jencks, "A New Breed of B.A.'s," *New Republic,* October 23, 1965, p. 17.

our view that the noninvolvement of so many students and their indifference to intellectual life is our most severe educational problem. Thus our dilemma: participation is a necessary spark for educational reinvigoration, but meaningful participation can hardly take place without such reinvigoration.

To these uniquely university problems must be added considerations common to any effort to induce rank-and-file participation in a large organization. Participants must be presented with genuine problems, and the process of participation must be one in which there can be a realistic expectation that views will be taken seriously enough to affect the decisions made. Obviously this will be a condition far easier to realize at local than at campus-wide levels.

Equally important is the opportunity for direct participation in the decision-making bodies themselves. Membership on an omnibus student-faculty relations committee is, at best, participation by indirection and leaves student participants uncertain as to how fairly or persuasively, if at all, their views will be transmitted to some higher authority.

Although no one doubts that student apathy is a widespread phenomenon, we think it is unwise to rely exclusively upon quantitative measures to assess its growth or decline. It may be unlikely that great numbers of a department's students and faculty members will attend an ad hoc meeting or assume active roles on a policy committee, but we do not believe that the indifference of a majority should serve as an excuse for excluding from the decision-making process the ideas and talents of those who are civic-minded enough to want to offer them. We believe that the change in attitude necessary to admit even a handful of students to a departmental committee has ramifications for the intellectual life of the university that go far beyond the effect of participation on those students who actually become active in the process.

While there are no easy ways out of our dilemma, we believe that what is most significant about apathy is the interpretation made of it. When the Academic Senate's Committee on Teaching last spring circulated questionnaires for student evaluation of faculty teaching, for example, it was announced after the returns were in that the experiment was a failure and would probably not be repeated because only 20 per cent of the students returned the forms. Although such a poor return is understandably disappointing, we think it was predictable in view of the kinds of difficulties we have discussed, and we believe that abandonment of the venture disregards a primary rationale for participation. Transmitting better information to faculty members that might result in better teaching is, of course, a significant motivation for such a questionnaire; but even more important, in our opinion, is the contribution that the institutionalization of such an evaluation would make in improving student confidence in our educational process. Knowledge that the opportunity to express oneself existed, and that student opinion was regarded as sufficiently important to be solicited, are not inconsequential features in building such confidence. One might draw a parallel with the Academic Senate at which attendance is usually correspondingly low and which at times has been unable to muster a quorum to consider the recommendations of the Report of the Select Committee on Education. One would hardly draw from this the conclusion that the tradition of faculty participation in governance should be discontinued.

Thus, rather than assuming that apathy requires dropping a worthwhile endeavor, one has to ask the much harder questions: To what extent is apathy the central problem, and to the extent that it is, what can be done to overcome it? A poor response to one method should not lead to the outright rejection of the enterprise. To use again the example of the course evaluation questionnaire, the Committee on Teaching might have considered methods other than distributing one centrally designed questionnaire in registration packets, and it might have reevaluated the form of the questionnaire. In designing and evaluating its project, the Committee might have consulted with students, through the ASUC's Student Education and Faculty Relations (SERF) Board, for example.

Instead of using apathy as an excuse to avoid our problem, we should recognize its pervasiveness, and then draw the appropriate conclusions:

1. It will be very difficult to devise methods for getting those students who *are* concerned onto appropriate committees.

2. Only long-term evaluation of the results of participatory experiments will have much significance, for no matter what selection methods are devised there will be repeated instances in which student committees or the students placed in joint committee roles will be uninterested, or awed into silence, or truant, or ignorantly bellicose. (Similarly, there will be instances in which students will find their faculty

counterparts uninterested, or overawed into silence, or truant, or obdurately complacent.)

3. The only course of action that holds out some hope of mitigating these problems is to open up genuine channels for students, to encourage development of student skills, and to persevere with patience when the results do not measure up to expectations. Self-government has never been justified on grounds of its superior efficiency or because it is foolproof.

PART THREE

THE FIRST STEPS

Chapter VII

※※※※※※

Faculty and Administration: New Relationships and Structures

The proposals that follow in this and ensuing chapters are not complete answers for the problems we have discussed, but instead represent essential beginnings in what will necessarily be a lengthy effort to achieve the basic redirection proposed.

The role of the Chancellor's office is obviously critical to this endeavor. A refocusing of its authority would be a major factor in creating a process of governance that would command the confidence of the community and would enable it to engage in debate and disagreement without jeopardizing the very existence of the institution. The authority of the office is constantly being eroded by what has appeared, to many, to be its major role: rule enforcement and representation of the "interests" of administrative efficiency and law and order (see page 28). We believe the future effectiveness of the office depends upon its ability to exercise leadership in the broadest sense, as spokesman for the whole community. This does not imply that the role of the Chancellor be reduced to that of titular monarch. It does, however, require that the Chancellor attain a certain kind of "distance" that is the necessary condition for evoking the constructive energy and idealism of the entire campus and directing it toward the common purposes of learning and education.

It is likewise clear that the faculty role in governance requires major restructuring if our basic premises are accepted. To develop an effective partnership in university governance, to help unify the campus in the face of attacks on university autonomy, to meet the necessity for reorganization incident to decentralization, and to respond creatively to the challenges and opportunities of student participation will require the highest kind of statesmanship.

ADMINISTRATION AND ACADEMIC SENATE

Some of the most important implications of the basic policy directions we have advanced relate to the Chancellor's relationships with the Academic Senate. At present, the Chancellor's formal, public contacts with the Senate are established through speeches that survey the state of the campus in a broad way or are directed to some immediate crisis. The response of the faculty tends to be one of frustration. The information conveyed by the Chancellor is usually fairly general, and unavoidably so, and yet no tradition of questioning has developed. Any system of questioning is considered undesirable if it leaves the Chancellor weakened and vulnerable. If the arrangements of the Senate, however, are not (and should not be) intended to topple the Chancellor, it is equally important that the forms of communication chosen by the Chancellor not force the Senate into the position of having to choose between helpless acquiescence and barren opposition.

The practice of asking the Senate for a vote of confidence originated in the crises of 1964–65, but the practice is dangerous and undesirable. It places the Senate in the position of being unable to consider alternatives the Chancellor opposes and to which, in some undefined way, he has committed his fate. To our knowledge, no one has ever answered the question of what would follow if and when the Chancellor were refused a vote of confidence. For its part, the Senate does not need the opportunity of expressing confidence in the Chancellor—its confidence should be taken for granted—it needs to be presented with clear policy proposals to which it can respond. This will encourage full exploration of policy alternatives without conveying any implication of lack of confidence. The speeches of the Chancellor should be framed to elicit such constructive discussion. At the same time it is important that the Chancellor's major assistants assume much of the burden of defending policies and responding to questions falling within their special purviews. This procedure would achieve two objectives: it would encourage forthright debate, yet it would protect the "distance" and comprehensive perspective that we regard as the essence of the Chancellor's leadership.

Budgetary policy is a vital area which, more than any other, deserves special attention in creating new arrangements for promoting informed discussion. The budget represents a translation of basic campus policies into concrete form. It is the method for assigning priorities and plotting the major directions of campus development. Despite the budget's crucial importance, it is a subject about which ignorance and misinformation exist in equal proportion among most members of the university. In the absence of accurate information and some grasp of the overall priorities, it is impossible to have intelligent discussion on matters such as the relative amount of resources being devoted to undergraduate instruction in general and to lower division instruction in particular, or to such areas of concern as research or construction.

A relatively simple device for promoting intelligent discussion would be to reserve a specific set of dates on the Academic Senate's calendar for the sole purpose of discussing the budget. On these occasions members of the Chancellor's staff would be prepared to explain and defend the policy decisions reflected in the proposed budget. The Senate's role should be to concentrate on the general policies and preferences and their implications, avoiding the temptation to divert itself by discussion of specific items and subheadings. Such discussions would enable the administration to allay such misconceptions as exist and to make clear what specific constraints are imposed by budgetary and fiscal decisions taken at the statewide level. To raise the level of this debate and to sharpen its focus, we also recommend that the proposed new Committee on Academic Planning, which is charged to consider budget policy,[1] submit in advance an independent analysis of the budget, stressing in particular the educational implications of the priorities and allocations proposed.

❧ ADMINISTRATION AND FACULTY COMMITTEES ❧

The primary agency for the faculty's participation in governance must come from a committee system through which it can maintain an effective working relationship with the Chancellor. At present this function is carried out through a dual system of "administrative committees" appointed by and reporting to the Chancellor and committees appointed by and reporting to the Academic Senate.[2] Wholly aside from any questions about duplication of effort or working at cross-purposes, we believe that such duality is wrong in principle.

In formulating policy proposals the Chancellor will presumably wish to solicit advice from many sources, including individuals in whom he has particular confidence. These will naturally include members of the faculty, but when they are consulted in this fashion their role should only be an individual one. Such informal consultation must be carefully distinguished from the method by which the Chancellor goes about consulting "the faculty" or establishing committees involving "faculty" representation. We agree with the Canadian Commission on University Government that in such situations he "must firmly resist the temptation to appoint the committee members"[3] or select the advisers himself. The Academic Senate has developed safeguards to ensure the representativeness and responsibility of its committees, including their appointment by an elected Committee on Committees and their duty of reporting to the Senate. We believe strongly that this

---

[1] Minutes, December 4, 1967, p. 6.

[2] There has been increasing reliance in the appointment of administrative committees on nominations from the Senate's Committee on Committees, which directly appoints all Academic Senate Committees. Under present practice the Committee on Committees submits a slate of two names to the Chancellor for each vacancy on an administrative committee.

[3] *University Government in Canada: Report of a Commission Sponsored by the Canadian Association of University Teachers and the Association of Universities and Colleges of Canada,* University of Toronto Press, Toronto, 1966, pp. 42–43.

should be the exclusive method of selection where advice representative of "the faculty" is desired.

Closely related to this problem is the need for a more definite method whereby the Chancellor can obtain an authoritative statement of the Senate's position on a policy issue. We believe that whenever a problem arises on which he wishes to obtain "faculty" advice that he should direct his request exclusively to the Senate Policy Committee.[4] The Policy Committee in turn can channel the request to the appropriate existing committee, or arrange for the appointment of an ad hoc committee, or consult directly with the Chancellor. The Senate, and only the Senate, should determine which of its committees has jurisdiction over a particular subject. The present practice is susceptible of great abuse, a point forcefully illustrated a few years ago at the state-wide level by the manner in which the Academic Senate was consulted when the quarter system was instituted.[5]

COMMUNICATION IN TIMES OF CRISIS

A major weakness in our system of governance has become evident during periods of acute crisis. At such times informal, unplanned consultation between members of the administration, faculty, and students is inadequate, and in the absence of defined responsibility in any

[4] The Senate Policy Committee has gradually evolved into the main center of faculty policy formulation and has established itself as the most important organ of the Senate. Of course the Senate may, if it wishes, delegate this function to another committee; the point of our recommendation is the importance of locating the responsibility explicitly.

[5] See *University Bulletin,* March 8, 1965, pp. 149–177, which collects all relevant documents surrounding this controversy. This history indicates that the critical decision to go to year-round operation was approved in principle by the Regents on February 17, 1961, before there had been any significant faculty consultation or discussion; thus the only issue debated at length was the choice between a quarter system or some variant of the trimester system. On this issue so many different committees were asked to comment and so many votes, usually not on comparable questions, were taken that the result was a mass of conflicting evidence from which almost any opinion could be supported. The flavor of the consultation is perhaps best illustrated by a letter in June 1963 from the Chancellor at Santa Barbara to President Kerr in support of the quarter system. The letter ends by noting that he had talked with various officers of the Senate's Santa Barbara Division, and adds: "None agrees with me, although all seem now to be a little tired of all the talk and probably would go along without much fuss." *Ibid.,* p. 170.

one agency, a maze of intermediary bodies and self-appointed groups have been frenetically active in seeking to press their views on the Chancellor and his staff. Some of the recommendations advanced later in this report should ameliorate some of this confusion, especially our proposals for emergency rule-making procedures (Sec. 308, Basic Regulations) and for emergency court hearings for testing allegedly invalid rules (Sec. 603, Basic Regulations). Nonetheless, there remains an important need for a body that has the responsibility of consulting with the administration in the handling of emergencies and that in turn would be the focus for establishing and conveying, as authoritatively as the circumstances would permit, campus opinion regarding the alternative decisions available.

It is probably impossible on this campus to define beforehand what form future emergencies might take. What we have in mind is a situation characterized by acute time pressure, the threat of imminent disruption of normal functions, or the intrusion of outside agencies into campus affairs. This kind of situation often results in a breakdown of communications at the very time when pooling reliable information is of critical importance. Therefore, we recommend the creation of a new agency that might be called the Emergency Advisory Committee.

We stress the importance of not using such an agency carelessly or needlessly to supersede normal processes. In particular, if the proposals we advance in Chapter Ten for the Rules Committee and for the creation of a Campus Review Court are adopted, many near-crisis problems can be handled by the specific emergency procedures those agencies will have at their disposal. We see the Emergency Advisory Committee functioning only when an emergency prevents the use of established procedures for the resolution of problems. We propose that either the Chancellor or any two members of the committee have authority to convene a meeting. The whole committee, in consultation with the Chancellor, would then determine whether to act itself as an advisory and fact-gathering agency, or whether sufficient time existed to route the problem to other established agencies.

The constitution of the committee should receive careful attention from all appropriate campus segments. Our suggestions for its membership are: (a) from the faculty: the chairmen of the Academic Senate, the Senate Policy Committee, the Committee on Academic Freedom, the Committee on Committees, and the cochairman of the proposed Rules Committee; (b) from the student body: the President and Vice-President of the student body, the chairman of the proposed student Committee on Academic Freedom, and the cochairman of the proposed Rules Committee; (c) from other groups of the campus community, a representative of the Teaching Assistants and a representative of the academic research staff.[6]

REFORM OF THE SENATE

We examined the persistent criticism of the Senate's existing campus-wide committee system and alluded to the numerous proposals for the reorganization of the Berkeley Division and for strengthening the position of this central organization (pages 29–35). A number of concrete recommendations were submitted to the Policy Committee by a subcommittee in the fall of 1966; a few have already been acted upon by the Senate, and presumably the study is continuing. We shall support some of these proposals below and add further suggestions along the same lines. Despite this, however, the Commission regards the direction of these proposals with some ambivalence.

As long as the campus is dominated by the statewide system and as long as the Regents prove ineffectual in protecting the freedom and integrity of the university, a powerful central Senate appears to be an essential instrument for the defense of the campus. Our uncertainty stems from the inconsistency of this stance with the imperative necessity for campus decentralization. It may even be argued that the effect of streamlining and strengthening the Senate will be to exacerbate many of the evils of the present arrangement. In the face of widespread apathy toward the Senate, it seems impossible substantially to improve the present method of selecting committees or to devise methods to tap the wide diversity of outlooks and abilities possessed by the faculty. Instead, strengthening the influence of the present committee system is likely to reinforce the present tendencies toward oligarchy and bureaucracy. The inherent conservatism of the system will be perpetuated and strengthened, and the opportunities for participation will

[6] There is no present method for selection of the last two representatives by the groups concerned. Nonetheless we think it important to emphasize the need for such representation, and presumably devising such methods would be part of the study suggested by the Senate Policy Committee and discussed on pp. 42–43. See also our proposed Commission on Decentralization, p. 72, where this same problem would arise.

become more constricted. A surrogate system may develop in which most of the faculty abandons all pretense of real involvement, leaving to a self-perpetuating group the task of speaking and acting for the whole faculty in the name of "self-government." Alternatively, the recently defeated proposal to delegate much of the Senate's deliberative function to a small representative assembly whose members would be elected by departments might have had a comparable effect. While the proposal was not without merit, one major weakness was that its elective procedure would probably have resulted in screening out diversity and in representing a narrow range of orthodox faculty viewpoints.

If the faculty is to achieve genuine participation in governance as distinguished from more effective faculty power, it must organize itself in ways that promote wider participation, more informed deliberation, and closer integration with other elements of the campus. These ends cannot be achieved by the reform of Senate committees or Senate procedures alone. They require not an improved and more powerful central forum for the expression of faculty interest, but a multiplication of forums at lower levels. We foresee senates at the level of colleges, schools, and small clusters of departments where issues are more comprehensible, more manageable, and more likely to evoke spontaneous participation. These local senates would offer the opportunity for more directly involving students in the decisions and deliberations. They could also bring about natural forms of cooperation with administrative officers, with the result that decentralized senates would reinforce decentralized administration.

Senate reform should follow the dual track implied above: simultaneously strengthening the existing structure to meet the immediate demands placed upon it, and pursuing methods of decentralization, to strengthen the faculty role in the departments, schools, and colleges. Neither the detailed nature of campus-wide reforms nor the precise shape of the local senates we envisage are matters in which this Commission has any special competence. The development of local forums, in particular, would have to be determined in the light of the special needs of the units involved. We therefore confine ourselves to matters immediately related to our charge and some suggested methods by which these general ends might best be achieved.

It should be noted that the Senate has not yet undertaken reforms commensurate with the diagnoses advanced by the Senate Policy Committee in several of its annual State of the Campus messages. Each of these messages has stressed the inadequacies of the present system, particularly at the committee level, and has stated a high priority for "a reorganization plan for the Berkeley Senate."[7] Nor does there appear to have been much progress to date of a planned study urged in 1965 of "how the 101 departmental faculty governments are organized . . . ,"[8] an undertaking of particular relevance to decentralization of governance. Similarly, plans for preparation of "a policy statement on the extent and form of campus autonomy best suited to the long-term needs of the Berkeley campus," launched with great emphasis in the first State of the Campus Message on October 11, 1965 and reemphasized by subsequent Policy Committees, have not advanced very far.

It may be time, therefore, to reassess the role of the Policy Committee and what can reasonably be expected of it on a campus periodically beset by crisis. If the Policy Committee is to continue as the major voice of the Senate in current affairs, to assume the channeling role vis-à-vis the Chancellor that we recommend, and to carry out the short-term planning and integrating functions with which it is charged, it cannot without assistance assume the additional burden of long-range planning. Yet such long-range studies as the following are most urgently needed:

how best to achieve campus autonomy, including local Senate autonomy;

the reorganization of campus-wide faculty government;

the decentralization of faculty governance, defining a relationship that strengthens and encourages local faculty autonomy;

how best to define and establish an appropriate governance role for teaching assistants, lecturers, researchers, and library personnel.

We hope that the Senate, when it again reaffirms the importance of the first two of these studies (as it presumably will), and if it also de-

[7] As we have already noted, the principal progress so far on these matters was a report presented to the Policy Committee on November 20, 1966 by its special subcommittee on Senate Government. This report was presented to the Senate in summary form the following March in the State of the Campus Message, but most of its recommendations have not been brought up for action.

[8] Minutes, October 11, 1965, p. 18.

cides to study the last two (as we hope it will), will couple these decisions with a realistic plan for their prompt execution.

Until long-range planning that incorporates decentralization plans for the Senate has been completed, it seems premature to reintroduce the proposal for a Representative Assembly that was narrowly defeated in a Senate vote in spring 1967. In addition to the doubts expressed above, we question the necessity of such a plan if the central Senate's major function is limited to campus-wide problems of major policy significance. The subcommittee that developed this recommendation did not concern itself with decentralization or the important problems of establishing a balance between a central Senate and the college and departmental faculties.

It is difficult at this point to project the most appropriate form of a central Senate once substantial decentralization of authority has taken place. If the concept of community governance were to be carried over to the campus-wide level, it is possible to contemplate, at least in theory, that the university of the future might find its apex of governance in something like the recently proposed Berkeley Campus Council or one University Senate, a legislative body that would represent faculty, administrators, students, research personnel, and nonacademic employees. In practice, however, it is impossible to reach any sensible conclusion about such a proposal until we have created the decentralized communities that would form the only possible constituency base for such a senate. Moreover, at this stage in our thinking about decentralization, it is not yet possible to state with assurance the functions such a central Senate might be expected to perform.

We hope the Academic Senate will devote substantial attention to the development of plans for decentralization and their successful realization. Until such proposals are ready, we hope the Academic Senate will concentrate on reorganizing its committee function into an efficiently coordinated system that integrates into the Senate structure administrative committees concerned with policy questions. It will obviously be important to such a venture to bring administrative representatives into committee deliberations where appropriate; to distinguish carefully between administrative and policy-making functions, restricting Senate committee work to the latter; and to build an increased awareness of committee responsibility for reporting regularly to the Senate.

⋈ *SENATE AND STUDENTS* ⋉

Several matters of immediate relevance to the Academic Senate should be noted here with regard to the relationship of faculty to students in the governing process.

1. The Student Affairs Committee has recommended that proceedings of Senate meetings be broadcast in an adjoining room or elsewhere for the information of interested members of the campus community who are not Senate members.[9] The matter was referred to the Policy Committee in June 1967, and the Commission hopes it will be acted upon favorably in the near future. The recommendation takes on added significance if the kind of discussion between the administration and the Senate proposed in the first section of this chapter can be developed.

2. The Senate in spring 1967 adopted a recommendation to create the office of a campus Ombudsman as a one-man Senate committee.[10] His function was limited to complaints from students "regarding decisions by members of the Division and other officers of the University which affect the student's academic status." Complaints "arising from the regulation of student political activity" were explicitly excluded from his jurisdiction. As of January 1, 1968, no ombudsman has been appointed.

There is no doubt that the Senate needs an information office to guide students with academic grievances to the committee having jurisdiction over the particular subject matter. It is, however, hardly necessary to create an ombudsman to serve this relatively simple secretarial function. Beyond this, the Commission is skeptical about the value of this approach. In its original Swedish conception, the ombudsman is a watchdog appointed by and responsible only to the legislative body to supervise administrative functions and recommend improvements. The current concept of this institution is for a much watered-down version in which both the essential independence of the official from the agency he watches and most of his power and prestige are lost or compromised. As a result, the institution becomes little more than a formality, harmless at best and at worst a diversion from

[9] Minutes, June 5, 1967, pp. 34–35, iii.
[10] Minutes, June 5, 1967, pp. 33–34, iii.

the underlying necessity for reform of governmental or administrative structures. If the Berkeley Senate committee system is properly organized, coordinated, and functioning, only an information office is required; if it is not, an official with much more power or prestige than that presently conferred on the Senate ombudsman will be required to accomplish anything of significance.

3. The role of the Student Affairs Committee needs to be carefully examined in view of our recommendations below on student participation in campus governance. The committee was originally established as an administrative committee, was converted into an Academic Senate Committee in October 1965, and had an exclusively faculty membership until three students were added in May 1966. The apparent assumption was that the committee should be *"the* logical focal point for student expression" (emphasis added) between students and the Academic Senate.[11]

We welcome this development, which reasserts a Senate concern for student affairs that has lain dormant since 1921.[12] We draw attention, however, to our discussion in Chapters Eight and Nine about omnibus student-faculty committees in general and this committee in particular, for it is important to recognize that such a device represents only a transitional step toward student participation rather than its final manifestation.

⅜ *FACULTY TIME* ⅜

One final general concern of the Commission relative to the Academic Senate and faculty committee work concerns the burden of time imposed on faculty members on this campus at present. For many faculty members the demands of administration consume as much time and energy as either teaching or research, and have no compensating good effect upon teaching. Our recommendations—those involving student participation in general and rule enactment and enforcement in particular—might appear to aggravate these burdens. Although this very critical problem must be faced, we believe that a solution that relieves the faculty of either essential policy-making responsibilities or

[11] Minutes, May 17, 1966, p. 5.
[12] Sevilla, pp. 460–462.

increased collaboration with students in policy-making would be regressive.

The nub of the matter, as we see it, is to relieve faculty committees of excessive administrative duties, delegate much of what they presently do to an administrator, and provide them with adequate staff assistance. Every department in the university is chronically understaffed in administrative assistants and secretaries—evidence that public officials and taxpayers prefer a system that compels the faculty to perform administrative chores and allows it to be accused of neglecting teaching. However, this is all the more reason why this campus should intensify its effort to inform the citizens and officials of this state about the actual costs of education and the consequences of not facing up to those costs. For many years the hidden costs of education have been borne by the students, in the form of a lockstep system of education; by the faculty, in the form of excessive administrative burdens, which at times have helped to make a mockery of the "house of intellect"; and by the administration, which has been overworked, understaffed, and generally harassed.

Chapter VIII

❧❧❧❦❦❦

Student Participation at the Departmental Level

Genuine and effective student participation in the full range of university affairs will not be achieved without a long period of experimentation with a variety of methods. In this chapter and the next, we offer a number of specific proposals for achieving greater student participation. While outlining basic structural principles, we are aware that these ideas may be put into operation in a variety of ways. We are hopeful that the reforms proposed here will engender further discussion and additional proposals.

Since this discussion emphasizes the formal structures by which greater student participation may be achieved, we wish here to reiterate our belief that such structures must be built on sound educational foundations. Significant, long-range development of student participation must ultimately rest upon informal individual absorption in the enterprise of education in an atmosphere of honest searching and mutual respect.[1] For this university and this society, a rebirth in education and the development of the student role in governance are closely dependent upon one another.

Although both the Chancellor and the Academic Senate have endorsed the concept of incorporating student views in policy-making in departments and other local units,[2] this goal has been realized only to a very limited extent. It is too soon to evaluate fully the programs recently undertaken, but our general findings are that significant participation, especially in matters of educational policy, is confined to graduate and professional students in several schools and departments;

[1] For a valuable discussion of this and many other problems, see Frank Pinner, "The Crisis of the State Universities: Analysis and Remedies," in Nevitt Sanford, ed., *The American College,* John Wiley, New York, 1962, p. 960.
    The existence of a community depends upon shared meaningful experiences. For education to take place, faculty and students on campus must be involved in activities important and rewarding to both. Coffee and doughnuts will not do; and no improvement is to be gained from switching to tea and petits fours. Half an hour's quiet conversation on a topic of real concern, if repeated over time, will do more than any number of monster receptions. Listening to music together, or making it together, or discussing the latest drama production, or politics, or religion, or the conceptual and ethical problems of the disciplines—these and many other humble acts of communication make up the academic communion for which we should strive.
    [2] The Chancellor urged each department to establish student-faculty relations committees in one of his first addresses after arriving in Berkeley in the fall of 1965. He argued that such committees would provide personal and informal settings in which students could "express their views about courses, instruction, student life in the department," and which would give faculty members "the opportunity to incorporate these views in the departmental planning." The Chancellor repeated this proposal in his address to the Academic Senate in June 1967. The Academic Senate itself endorsed on May 17, 1966, Recommendation No. 8 of the Select Committee on Education specifically charging departmental chairmen and faculties with responsibility for initiating regular consultation with students on educational policy and other departmental affairs. The Senate further indicated support for this position in one of the charges to this Commission, which asks us to "assess what steps might be taken at college and departmental levels to increase and improve the appropriate participation of students in the formulation of educational policies, including measures for the improvement of teaching and the advancement of scholarship."

that few, if any, channels exist for undergraduate, nonprofessional students; and that, in general, the campus still lacks a widespread commitment to experimentation in this field.[3]

If students are to be integrated effectively into the workings of the department in order to ensure that decisions of importance to students are made only after prior discussion and consultation with student representatives, the Commission believes that the most direct and simplest method is first, to provide membership for students on regular departmental committees in which problems are discussed and policies formulated; and second, to invite nonvoting student representatives to attend and to participate in departmental meetings at which decisions are finally made. We do not regard omnibus student-faculty relations committees as an appropriate solution to this problem. They have served useful functions in some smaller departments, and we recommend their establishment where they do not now exist as effective agencies for developing *plans* for comprehensive participation, but we do not consider them to be adequate permanent institutions themselves, for reasons to be discussed below.

Participation in regular faculty meetings and in the operations of one or more regular faculty committees has occurred (or was scheduled for fall 1967) in one college, five schools, and seventeen departments. Some examples will illustrate those areas in which this approach has already shown promise:

1. Two students with voting rights, chosen by a "Student Action Group" of both graduates and undergraduates, now function as members of all standing committees in the College of Environmental Design; a student representative with speaking privileges is also invited to all faculty meetings of the College and its four constituent departments.

2. In the School of Social Welfare, representatives of the Associated Students of Social Welfare now sit on all of the School's administrative committees except the faculty personnel committee. This includes admissions, curriculum, policy, financial aid, and the School's

---

[3] In addition to a Commission survey of departments in mid-1967, we have been assisted in gathering background information by interviews with each department chairman and dean conducted in 1966 by the ASUC's SERF Board, and by questionnaires circulated in spring 1967 to each department chairman and graduate student organization by the Graduate Student Subcommittee of the Graduate Council.

Executive Committee. In addition, there are a Grievance Committee and a Student-Faculty Liaison Committee; the latter meets regularly with the dean and a faculty committee and handles extracurricular matters as well as mutual problems such as library policies. The School also has an annual three-day educational and social student-faculty conference at Asilomar.

3. During spring 1967, six students chosen by the Boalt Hall Student Association joined five faculty members in a Committee on Increased Student Participation in Law School Decision-Making. All law school faculty committees were interviewed to determine the kinds of decisions each made and the appropriateness of student participation in each. Recommendations of the Committee were adopted by the Law School faculty in June 1967 and are now being implemented. Five parallel student committees, to consult and meet jointly with faculty committees as needed, will be appointed by a BHSA Committee on Committees on which the Dean sits as a nonvoting member: these are the committees on Educational Policy, Library, Admissions, Financial Aids, and Physical Facilities. Two members of the Student Educational Policy Committee will be regular voting members of the faculty Curriculum Policy Committee and two will be regular voting members of the Faculty Summer Session Committee. The faculty's Courses Committee and the Academic Relations Committee will submit all proposals to the Student Educational Policies Committee before they go to the faculty. No recommendations were made for student involvement in the Budget, Graduate Studies, Alumni Relations, International Legal Studies, or Earl Warren Legal Center Committees.

4. In Letters and Science departments, three graduate students sat on a faculty committee to revise the graduate program in the Classics Department and will continue to meet this year on the committee of courses and curriculum. In the French Department, teaching assistants are now serving on a faculty committee on the lower division program. In the Linguistics Department, one graduate student is on the Department's Library Committee and another on the Graduate Studies Committee; the Department plans to place an undergraduate student on the Undergraduate Program Committee. In the Mathematics Department, the Mathematics Graduate Student Association is represented at all full faculty meetings as well as on a qualifying exam reform committee. Group I (Clinical, Social, Personality) in the Psychology Department has added two graduate and two undergraduate

students to its Curriculum Committee. In Biochemistry, graduate students in each laboratory elected representatives to a student executive committee, which has discussed problems on courses, graduate teaching, financial aid and undergraduate education with appropriate faculty committees and the departmental chairman.

While these examples indicate ample precedent for suggesting that students be given membership on departmental committees, several cautionary notes should be added. First, most of these experiments are quite recent, and it is too early to evaluate the results. Such innovations must withstand complaints of student apathy and overcome the risk that such participation will be kept token and peripheral. To date, however, much of the student reaction has been enthusiastic, and we have received faculty comment describing student participation in curriculum committees as *"very* useful," with students adding "a new perspective highly relevant to the issues discussed."

Second, we have encountered the opinion that in certain (but by no means all) natural science and professional disciplines there is little felt need for instituting methods for greater student participation in educational matters. Our data suggest that in some small departments informal rapport between students, faculty, and administration is excellent. Among the factors that contribute to this apparently successful situation are small department size, a favorable faculty-student ratio (especially in disciplines where substantial nonstate funds are available for teaching purposes), or special circumstances that induce close contact between students and faculty—such as laboratory work in the sciences, field work in forestry, studio work in art, and rehearsals in dramatic art and music. Obviously new structures of participation should not be imposed where they do not appear to be needed. We stress, however, the inadequacy of existing data; even in these "happy" departments we have encountered few serious attempts to evaluate student opinion or to reconcile apparent discrepancies between faculty and student reactions, or to take seriously critical comments from a minority if a majority of students seems satisfied.[4]

[4] One student-faculty relations committee circulated a questionnaire, to which one-sixth of the school's students responded, posing rather limited choices (a monthly public forum, a student committee elected or chosen by lottery to meet with faculty members, regular luncheon meetings, or informal coffee hours); the committee report concluded that there was no need or student desire for formal arrangements, and proposed instead occasional student-

Third, these ventures underscore the importance of substantial faculty initiative and support. Our survey of departments revealed, on the one hand, strong student opinion that faculty responsiveness and encouragement were the key to successful student participation. On the other, it elicited frequent faculty responses along these lines: that increased student participation was not a worthwhile goal,[5] or was not desired by the students, or in any event was not important enough to warrant the diversion of limited resources from other functions, or that the department was too harassed to take on any additional burdens.[6]

---

faculty luncheons and possible coffee hours, with a note that steps must be taken to assure faculty attendance. The committee specifically rejected student proposals made in response to the questionnaire for a faculty ombudsman to hear student grievances, for dean-sponsored quarterly forums to hear student opinion and for a bulletin board for expressions of student opinion in the lounge. In another unit, official responses to our inquiries about the advising system indicated great satisfaction, but student responses to a questionnaire gave a mediocre rating to the quality of the advising system.

[5] The chairman of the graduate studies committee of one large department reported that the channels for student participation in that department were "personal discussions, TA Union." Asked what additional methods would promote effective communication and cooperation, he replied: "At present, the information provided in response to the previous question represents, in this department's opinion, the full range of possible and meaningful graduate student-faculty patterns of relationship outside the classroom."

[6] The response of one chairman was an elaboration, at much greater length, of this point: "Until funds are provided for adequate staffing of the faculty of this department and for its educational activities, until adequate space is provided for their conduct, and until the administrative offices of the University provide real service to departments, such plans [for increased advising and participation] are mere intellectual exercises. . . . The Chairman and the Vice Chairmen of the department must spend so much time battling with various administrative offices of the University to get books ordered for classes, leaky walls in the building mended, and supplies and equipment purchased, that the only student conferences they hold are with emergency cases. As a consequence our concern is not so much with how our educational program can be improved, but rather with how it can be maintained at all. . . . Since the number of undergraduates assigned to us to advise runs about 80 per faculty member, and on top of this graduate and special students must be advised, it is apparent that the task confronting us is not how better advising can be accomplished, but how any advising can be done. . . . I am sorry to be so negative . . . but the practicalities of the situation are such that I see no chance for improvement. Nor, indeed, do I see any possibility of providing an opportunity for increased student participation in the planning of educational programs in this department. When I was a student, I was able to spend several hours a semester with my adviser, and as a consequence of his counsel my education was greatly enriched by courses in such diverse areas as the Spanish ballad,

When the officers of graduate student organizations were asked to characterize faculty reactions to student participation, many agreed with this assessment, using words like "condescending," "indifferent," "paternalistic," and "skeptical."

The imposition of structures of participation in the face of these objections is unwise, for it is likely to produce nothing more than token compliance. In urging departments to adopt measures for incorporating student views into policy-making, Chancellor Heyns has wisely warned against "window dressing or toys, which will simply irritate the caliber of students in a University like this."[7] Some of these obstacles can be eased by supplying additional funds, and some faculty resistance may be lessened if more sophisticated survey data on current student opinion are made available and if, as experience accumulates, there are periodic evaluations of existing experiments. The cumulative effect of improvements in teaching and educational reforms may also create greater willingness to engage in policy discussions with students.

Once a department has determined to test methods of increased student participation, it faces many problems in devising structures that will permit genuine and sustained discussion. In this connection, we wish to emphasize the limited utility of omnibus student-faculty relations committees, which we believe can best function as initial agencies for planning and executing the most effective forms of student participation in departmental affairs. As permanent, continuing groups, such omnibus bodies tend to become irrelevant adjuncts to the policy-making process. Most matters of consequence raised in such groups obviously must go before regular departmental committees, and a student-faculty relations committee all too frequently becomes either an unnecessary filter or is looked upon as a dead end.

We do believe that those departments which have not yet taken measures to increase student participation might find an omnibus committee to be a useful first step. The role of a student-faculty rela-

civic government and forestry; but my adviser did not have to spend his time seeking extramural funds to educate me. The chairman of my department conferred regularly with those of us who were undergraduate majors, seeking to discover our educational needs and desires; but he did not have to argue with Buildings and Grounds for repairs, for the comparable department then conceived of its function as providing service to academic departments. Those were happier days for the undergraduate student and the faculty alike. A university was an educational organization and not a factory, and an institutionalized factory to boot."

[7] Speech to department chairmen, October 1965.

tions committee should go beyond occasional meetings, the creation of lounges, or the improvisation of a hot line from students to chairman. Its primary task ought to be designation of the faculty committees to which students might be added, the methods of selecting students for these and other participatory roles which will be most effective considering local conditions, and the procedures for evaluating the operations of the various structures established.[8] A student-faculty relations committee might be disbanded when the formal and informal participatory institutions created by it progressively render its own role superfluous.

Although modifications will obviously be required to fit general proposals to specific circumstances, we think it useful at this point to offer suggestions for attacking two major problems: the selection of student representatives, and the delineation of the scope of departmental concerns in which they should participate.

SELECTION OF STUDENT REPRESENTATIVES

The choice of students who will participate with faculty members in the formulation of educational policy at the department, school, and college level should, of course, be made by students. However, no ready-made vehicles now exist that enable each segment of the student population to make such choices effectively. Participation at this level requires student groupings small enough in size to permit wide networks of acquaintance and shared interests among members. Such constituencies are also necessary to encourage continuing interchange of ideas between selected delegates and the students they represent.

For lower division students there are virtually no existing groups that meet these qualifications of manageable size and common intellectual interests. The Lower Division Colleges we propose (see Chapter Five) would, if adopted, provide an acceptable basis for participation. Short of the development of these and other such intellectual communities, we see little chance of devising meaningful methods of representation for lower division students.

Securing constituencies for graduate students poses fewer prob-

---

[8] For an example of work of this nature, see "Report of the Committee on Increased Student Participation in Law-School Decision-Making," adopted by the Law Faculty on June 6, 1967.

lems. In most departments the problem of numbers is far less acute and students tend to be well aware of their problems and of the need to establish closer relations with their respective faculties. Approximately fifty graduate student organizations now exist and could potentially develop into effective constituencies out of which representatives to departmental committees might be chosen. In addition, there exist natural subgroupings, such as teaching assistants or doctoral candidates, which could provide delegates for specific policy groups. Only in a few departments with very large numbers of graduate students are there serious organizational problems to be resolved, and in such cases, divisions inherent in the discipline might provide possible solutions.

Between these extremes are the approximately 10,000 upper division undergradutes. All have chosen a major, which in theory gives them a departmental home base. This selection, however, in many cases represents the mechanical fulfillment of a requirement rather than a significant intellectual commitment to the particular discipline. The lack of undergraduate organization, in contrast to that of the graduate students, reflects this lack of attachment. Particularly in large liberal arts departments, most students tend to be less certain of their goals, more remote from their professors, less attached to their departments, less engaged in their education, and much less likely to seek and find, on their own initiative, organizational means through which their needs and opinions can be formulated and expressed.

Some departments are, of course, small enough to permit students to vote intelligently in a direct election. In the large departments, such a direct election would be meaningless. Here, intermediate student groups are needed to reduce the amorphous collection of majors into communities of manageable size capable of choosing representatives, able to interest students in educational policy, and suitable as forums where matters of student concern can be discussed before being translated into proposals for departmental consideration.

In our view, these problems cannot be surmounted in the larger departments without greater initiative on the part of departmental faculties because a special departmental structure for student representation must be created. The Commission has discussed and rejected a proposal to create new at-large student membership organizations in each department. Such organizations among undergraduates have generally been the products of political crises and have always dissipated when the immediate crisis passed. We are convinced that the interests of educational improvement, student morale, and departmental cohesiveness would best be served if the participation of upper division students in departmental affairs evolved from institutions that were closely related to their intellectual interests and academic needs.

≫ DEPARTMENTAL ADVISING PLAN ≪

One existing institution that could be adapted to such a purpose (and which, as presently structured, is not operating satisfactorily in many large Letters and Science departments) is the departmental advising system. The Commission proposes—and departments could of course tailor the plan to meet their particular needs in any number of ways[9]—that students be offered the option of joining an advising group of perhaps fifteen juniors and fifteen seniors with a faculty adviser. The groups could reflect common choice of a definite academic concern within the broad field of the major, or they could reflect post-college plans—math students, for example, might be divided into future graduate students, computer workers, or math teachers. These groups would meet as needed to assist the students in planning a rational and coherent major program and would hopefully develop, to a greater or lesser extent, into coherent, small communities united by intellectual preoccupations, offering an opportunity to acquaint faculty members and students with each other's views on the academic program of the department. They would also provide a setting in which students would be better able to share experience and knowledge with each other. Finally, the criticisms and suggestions that would flow from such groups could be more easily assessed by the faculty, because the information on student opinions would not be of the vague sort usually introduced into faculty discussions, but would issue from an identifiable source whose experience and ability would be taken into account. With these groups as nuclei it would then be possible to establish at the departmental level a system of student participation into which these groups would "feed." Each group's elected chairman might join other chairmen to constitute a departmental council of majors that would formulate student proposals and nominate their representatives for various departmental committee assignments. Conversely, the majors council would itself serve as a forum to which the

[9] A detailed description of one possible model for a large department in the humanities or social sciences is offered in Appendix D.

faculty could bring proposals or problems in order to elicit student responses. The council would thus provide a setting where curriculum, teaching, and problems related to the major could be discussed with the expectation that the students involved would have some fund of experience and knowledge, as well as a strong disposition to cooperate in improving the intellectual level of their common endeavor.

Difficulties of faculty staffing constitute the major objection this plan has met. The chairman of undergraduate advisers for a department with 800 majors suggests that the plan be voluntary for students, the incentive offered them being contact with faculty in small groups plus the opportunity to have a representative on the majors council; the incentive for faculty participation might be a significantly smaller number of advisees.

There are other ways a departmental majors council might be formed, of course. One department is planning to have sections of one required course for juniors and one required course for seniors each elect a representative. A science department might use laboratory groups as units. Graduate students in departments with well-developed graduate student organizations, especially teaching assistants having close contact with majors, might be helpful in working out methods from department to department.[10]

Various transitional forms are also possible. Graduate student representation can be worked out easily and quickly[11] and could be-

[10] One science department held an open meeting to which all undergraduate majors were invited, and worked out its own modification of this advising and council of majors proposal. The plan included holding open discussion meetings regularly. The chairman reported that the meeting was useful in dispelling certain widely held faculty folklore and "was constructive in tone, critical and valuable to me and the other faculty present."

[11] Graduate student organizations and departments have worked out many different techniques of selecting graduate student representatives for faculty committees or for student-faculty relations committees. In Education, for example, student members and alternates for the Student-Faculty Council are chosen by election in each of the eight divisions of the School and by any school-wide student organizations. The Council has a standing committee on committees of five student members to review applicants for spots on faculty committees; the committee recommends, the Council appoints. The Boalt Hall Student Association also has a committee on committees (on which the Dean participates without vote) which appoints students to its own parallel committees as well as to faculty committees. In Biochemistry, representation in the Graduate Students Organization is achieved by an annual election of one student from each laboratory to an executive committee, plus four first year graduate students who do not join labs until later. In Zoology, students for

come operative while work proceeds toward developing methods for undergraduate representation. Furthermore, we hope other educational innovations, some stemming perhaps from our report, will produce new interdisciplinary units, settings, and areas of focus for those students who have never viewed departments as satisfactory intellectual homes.

☙ SCOPE OF PARTICIPATION ❦

Most of the committee seats already given to students involve aspects of work on the curriculum, although instances of students serving on admissions, library, and financial aid committees also exist. Committee participation in curriculum matters should range from long-range academic planning and continuing general evaluation of both undergraduate and graduate programs to special groups considering such matters as the reform of major requirements, policies concerning teaching assistants, qualifying examinations, and graduate admissions. Students should participate directly in the committees considering such matters, and when committee proposals are discussed in departmental meetings, student members should be invited to attend and speak. Other questions of educational policy—such as the appointment of visitors, or the priorities to be assigned to meeting teaching needs in different fields—could be discussed in the graduate and undergraduate councils or through the inclusion of students on ad hoc committees considering such proposals.

Students should also be included on committees dealing with use of the department's physical space, especially in the design of commons rooms, special library collections, and service facilities. To the extent that auxiliary services such as placement and financial aid become further decentralized, students should be included on policy and planning bodies for such activities.

One of the most controversial areas of proposed student participation concerns the proper role of students in matters of faculty promotion and tenure. Controversy has had the effect of obscuring a surprising amount of agreement on the subject. Few students will dispute that faculty should have final authority to decide promotions and ap-

the Joint Advisory Committee (three members, three alternates) are elected by a mail ballot to the 120 graduate students.

pointments, while few faculty will assert that student opinion ought to be wholly disregarded in evaluating the performance and promotion of the faculty. If we accept the assumption that student opinion should play a part in these decisions, four main questions emerge:

1. How much influence should students be allowed?
2. Is the same weight to be given to student views on all of the various criteria that constitute the basis for evaluating the performance, promotion, or tenure of a faculty member?
3. By what means are students to be given the opportunity of participation in these matters?
4. What sort of safeguards should be established to protect the careers of faculty members against abuses, either by students or by faculty members?

The first and second questions should be combined, because, in our view, the value of student opinion varies according to the criterion in question, so that the weight assigned to that opinion should also vary. If it is granted that students and faculty share the view that the university should seek excellence in teaching and research, then it is appropriate to ask in what respects is student participation likely to improve the quality of the faculty's various activities. According to formal university policies, faculty members are judged by numerous criteria, of which research and publication have been the most important, teaching next, and community or public service last. It is important to recognize, however, that other considerations are usually introduced also, even though they may lack the weight and specificity of those mentioned. Each faculty member is expected to share in the administrative burdens of the department, to take some part in general university affairs, to supervise and guide graduate students, to gain outside recognition by participating in conferences, in the editorial work of learned journals, and in the evaluation of manuscripts submitted to publishers. This list could be multiplied almost endlessly, but enough has been said to illustrate that when a faculty member is being judged, many sides of him are put under scrutiny. A whole person is being looked at and the possibilities of abuse and personal hurt are almost as numerous as the facets under examination.

The vast majority of undergraduates primarily observe only one aspect of a faculty member, his performance as a teacher. Graduate students enjoy a greater advantage, for they come into contact with him in various settings, and hence have a fuller sense of him as a whole person. It might be noted, parenthetically, that many faculty members are ignorant of many aspects of a colleague's performance. Generally they have no firsthand knowledge of his teaching ability and even less of his skill as an adviser and supervisor.

It follows that on many matters relating to the promotion and tenure of faculty, student participation, especially of undergraduates, would be undesirable. But student views may be of great value regarding teaching, advising, and supervising of individual work, particularly if they are able to promote a greater emphasis on these functions as criteria of faculty performance. Student influence, then, should be strongly weighted in reference to these matters. If effective procedures can be developed for this purpose, existing methods, which rely largely on hearsay, can be replaced to the advantage of faculty and students alike.

There are various methods of achieving these ends. Panels of representative students (selected by the department chairman from a list submitted by graduate and undergraduate councils) might be asked to prepare evaluations (including a description of the methods used and recommendations) of candidates for promotions, which the department chairman would include in the person's dossier. The faculty member in question ought to be shown the entire evaluation and be allowed to enter a rejoinder. He should be allowed to request that his chairman return the evaluation and his rejoinder to the student panel and ask for a response to his exceptions. This procedure might well be extended to evaluating the teaching assistants in a department. It might also be possible to establish a joint student-faculty committee to undertake surveys and interviews of graduating seniors and recent graduates of the department to gain both immediate and retrospective views on both the curriculum and teaching. Our point is simply that possibilities for including a significant measure of student opinion in the selections and appointment process are varied, and experiments can proceed in this field without undermining the preeminent responsibilities of the faculty for such decisions.

Although we have emphasized formal structures for participation, we certainly do not wish to understate the value of the informal student-faculty relationships that social and educational settings can encourage. Methods of study in some fields (dramatic arts, music, art, forestry, or small science departments, for example) facilitate such contact; but most undergraduates, and graduate students in some large and understaffed departments, have few opportunities for personal exchange with faculty members. Some departments are promoting bag lunches, coffee hours, seminar social hours, and student-faculty lounges, but others complain of lack of space and money. Other departments have sponsored frequent colloquia at which students can hear and discuss the research of their professors.

In 1966–67, a great many more undergraduates participated in seminars and tutorials than during the previous year,[12] although much of the student contact was with teaching assistants, not regular faculty members. The emphasis on more small group instruction ought to be extended, as should the Board of Educational Development's program for more student-initiated courses. Efforts to improve the preparation and performance of teaching assistants (as in the Physics Department) should be widely publicized and imitated, with both faculty and student credit offered for training and evaluation seminars. Finally, our proposals for revision of the advising system, for lower division colleges, and for other teaching units of manageable dimensions will all assist in supplying greater opportunities for informal faculty-student relationships. We also urge the administration to solicit support, perhaps from the Centennial Fund or from foundations, to help departments (especially the larger ones) undertake experiments in improving or initiating advising plans, tutorial programs, senior seminars for majors, or other constituency plans.

➤ *A SENATE BOARD* ➤

It is extremely important to develop procedures for analyzing and evaluating the experimental methods discussed here and for aiding their initiation in recalcitrant departments. Accordingly, we recommend that the Student Senate create a Board for Student Participation in Governance (on which, at least initially, graduate students should predominate). A small number of faculty members should be invited to sit with this Board in an advisory capacity, and we urge the Vice-Chancellor for Academic Affairs to cooperate closely with it. The

[12] These were arranged largely through the efforts of the Board of Educational Development, The Tutorial Advisory Committee, and the Mathematics Graduate Students Association. See "Small Group Instruction at Berkeley," a report prepared by the Board of Educational Development, Spring 1967.

Board should survey departments and schools on a systematic and periodic basis (with administration help in collecting data) to determine the extent and the modes of student participation; it should evaluate the effectiveness of various experiments; it should learn as much as possible about comparable experiments in other institutions; it should publicize (through newsletters, forums, and other means) its findings, both good and bad, to facilitate a wide exchange of a variety of experiences; and it should provide experienced advice to local units planning participatory experiments. To accomplish these ends, the Board will require sufficient financing to maintain a small staff and employ part-time or summer student researchers. This financing could be supplied from the Student Senate budget or from a foundation grant obtained for this purpose.

Chapter IX

☙☙☙☙☙☙

Student Participation Campus-Wide

Although we have emphasized our belief that the promise of student participation can best be realized as one dimension of the growth of decentralized educational communities, we recognize that in the years immediately ahead many important policy decisions (including questions of decentralization) will be made at the campus-wide level. We consider it essential to incorporate students into those aspects of decision-making that remain centralized. The proposals discussed below first suggest the structure of a viable, representative, campus-wide student governing agency and then deal with the institutional modes through which students (and their governing agency) can share in the policy-making process.

✑ *DISSOLUTION OF ASUC AND NEW INSTITUTIONS* ✐

"Student government" on this campus is presently mired in a Serbonian bog[1] from which there can be no escape. Its legal standing is ambiguous; its political power in nonexistent; and the miasma of conflicting theories, incompatible functions, contrary procedures, and impossible rules that envelops the terrain makes it impossible for even the most earnest pilgrim to find his way to higher ground.

We have already indicated our conviction that abandoning the conception of a separate student government offers fresh possibilities for clarifying the role of students in university governance. In order to develop the institutions through which students can participate in co-operative discussion and policy-making at all levels, it will be necessary to dissolve the existing organization known as the Associated Students of the University of California, to reassess the functions that organization has been expected to perform, and to begin *de novo* to build the structures required to perform these assorted tasks.

As an unincorporated association presumably set up to represent the student body, yet set within the university hierarchy and assigned the management of certain properties it does not own, the present ASUC occupies an impossible position—that of an administrative holding company dressed in the garb of a constitutional government. The conflicting pressures of these two roles have paralyzed the ASUC, rendered it an arena for aimless and frustrating sham political battles, earned it the indifference of most students and faculty, and severely entangled its financial and managerial arrangements to

---

[1] A Gulf profound as that Serbonian bog
Betwixt Damiata and Mount Casius old,
Where armies whole have sunk; the parching air
Burns frore, and cold performs the effect of fire.
Thither by harpy-footed Furies haled,
At certain revolutions all the damned
Are brought; and feel by turns the bitter change
Of fierce extremes, extremes by change more fierce,
From beds of raging fire to starve in ice
Their soft ethereal warmth, and there to pine
Immovable, infixed, and frozen round,
Periods of time; thence hurried back to fire.
John Milton,
Paradise Lost, Book II, 592–603

the point that only the full-time administrative staff has any degree of control over "the students' affairs." Given the prevailing confusion, we do not consider it likely that the ASUC monster can be sufficiently reformed internally to serve our primary goal of creating a representative, central student agency that undertakes certain policy responsibilities directly, while promoting and coordinating student participation in policy-making that takes place outside the agency itself.

We here propose several new institutions (most significantly, a large representative Student Senate and an independent Student Union Board of Directors) to replace the ASUC. These proposals are designed to initiate a searching, public discussion of alternatives to the present chaos. The Commission did not sit as a student constitutional convention, therefore our proposals do not offer complete blueprints for change, but rather suggest the broad outlines of the reforms—in both structure and spirit—that we consider necessary to achieve genuine student participation in governance. We cannot insist too strenuously that these proposals must receive thorough public investigation before any attempt to enact them can be made. We also emphasize that no change of this magnitude can be accomplished without submitting the specific plans derived from these proposals to a student plebiscite. Indeed, the most significant changes we envision cannot be accomplished without a far greater degree of student interest and involvement in these affairs than presently exists.

⊱ *NEW STUDENT SENATE* ⊰

We propose the creation of a campus-wide, representative Berkeley Student Senate of approximately 75 members elected from constituencies, with its student body executive officers elected on a campus-wide basis. This central student organization will have a role somewhat analogous to that of the Academic Senate, the agency through which faculty participation in governance is organized, but which is regarded as an integral part of the community, not an isolated government. Like the Academic Senate, the Student Senate should primarily be a forum for discussion of diverse opinion, an agency for research and assessment of university policies, and the instrument for injecting student viewpoints and representatives into the process of campus-wide policy-making. Like the Academic Senate, the central student organization should function as an institution for overall *policy* determination, not day-to-day administrative management. Just as regular faculty members can participate in the Academic Senate by virtue of their status, so status as a student should be the only prerequisite for voting and other participation in the Senate and all student elections. The operating costs of the central student organization should be financed in the same manner as the comparable costs of the Academic Senate; as both perform essential governance functions in the modern university, their cost should be regarded as a necessary university expense and should be provided on a contract basis by the Chancellor's Office from general funds. A variety of measures could be used to finance programs sponsored by the Student Senate.

An enlarged Student Senate elected from constituencies offers an opportunity to increase the representativeness of the body and enhance ties of communication and responsibility between the Senate and the student body. Although the new process of preferential proportional voting (PPR) has made the electoral process more equitable in representing minority interests, it has exacerbated the problem of maintaining communication between elections. While each representative was elected by a certain fraction of the student body, it is unclear to students and representatives alike just which students elected which representatives. Political parties are necessary for organizing a PPR election, but they appear to be shadow groups with few signs of continued existence between elections. Furthermore, campus-wide political parties perpetuate centralization to an unfortunate extent. A central student government ought to provide a measure of coherence and coordination in an essentially decentralized system, but political parties tend to limit the direct ties between local groups and the central governing agency.

The choice seems to be between a large representative assembly which, on a continuing basis, derives its strength and direction from the student body, and a small body such as the present ASUC Senate, which functions as an executive to which students have delegated substantial authority to run student affairs on the campus. In keeping with our belief that decentralized settings strengthen and sustain the quality of participation, we see more promise in a large Senate that would draw representation from viable and reasonably well-defined local constituencies. (The creation of such constituencies is discussed in Appendix E.) On such a basis it would be possible for a representative to know personally and have good communication with the students electing him. It would be reasonably easy for the members of a constituency to meet frequently to discuss current questions, to evaluate the performance of their representative, and to inform him of their views on particular issues. It would also make it easier for the Senate to recruit more qualified volunteers for special projects.

The new Senate's role in the process of formulating policy may be realized in a variety of ways. The Senate could make certain central policy decisions by itself—for example, taking actions to protect student academic freedom or political rights, expressing student opinions on issues that concern them, and accepting a delegation from the proposed Campus Rules Committee to administer the process by which student organizations are "recognized" and their use of campus facilities is controlled. The Student Senate could also provide assistance in coordinating the work of students in decentralized governing agencies such as dormitory units or departmental student councils. This work might include the circulation of ideas developed in a local group or the formulation of general policy suggestions when a particular set of local groups faces a common problem. Aiding the creation and growth of such local units could well be the most significant activity the Senate could perform over the next few years. The Senate could also make provisions for sharing governing responsibilities with other groups and governing units in the university; it could participate, for example, in the establishment of rule-making and judicial bodies in which students form a portion of the membership. It could make arrangements through which students can share fully in policy-making in certain areas of joint responsibility by creating (in conjunction with the Academic Senate) joint committees on specific areas of mutual concern. The Senate could be the agency through which students assert a voice in the making of decisions that affect them, such as academic planning, but for which primary responsibility lies elsewhere. The Senate could act on resolutions brought to it by the student representatives on all of these committees and could also adopt resolutions of advice on its own initiative. In all these endeavors the Senate's committee on committees would have the crucial responsibility for selecting student delegates and placing them in the arena in which policy is determined. The Senate would also have the job of developing a workable pattern of communication and responsibility between such delegates and the student body. Providing these delegates with intelligent public support and a steady flow of information, policy ideas, and critical evaluations of existing policies are tasks that could be stimulated and coordinated by the central Student Senate.

As the central student organization, the Senate should become an effective leader in shaping intelligent public opinion on questions of general importance and in fostering a spirit of critical inquiry and innovation in university affairs. Its committees should develop a tradition of conducting hearings in public, both to assess proposed legislation and to investigate problems for which no legislative solution has yet been suggested. The Senate ought to reserve ample time for public questioning of the student body executive officers and student delegates to joint committees. As was previously recommended for the Academic Senate, the Chancellor or other principal administrative officers should deliver policy addresses to the Student Senate and engage in open question periods with it on policy proposals.

The Senate should also arrange for the publication of committee reports, working papers, important debates, and research studies. It might also use the resources of campus radio and television to promote community discussion. Such extensive open discussion on matters of common concern could provide a measure of cohesion and coordination in the varied, decentralized governing process. Discussion of special issues at the local level could in this way be placed in broader context, and reports on local problems and solutions could be brought to bear upon general discussions.

A Student Senate research staff could be an effective means of developing a more enlightened public opinion and creating a spirit of critical inquiry with respect to university policy. Student-initiated policy studies (perhaps undertaken in conjunction with academic programs such as student-initiated courses through the Board of Educational Development) could serve as a fruitful source of new policy ideas for student representatives and promote broader and higher quality discussion of these issues in the university. The development of informed, well-documented criticism and policy proposals through organized research into housing problems, rising food and rental costs in the community, the realities of the advising system, or changing patterns of student employment and career interests would be a valuable source of criticism and innovation.

To facilitate studies of university policies, the Student Senate might develop the present ASUC Library in Eshleman Hall into a center for the collection of materials related to problems of university governance and educational reform. Such facilities would have, readily available for student reference, local documents such as the minutes of various governing bodies, including the Student and Academic Senates, the Academic Assembly, campus-wide committees, and the Board of Regents; the *University Bulletin;* materials from other universities and national organizations such as the National Student Association, the American Association of University Professors, and the American Council on Education.[2] Students serving on Academic Senate, departmental, and administrative committees could turn over their files to such a collection at the end of their terms, a practice that would help to alleviate the problems of transiency and orientation referred to elsewhere in the report.

✣ STUDENT BOARD OF DIRECTORS ✣

We propose the creation of an independent Student Union Board of Directors with final policy-making responsibility for management of the Union facilities and direction of its program of extracurricular activities and services. The Board should be composed of the following voting members, each serving two-year terms, with appointments staggered to ensure continuity: eight students, four of whom to be appointed by the President of the Student Body, and four to be appointed by the Student Senate; two members appointed by the Chancellor; two faculty members appointed by the Academic Senate; one representative of full-time research personnel who are not members of the Academic Senate; and one representative of the nonacademic staff (means of appointment for these two positions to be determined); *ex officio,* nonvoting members of the Board, to include the President of the student body, the Dean of Students, and the President of the Alumni Association (or their designates). The Board of Directors should each year appoint a student to be Union Program Chairman, who should then also serve as chairman of the Board of Directors for the year, voting in cases of a tie. The Executive Director of the Union should serve as secretary of the Board. Such an arrangement appropriately entrusts students with primary responsibility for the poli-

[2] Appropriate materials assembled by this Commission might well be turned over to such a library collection.

cies and programs of the Student Union, but it also encourages the substantial presence and influence on the Board of other members of the community.

While it is difficult to draw a precise line between Student Union activities and programs that fall under the purview of the Student Senate, the following guidelines seem appropriate. The Student Union should be the major organizer and promoter of extracurricular, leisure activities of a general, recreational nature—games, music and television lounges, foreign students' hospitality, films, dances, athletic and spirit groups, musical groups like the Glee Club and the Band, and certain facilitative services such as check cashing booths, theater box office, and information desk. The Senate should promote and coordinate programs involving academic and community affairs, such as teacher evaluation, community service projects, orientation, tutorial groups, policy research and evaluation. Those auxiliary enterprises that are operated as part of the Union's recreational program or services (bowling alley, games room, ski lodge, cap and gown rental) should be under the jurisdiction of the Union Board of Directors and income from them should be applied to Union program expenses. Other enterprises, such as the bookstore, which are located in the Union building but whose functions extend beyond the scope of Union programs, should be administered separately, with different arrangements for the use of income generated by them. The Union Board should also have the responsibility for interviewing and appointing the Union's professional staff.

⅍ FINANCES ⅋

Dissolution of the ASUC will require a thorough public investigation of its fiscal and business affairs in order to determine procedures for liquidation and transfer of its responsibilities and resources to new administrative units. A great deal of study is also necessary for developing the most appropriate arrangements for securing and administering revenues for the new Senate, the Student Union Board of Directors, and other agencies. The Commission could not attempt the detailed investigation required to formulate final plans for these matters; we offer here a series of guidelines and suggestions which we hope will be useful in the preparation of specific agreements.

One principle underlying our proposals is a recognition that it is merely a convenient shorthand to label a portion of the student incidental fee an "ASUC fee," or a "Student Union activities fee." We think it more realistic and helpful to acknowledge that the income from all student fees forms one general sum that is allocated in a variety of budgeting procedures. The task with respect to "student government" is to devise ways of channeling necessary funds from this general source to the appropriate agency. Both the Student Senate and the Union Board of Directors will perform necessary functions in the campus governing structure, and it seems justifiable to support their work out of general campus funds without levying a separate "compulsory fee" for student government.

Some specific suggestions for the various agencies and activities are suggested below:

1. *Necessary operating expenses for the Senate and Executive.* Money for salaries, secretarial staff, telephone, postage, and printing should be secured on a contract basis from general campus funds. The central student agency could draw up an operating budget and contract either annually or biennially for the needed sum. This is the procedure followed by the Academic Senate and it is equally appropriate that general funds be used to finance the necessary governing functions of the student agency.

2. *Operating expenses for the Student Union.* Continuing administrative expenses for the Student Union should be drawn, as they are now, from a combination of general campus funds (that part of the student incidental fee known as the "ASUC membership" fee) and revenues from auxiliary enterprises related to the Union program. The Union's staff (professional and nonprofessional alike)[3] should become university employees, with the Union Board of Directors as their administrative supervisors.

3. *Programs and activities.* (a) Certain activities might se-

---

[3] ASUC staff expenditures have been handled under two separate rubrics. Most of the staff expenditures (Executive Director, Controller, secretarial, custodial) are considered part of the ASUC administrative budget, totaling nearly $500,000 and prepared primarily by the Executive Director. Of the approximately $267,000 activities budget prepared directly by the ASUC Finance Committee and Senate, almost one third is appropriated for professional staff advisers: Publications Administration ($24,000), Activities Office ($31,000), and Musical Activities Administration ($32,000). (All figures are approximate. For details, see ASUC Finance Committee, Budget Requisition and Analysis, budget code items 251,321,331, May 1967.)

cure independent financing. The *Daily Californian,* for example, has developed alternative plans for independent operations, and such independence should be encouraged. One possible plan calls for the collection of a subscription fee as part of the general student fee schedule, another for independent sale of subscriptions. The California Band might also secure independent financing from the Department of Intercollegiate Athletics or a special alumni fund. (b) A student-faculty Committee on the Incidental Fee could be established to examine the general problem of student fees and how they are appropriated for various university expenditures. The central student agency—through this committee—could receive a block budget (based on a per capita student formula) which it would then allocate among its various activities. A similar transfer (based on a per capita formula) would be made to the Student Union Board of Directors for use as it desired in Union programming. (c) The central organization should charge its Finance Officer or Appropriations Committee with soliciting supplementary funds for research and programs from the Regents, the President's Office, and foundations. (d) At present the ASUC Controller's Office maintains trustee accounts for a large number of student groups such as honor societies, class officers, various contest and charity groups. A student accounting service might be established by either the Student Union Board of Directors or in the campus Accounting Office directly, to provide such services for these groups.

ASUC STORE

At present the ASUC Store performs a variety of roles. It stocks books required for courses, maintains an additional selection of general books, and purveys a wide variety of school supplies, souvenirs, sweatshirts, toilet articles, greeting cards, and other items. The net revenue from these assorted enterprises provides a considerable amount of the ASUC operating budget. As a potentially significant element in the intellectual life of the community, a university bookstore should be looked upon as more than a supplementary source of revenue. Certainly its functions should transcend the primarily extracurricular role of the Student Union, even when (as is the case on our campus) the store is located within the Union building. In local practice, however, the complexities of ASUC affairs make it difficult to make immediate changes in the fiscal relationships between the store and the Union operations. Accordingly, we offer both short-run and long-range proposals.

We recommend that a joint policy board be established for managing what is now known as the ASUC Store and recommending plans for its future development as the university bookstore. The Board should be composed of an equal number of students and faculty (appointed by their respective Senates), representatives of the Vice-Chancellors for Academic and Student Affairs, and several members representing the library staff and full-time research workers. Among the Board's immediate tasks will be the evaluation of existing plans for remodeling the store's facilities and the consideration of proposals for creating a bookstore more appropriate to a university community.[4] The Board will also have to assess various possibilities for the use of the bookstore's revenue, including reinvestment in the enterprise itself, patronage refunds, or application to other community activities. The Board might explore with the Union Board of Directors the possibility of establishing a separate store within the Union to sell supplies, souvenirs, and other merchandise and thus provide additional income for the Union. Pending these long-range proposals, some temporary arrangements for allocation of store revenues to the Student Union and Student Senate will have to be worked out as part of the plans for dissolution of the ASUC.

⇘ GRADUATE REPRESENTATION ⇙

One significant advantage of these proposals is that they offer an opportunity to bypass the thorny but irrelevant disputes over "student government" powers and functions that have preoccupied students and administrators for a number of years.

The misapplication of the concept of "government" to ASUC affairs has severely tangled the separate questions of voting rights in the association and methods of raising revenue. The obfuscation produced by this unfortunate confusion is a significant cause of the apathy and frustration that prevails toward the ASUC. The trouble stems from the erroneous assumption that the ASUC is a "government" that has the power to levy a compulsory tax on all students. It is held that

---

[4] See interview with Carl Schorske in *Daily Californian,* October 1, 1965, p. 1.

payment of that compulsory fee is an act of "membership" in the government and determines the right to vote. It is further held that because "membership" implies the payment of a compulsory fee, a "substantial number" of students must approve "compulsory membership" before the fee that will entitle the student to vote can be levied. On the basis of this theory, several attempts to secure ASUC voting rights for graduate students have been frustrated by pettifogging delays, interference in elections, and eventual demoralization and failure.

There are several fallacies in the "compulsory membership" approach. The question of voting rights and representation in an organization charged with governing responsibilities takes precedence over the question of raising revenue for that organization. The concept of "compulsory membership" is a specious one, for voting should be a voluntary affair and should not be arbitrarily restricted or compelled. To require the payment of a fee as a prerequisite for voting may be appropriate for a private club, but it is obnoxious when applied to voting for a representative governing agency. To assume that a special compulsory tax is the only means of financing the work of a student agency is an error, and to make this particular method of finance the basis of the right to vote is an absurdity. The entire problem results from the mistaken notion that the ASUC is a separate constitutional government with the power to levy taxes. Only the Regents have the power to impose obligatory fees, and they have done so in many instances without requiring votes of approval from the student body. To pretend that the ASUC "membership" fee is the tax of a student "government" that requires formal ratification according to special electoral criteria before representation can be extended is to create a false social compact which, despite its symbolic uses, bears no relation to the realities of the situation.[5] Such theoretical confusion only serves to try the patience and exhaust the energies of those who would like to see students develop a representative institution through which they might play a role in campus governance.

No one has seriously argued that graduate students should remain unrepresented in campus governance. Some have questioned the wis-

[5] The emptiness of the compact theory of membership and taxation is emphasized by the Chancellor's recent reassignment—without the approval of two-thirds of a substantial number of the affected population—of the power to collect and appropriate student fees and other ASUC revenues to an appointed 16-member board, including six undergraduates and two graduate students. (See *Daily Californian*, November 30, 1967, p. 9.)

dom of incorporating graduate students into the undergraduate organization, arguing that the different interests of graduate students would
compel the creation of a separate association for them. We are not persuaded that graduate and undergraduate interests are so incompatible
that their representatives should be divorced from each other. Many
of the policy questions before the Student Senate would affect graduates and undergraduates here equally, and both groups have substantial concern in the quality of education at Berkeley. The changing
nature of the curriculum and the increased economic and social importance attached to higher degrees, moreover, are rendering the distinction between undergraduates and graduates somewhat arbitrary.
Most graduate students are presumably less interested in traditional
extracurricular activities than are some undergraduates, but the distinction is an irrelevant one, since the proposed Student Senate would
not be concerned with such matters. To the extent that graduate students do have different problems, it would seem likely that the representatives of graduate constituencies in the Student Senate could secure
expression for them. Such special needs may also be met through expansion of the graduate professional associations in each department.
Professional associations, however, are not a sufficient substitute for
representation in the student government on the many issues and policies that transcend departmental and professional lines.

The conception of a central student organization advanced in
this report poses no theoretical or practical barriers to the enfranchisement of either graduates or undergraduates. All students will be represented directly in a Senate and through an Executive without having
to take out "membership" in an intermediate association, a device that
permits the present, misleading segregation of the "ASUC fee" from
the rest of the charges students pay each term. How a portion of the
student's total fee can be utilized for financing the work of central
student governing agencies is a question distinctly subordinate to the
question of representation.

A campus-wide Student Senate that can represent both graduate and undergraduate students is a prerequisite for effective student
participation in governance, and the Commission sees no reason for
delaying its establishment. The statewide policies embodying the du-
bious notion of "compulsory membership" do not seem applicable to
the proposals advanced here, especially since the use of a student "government" as a managerial unit of the university is explicitly aban-

doned. If existing statewide policies are held to prevent the formation of a representative Student Senate as outlined in this report, then such policies must be modified immediately. If the Berkeley campus does not now possess enough freedom to establish appropriate institutional means for student participation in governance, then it is faced with a crisis of most severe proportions.

⊁ *"PRESERVING THE BUILDINGS"* ⊱

A second important advantage of these proposals is that students continue to have primary responsibility for the Student Union program and extracurricular activities, at the same time that the new Student Senate is freed to act on a much broader range of issues than the ASUC could do while saddled with direct responsibility for Union management and recreational programs. There is the further advantage of resolving the inherent conflict in the role of the ASUC Executive Director, since that position properly becomes that of Student Union Director. Finally, the confusion created by assigning the student "government" a physical area of the campus to be administered separately from other campus facilities is resolved. This assignment has necessitated the creation of an elaborate ASUC bureaucracy in which students have difficulty exercising genuine control and has obscured the far more important functions a student governing agency ought to perform. There is no more reason for the Student Senate to have the job of maintaining the Student Union than for the Academic Senate to bear administrative responsibility for the upkeep of its offices in California Hall.

The extent of the ASUC's financial enterprises, its sizeable budget, and its elaborate facilities have fostered the illusion among some students that these trappings of wealth and power actually signified the existence of substantial student responsibility. Over the years, some of the students most active in the ASUC have believed that the source of whatever power and prestige the organization possessed lay in occupying and managing the Student Union facilities. Some student leaders, frustrated by the actual restraints placed upon student management of these facilities, have sought genuine control of the facilities by attempting to establish a legal case for student ownership of them. Despite some ambiguities in the law and certain claims for equity in property transfers over the years, this approach does not seem to be a fruitful one. Other students have looked upon the buildings as a "sandbox" in which the students are allowed to play at government but are restricted to trivial matters while real control lies elsewhere.[6]

The concept of a separate government with a uniquely defined physical jurisdiction has kept students isolated from genuine policy-making, has obscured the distinction between management and governance, and has left students either with the illusion that their carefully restricted management of expensive physical facilities constitutes "self-government" or with profound resentment of the discrepancy between the symbols invoked and the power actually extended. We are convinced that the amount of influence and power students can exercise in university governance is in no significant way related to the amount of money in the "students' budget" or the net worth of campus edifices designed for student extracurricular use.

Our hope instead is that the Student Senate will develop into an integral and creative part of the campus governing structure, thus providing opportunities for students to share directly the responsibility for university policy-making. At the same time, the work of the Student Union Board of Directors and its program committees will afford opportunities for students to continue to direct extracurricular facilities and activities as they see fit.

⤳ COMMITTEE SERVICE AND COORDINATION ⤳

In addition to a representative and effective central organization through which the student body may express opinions, initiate programs, and assume significant governing responsibilities, measures must be devised that will enable students to participate directly in shaping policies that concern the entire community but for which the

[6] During the discussion of constitutional reform proposals in 1966, for example, the *Daily Californian* argued that the delegation of authority to manage buildings and activities placed severe intellectual and physical limitations upon the ASUC and effectively prevented it from addressing itself "to education, to the clarification of student rights, to the relationship between the students and the community." The editorial doubted that "students have seriously considered the destruction of traditional student government and the consequences it would have as regards student influence on the University" and argued that "only if the trivial is stripped from the students' control can the students ever hope to exercise some real influence over their educational fate." (*Daily Californian*, April 27, 1966.)

Chancellor's Office and the Academic Senate bear predominant responsibility. Inevitably, the search for such measures focuses upon the network of advisory and legislative committees, which, despite its many shortcomings, offers some promise of becoming an effective center of policy formulation and discussion.

The concept of student membership on administrative and faculty committees is not a new one. In the past few years students have served on nearly a score of administrative committees ranging from supervision of the Federal Work Study Program through a subcommittee on Parking Utilization to the Centennial Celebration Committee. In addition, student members were added last year to the Academic Senate's Committee on Student Affairs.[7]

This form of participation, while laudable as a first step, is not sufficient, and as presently organized, it is not an effective means of incorporating students into the process of policy formulation. Interviews conducted for the Commission with a small sample of students appointed last year to twelve committees give the impression that on only two or three of the committees covered in the sample were the students effectively integrated in the work being done. The reports illustrated the kinds of obstacles one might expect to encounter in such a program: a committee never met, or met only once or twice, or met at times when the student could not attend, or met when he was not notified of the meeting; the problems with which students thought they should be dealing were declared to be under the jurisdiction of some other committee, or had been decided before the student was appointed, or were thought by the students to have been decided by the faculty members outside formal committee meetings; certain faculty members did not ask questions, were willing to "sit tight" until some

[7] At UC Irvine, students participate extensively in the work of Academic Senate committees. Students (one each except where noted) serve on the following committees: Athletics, Education Abroad Program, Graduate Council (2), University Welfare (2), Privilege and Tenure, Academic Freedom, Undergraduate Admission, Scholarship and Prizes, Budget, Educational Policy, Library. The representatives are chosen by the Associated Students and make periodic reports to that body. Two student representatives have floor privileges at regular Senate Meetings. At UC Santa Cruz, the Academic Senate authorized its chairman to invite students at his discretion to attend Senate meetings (spring 1967). Six students were invited to attend the May 1967 meeting at which the question of tuition and fees was discussed. Students also meet with certain Academic Senate committees at UC Santa Barbara, and studies are in progress at Davis and UCLA.

problem "blows over and they won't have to make any changes"; or the student appointed knew nothing about the problem with which the committee dealt, or (a common complaint) he never received adequate briefings about the committee's work. Most of these complaints, of course, reflect the sorry state of much of a university's committee system rather than any new problems posed by the students' presence; indeed, in only a few instances did students report feeling that they or their ideas were not welcome. Student expectations were probably unrealistic, especially when compared with the expectations faculty bring to committee assignments. Thus while one draws the impression that the participation of this particular sample was not very effective, much of the difficulty stemmed from the committee process that happened to be involved.

We have previously suggested some measures for remedying these general problems by eliminating a number of committees, clarifying the responsibilities of those that remain, and specifying procedures for open discussion and the reporting of proposals and analyses that will more fully integrate this work with other steps in the decision-making process. However, one special problem connected with participation by students that must be taken into account is the diffuse and isolated character of such participation at present. Both student appointees and ASUC officers have emphasized for us the severe shortcomings created by the lack of well-defined constituencies and procedures through which delegates can report on their work, present proposals for criticism, and solicit new ideas. Without such ties to a broader spectrum of student institutions and opinion, the appointees tend to become either lost or dispirited in the committee process. It is apparent that simply adding students to existing committees is not a satisfactory solution. The Commission's approach here is, as in most other areas, an experimental one which suggests several plans for achieving an effective structure for student participation in policy formulation at the campus-wide committee level while simultaneously improving the operation of the overall process.

In order to expand student participation in the formulation of educational policies, the Commission recommends that two students (one undergraduate and one graduate, to be appointed by the Student Senate's Committee on Committees) become voting members of the following Academic Senate committees: Educational Policy, Teaching, Admissions and Enrollment, Board of Educational Development,

Council on Special Curricula, Committee on Courses, and Academic Planning (a new committee proposed by the Senate Policy Committee now before the Academic Senate). The Student Senate should nominate at least two graduate students to serve on the Graduate Council. To coordinate the work of these delegates, the Student Senate should create a Council on Educational Policy, to be composed of the representatives to these committees, four or six senators, several delegates from departmental student councils, and several at-large members (drawn from student organizations active in educational programs and evaluation, such as SERF Board). This Council would serve as a forum for discussing reports of committee representatives, facilitating the exchange of information and ideas among the various committee members, channeling new proposals and evaluations to the various delegates, and serving as a nucleus for students generally interested in educational reforms.

We believe that this combination of student representation on faculty committees and a separate student coordinating council offers fruitful opportunities for creative participation, responsible reporting, and maximum discussion of problems and proposed solutions. Direct participation on committees is necessary if students are to have effective opportunities to express their views, and a coordinating council seems advisable to ensure that student discussion will be well informed, comprehensive, and creative. We disagree with the suggestion of the Select Committee on Education that students be excluded from campus-wide committees on educational policy, but that faculty committees consult with counterpart student groups.[8] Such consultation tends to be diffuse and ill informed; "student groups" are likely to be amorphous, shifting entities, and so vague a procedure is an ineffective substitute for sustained discussion in a context of directly shared responsibility.[9]

[8] The Committee's argument (see p. 62, *Education at Berkeley*) that such a situation might lead to polarization and mistrust, that students lack competence and experience at this level, was discussed in Chapter Six.

[9] Students, for example, did not serve on the Special Committee on Academic Program of the College of Letters and Science. After its report was published (*The Undergraduate Program in Letters and Science,* 1967), a group of students connected with SERF Board produced a thoughtful and intelligent critique that offers a number of alternate proposals ("A Student Proposal for an Undergraduate Program in Letters and Science," SERF Board, ASUC, November 1967). It will be difficult for this document to secure the full hearing it deserves, since it is an unofficial report and on the agenda of no

The approach outlined above is also applicable to other areas of campus-wide policy-making, especially campus development and environmental design, and cultural affairs. Moreover, the experience of students in intellectual disciplines related to these questions can be drawn upon directly.[10] We therefore recommend:

1. That student representation be instituted and/or expanded on the Building and Campus Development Committee and its subcommittees, the Campus Planning Committee, the Chancellor's Advisory Committees on Development, and on Housing and the Environment. The Student Senate should create a Council on the Campus Environment to be composed of delegates to these committees, several Senators, and a number of at-large student members, drawn from the College of Environmental Design and other areas of potential student expertise, including (on a rotating basis) representatives from departments and colleges currently involved in planning new facilities.

2. That student representation be instituted or expanded on the Committee for Arts and Lectures, committees on art exhibitions and the Art Museum, the proposed Auditorium-Theater Policy Committee, the Regents' Lecturer Committee, the Public Ceremonies Committee, the Chancellor's Advisory Committee on the Creative Arts, and other standing or special committees on cultural affairs. The Student Senate should create a Council on Cultural Affairs, to be composed of delegates to these committees, several Senators, and a number

---

deliberative body. The student creativity and energy that went into the preparation of this critique might have been used more effectively if students had served directly on the committee and produced proposals for discussion by it; but more important, general discussion of the problems (and the final report itself) would have been greatly improved by expanding the perspectives and the bases from which they were examined.

[10] See the remarks of President William R. Keast to the Wayne State University Student Assembly, May 12, 1967: "We have recently had an instructive example of how valuable and decisive the contribution of students can be when their special knowledge and interest in the improvement of the learning process can be brought to bear. In planning the new Basic Science Building for the Medical Center, Dean Gardner called upon the Student Council of the Medical School to make recommendations about space arrangements, laboratory layout, and the like, from the special vantage point that their own experience as medical students had given them. They took their assignment seriously, worked hard and imaginatively, and came up with a large number of suggestions, most of which would not have been put forward otherwise. Almost all of their proposals were adopted." Keast, "The Student and University Government," May 12, 1967, reprint.

of at-large student members drawn from various fine arts departments, the University Theater, Orchestra, Chorus, the ASUC Studio, and Union Program Board.

3. Predominant responsibility in formulating policies for the various services related to student housing, employment, and welfare should rest with the Student Senate, with substantial participation by the administration and faculty. We propose that the Student Senate establish a Student Services Policy Board to develop innovations, evaluate existing policies, and interview and approve candidates to fill vacancies in staff director positions for the various services (for example, Student and Alumni Placement Center, Housing Services, Student Health Service, Food Services, Work-Study Program, Residence Halls, Foreign Student Services, and Recreational Facilities). The Board should be composed of a majority of students (including some Senators appointed by its committee on committees and nonsenators appointed by the Student President) and representatives from the Academic Senate and the Office of Vice-Chancellor for Student Affairs. Staff directors of the services should be nonvoting, liaison members of the Board. We suggest that the Board establish a series of subcommittees (including both Board members and additional appointees approved by the Senate) for each service agency. These subcommittees should be responsible for visiting facilities, preparing evaluations of existing programs, and recommending policy changes and program innovations to the entire Board.

4. Administrative expenditures, including printing and secretarial services, for the Councils and Boards proposed above should be included in the general operating budget of the central student organization.

5. Although we have expressed doubts concerning the effectiveness of an unspecified process of "consultation" with an equally vague array of "counterpart student groups," we do believe that properly structured, parallel committees might in some cases serve as useful devices, and we would like to experiment with such an arrangement. Accordingly, we propose that the Student Senate establish a Committee on Academic Freedom and Student Rights, and a Committee on Library Facilities and Services. These committees shall exchange agenda and reports with the corresponding Academic Senate committees, and upon the initiative of either the student or faculty chairman, shall meet jointly to consider problems or proposals of mutual concern.

For example, while the academic freedom committees might meet separately to consider individual grievances, they might meet together to attempt to prepare a report and resolutions for their Senates on issues such as the directive against striking teaching assistants and faculty. (The committees could issue separate reports in the event of disagreement.) Similarly, the Student Library Committee might undertake its own comprehensive review of library services and then request the faculty committee to meet for discussion, revision, and possible joint endorsement of proposals based upon that study.

6. As student participation on these committees broadens, the role of the Academic Senate's Committee on Student Affairs will need to be reconsidered. At present it is responsible for consulting relevant student opinion and bringing student views to the attention of the Senate, but like omnibus committees at the departmental level, such a group is useful primarily in establishing more broadly based, well-focused, continuing bodies. We hope that the Student Affairs Committee will take an important role in encouraging, refining, supervising, and evaluating the proposals we have made. When it is satisfied that more specific arrangements are functioning well, we anticipate that it may then choose to dissolve.

7. In recommending that students become members of Academic Senate committees, we intend that they receive the same privileges accorded faculty committeemen, including the right to vote and to submit minority reports. At present, the question of extending such privileges to students is clouded by Ruling 4.67A of the Committee on Rules and Jurisdiction of the statewide Academic Assembly.[11] It states:

> Only members of the Academic Senate may be members of Faculties or other committees of a Division which are instructed in Divisional legislation to act for the Division, or which are empowered by the Division to give advice to University officers or to non-Senate agencies of the University in the name of the Division. Therefore, only those committees of a Division whose charge does not conflict with these principles may include persons who are not members of the Academic Senate; in all instances the legislation establishing such a committee must explicitly provide for the appointment of persons not members of the Senate.

[11] *Rules and Jurisdiction, Ruling 4.67.A* (Report of the Committee on Rules and Jurisdiction, in the Notice of Meeting of the Assembly of the Academic Senate, May 22, 1967, p. 55.) The ruling was a response to the inclusion of students on Academic Senate committees at UC Irvine.

We find the wording of this ruling highly ambiguous, and we are not at all convinced that it bars students, as some have alleged, from voting membership on committees. If the committees do not have final legislative authority, and if they issue public reports in the name of the committee, subject to the approval of the Division, student membership would seem permissible in terms of the resolution. The Commission urges the Berkeley Division, however, to seek the repeal of this ruling and to secure specific authorization of voting membership for students.

We urge this step in order to underscore the community's commitment to enhancing the status of students and to draw attention to the power of the statewide system to complicate needlessly the resolution of campus problems. We do not, however, wish to exaggerate the importance of voting in committees. Most committees operate informally without taking binding votes, although a slavish pursuit of unanimity sometimes impedes their work. In our own deliberations, too, formal votes were seldom taken, with either a common position being established after extensive discussion or a frank recognition being made that more than one point of view could be expressed in the public reports of the body. We thus regard student participation on Academic Senate committees as important for the opportunity it offers for full and open discussion and analysis of problems, and we hope that, should voting be temporarily unfeasible, full student participation in every other aspect of committee activities may begin as soon as possible.

Chapter X

☙☙☙❧❧❧

Law in the Campus Community

The content, enactment, and enforcement of rules regulating student conduct have posed something of a puzzle on this campus in recent years. Although the rules have been the storm center of recurring crises, the chief protagonists have repeatedly depreciated their significance. The administration has lamented the controversy over the rules as a diversion from the problems of education, while student activists have deplored the tendency of regulatory disputes abruptly to steer the pattern of student protest off its intended course.

Such diversions are not the only unfortunate consequences of this preoccupation with controversies over rules. The persistence of these controversies also symbolizes the partial failure of a significant experiment in campus law and order, of which the rules involved were intended to be an important part. These rules were drafted as an (originally) provisional implementation of the Academic Senate's resolution of December 8, 1964. Coming at the climax of the Free Speech Movement, that resolution linked a guarantee that "the content of speech or advocacy should not be restricted by the University" with the limitation "that the time, place and manner of conducting political activity on the campus be subject to reasonable regulations to prevent interference with the normal functions of the University. . . ."

To a limited extent the rules derived from this resolution have had constructive results. Since the fall of 1965, when the rules were enacted, political advocacy has had a vigorous existence on the campus. The three aspects of Berkeley's "free forum" have been regularized: student-sponsored indoor meetings and forums have been given wide scope, provision has been made for amplified rallies at Sproul Hall plaza, and other regulations have offered student organizations the opportunity to maintain tables in specified locations for fund-raising and the distribution of noncommercial literature. As might have been expected, the intellectual quality of these activities has ranged from highly stimulating to embarrassingly inane. On the negative side of the ledger, there have been some unfortunate instances such as the interruption and disruption of outside speakers[1]; moreover, there are still many unsolved problems concerning the scheduling of rallies, the range and diversity of viewpoints presented, and the general intellectual quality of the noon rallies.[2] On the whole, however, it is our opin-

---

[1] We agree with the Academic Senate's Committee on Academic Freedom that "the key question" is whether the protest expressing hostility to the views voiced by certain speakers "interferes with the original communication." The Committee distinguished "permissible, albeit strong, forms of expression" from "interference with the rights of those seeking to present their views and of those interested in hearing them." Minutes, Academic Senate, June 5, 1967, pp. 25–26 n. We agree that free expression is a normal function of the university and that interference with it is punishable under the December 8 resolution. We are encouraged that no instances of this kind have been reported in 1968 despite a highly charged atmosphere resulting from the war and a series of campus crises.

[2] We emphasize, however, that the quality of the noon rallies should remain the ultimate responsibility of the participants; any effort to change their character by coercion is wrong in principle and would only generate further bitterness and distrust.

ion that the cumulative impact of this diversified free forum has contributed greatly to lively dialogue on the campus.

In a broader sense, however, the policy of December 8 has not
provided the intended basis for achieving a consensus about campus
law enforcement. Instead, that policy is in danger of being corroded
by the conflicts it has failed to prevent. The germinal assumptions
about law and order that were implicit in the December 8 resolution
and that had the potential of creative development have instead become a casualty of crisis. It is important to analyze the causes of this
failure. While the underlying assumptions of the resolution still seem
to us to be sound, it is our belief that it has never been given a reasonable chance to work. The resolution envisioned more than a new policy
and a new set of rules. It sought a fresh approach to the regulation
of our affairs. The promise of December 8 was that the highest ideals
of our legal system, too long considered a realm apart, would be
brought to the campus and adapted to its spirit and its needs. To fulfill
that promise, there had to be something more than the resolution itself
and the provisional rules. Beyond these were two important needs:
the establishment of a number of prerequisite conditions for a supporting system of campus legality; and a more searching examination of
some of the unresolved problems and ambiguities posed by the December 8 resolution.

1. It is clear that in retrospect the establishment of a number
of conditions, each involving a substantial reform of our institutional
machinery, was needed in order for the resolution to have become the
effective basis for a real consensus regarding campus order and justice.

(a) As the December 8 resolution nowhere determines what
constitutes a "reasonable regulation," that concept must be defined by
legislative means. This in turn requires viable and flexible channels
for rule-making and rule-amendment that involve students in a significant way. The original rules, which were drafted with informal and
limited student involvement, were intended merely to be provisional.
Since the time of their enactment, neither the structure nor the spirit
required for realistic resolution of the legislative problems has ever
evolved. Thus the sense of legitimacy essential to any pattern of rules
has not been realized.[3]

---

[3] A reading of the minutes of the Campus Rules Committee is depressing
evidence of this failure.

(b) The development of community confidence in the legitimacy of the rules has been retarded by the absence of adequate mechanisms for adjudicating the alleged invalidity of a particular rule. This requires that invalidity be a defense that can be fully litigated in the same manner as any other defense. A system that denies this right offends basic feelings about justice and tarnishes the popular conception of the fairness of that system. The right to claim invalidity as a defense was acknowledged belatedly and ambiguously[4] and its implementation is entirely inadequate.[5] It is also desirable, given the urgency of minimizing the incidence of confrontations, that there be some method of resolving questions concerning the validity of rules or administrative enforcement policies by peaceful means before a rule violation or disturbance eventuates. Yet no avenues now exist by which a declaratory judgment determining a rule's validity can be obtained.[6]

[4] The September 1966 Berkeley Campus Regulations provide that challenges to the legality or constitutionality of a rule can be submitted in writing to the Chancellor as part of the Chancellor's review of a disposition recommended by the Dean of Students, Student Conduct Committee, or Hearing Officer; the Chancellor will refer the submission to the Office of the General Counsel of the Regents. Until December 5, 1966, there was no provision for review of an allegation that a rule violated Academic Senate policy, which has been the chief complaint of students, many of whom have claimed that a rule was inconsistent with the December 8 resolution. On that date the Chancellor announced that, as part of his final review of a case, he would refer to the Senate Policy Committee an allegation that a rule violated Senate policy. *Daily Californian*, December 6, 1966, p. 5. The effect of these methods of review is not stated; it remains uncertain whether or not the Chancellor is bound by the advice he received from University Counsel or the Senate Policy Committee, or whether a finding by the Chancellor that a rule is illegal, unconstitutional, or violative of Senate policy will result in acquittal.

[5] First, it is clear that validity of the rule should be adjudicated initially in open proceedings before the court of first instance, prior to or in conjunction with the factual evidence. Second, the role of the Senate Policy Committee or the General Counsel of the Regents is unclear; for example, will they obtain opposing written submissions from spokesmen for the administration? If so, will there be an opportunity to answer it? Third, referral of an important Berkeley campus rules question to the General Counsel of the Regents is inconsistent with any reasonable measure of campus autonomy.

[6] On December 5, 1966, the Academic Freedom Committee offered its services in this area: "We will consider any request to examine whether a campus rule is in conflict with academic freedom principles, and if we so find we will take whatever steps we deem appropriate to secure a change." Testimony of Professor Leon Henkin, Chairman of the Committee, before this Commission. This is a constructive gesture, but the Committee itself recognizes that it has no power to effectuate its opinion and to declare a rule invalid; when asked in

(c) Implied in the December 8 concept of law and order is the necessity that fair trial procedures be guaranteed. The rules recognize this necessity and embody many important elements of due process. That the existing system has failed nonetheless to win the confidence of large numbers of students is largely due to five critical problems in the established procedures: the failure to separate legislative and executive from judicial functions, so as to create an independent judiciary; the failure to provide formal finality for the judgments of the judicial system; the conflicts of interest built into the role of the Dean of Students, who under present procedures may be a student's confidential adviser, or become his prosecutor, or be an investigating magistrate, or serve as a trial judge using procedures of his own devising,[7] or impose sanctions which may or may not be reviewable by anyone else; vagueness, confusion, ambiguity, or omission in some important areas that concern disciplinary procedures; and the practical un-

---

testifying before us whether the Committee's judgments were authoritative, the chairman replied: "I don't have the imagination to conceive of a world in which we are that powerful."

[7] The Berkeley Campus Regulations currently in effect include a section headed "IV. Regulations Concerning Procedural Fairness and Disciplinary Proceedings," which contain the due process protections to which reference was made in the text. There is no indication in the Regulations that this section is not generally applicable to all disciplinary cases, but in his testimony before the Commission, Professor Steven A. Weiner, Chairman of the Committee on Student Conduct, insisted that he had been informed by the Regulations' draftsman that the due process protections applied only to political cases. Professor Weiner stated that he had been "plagued" by this "ambiguity," and had recommended that the rules be "clarified" by a statement that the protections in part IV apply to political cases only and that new rules should be drafted for non-political cases "so that all is in writing." Thus far, no changes have been made (Professor Weiner testified on March 2, 1967). If Professor Weiner's interpretation is accepted, there are no published procedures binding the Dean in his handling of disciplinary cases.

A number of other points relating to the inadequacy of existing procedures were brought out in our investigations or in testimony before us, for example, Professor Weiner's statement that there are no guidelines, published or otherwise, for the use of interim suspensions even though that procedure "should be used with great care, since it is a summary determination of guilt"; or Dean Williams' statement about the lack of specificity in the university-wide standard of conduct, which he acknowledged did not meet AAUP standards. We see little value in pressing such points, for we think there is little basis for disagreement with the proposition that campus disciplinary procedures require substantial revision.

availability of the defense of a rule's invalidity noted in paragraph (b) above.

(d) The cumulative impact of the circumstances just described has contributed to an inability to achieve a sensible accommodation on the nature of rules and rule enforcement. This has been seen in a tendency for both enforcement of rules and resistance to rules to move from the actual issue at stake to a concentration upon the importance of obedience or disobedience as moral imperatives for their own sake.[8] One result of this distortion has been periodic repudiation of essential elements of any rule of law. It is not difficult to see this process transforming an essentially low-level rules problem into a decisive challenge to all authority. It is also evident, however, in the challenge to some essential prerequisites of any rules system. A rule that restricts the use of loudspeakers which in general is reasonable under the December 8 resolution is applicable to any amplified speech at an unauthorized time or place, whether or not under the particular circumstances of the violation there was any interference with normal functions of the university. Similarly, a rule establishing maximum size for posters, if generally reasonable and therefore valid, is technically violated by display of a poster which to any degree exceeds that size. It is essential that we establish attitudes that acknowledge the legitimacy of such rules and that keep enforcement in a temperate context appropriate to their narrow scope and relative insignificance.[9]

The conclusion is inescapable that because none of these problem areas has been adequately dealt with, the philosophy and policy of the December 8 resolution have never been given a reasonable chance to work. It is perhaps impossible, and for present purposes

---

[8] It is significant that the first rules conflict subsequent to the enactment of the provisional rules in the fall of 1965 involved just such a lack of mutual restraint. The issue was an oversize VDC poster. To the administration, a somewhat oversize poster represented a major challenge to law and order. To the VDC, a reasonable regulation governing the size and location of posters represented a major challenge to political rights. Since that time, the same attitudes have manifested themselves on numerous occasions, much to the detriment of the functioning of the December 8 resolution.

[9] Compare, for example, violation of a 35 mph speed limit. If the limit is generally reasonable, it is no defense to allege that 40 mph was a safe speed under the circumstances existing at the time of the violation. On the other hand, enforcement policy and the sanctions imposed for such violations would be tempered in such cases.

probably irrelevant, to allocate blame for these failures. Nor has the campus achieved the historical perspective required to establish responsibility for the sad fact that rules controversies have assumed an importance so vastly out of proportion to their intrinsic merit. We see these events rather as indicative of profound uncertainties in our thinking about the nature of campus law and order.

2. The unresolved fundamental problems stem from the widespread tendency to appeal to the principles of December 8 without acknowledging and attempting to clarify their underlying ambiguity.

The most important of the problems posed by this ambiguity has to do with the conception of "the normal functions of the University." In the resolution of December 8, that phrase cut two ways. On the one hand, "normal functions" was a way of affirming the sovereignty of institutional purpose. It was a reminder that this is a community of scholars, and that the integrity of that community should not be subordinated to the special needs of political activity where the two happen to conflict. On the other hand, because the concept originated in an attempt to limit the area of disciplinary control, it was read as excluding an approach to the making or administering of rules that was based on criteria extraneous to our institutional purposes. Outside political attacks were presumably to be unacceptable considerations in rule-making and rule-administering, and administrative convenience was not to be given high priority in regulating campus political activity.

The fact that both views represent plausible deductions from the resolution highlight its ambiguity. The debate becomes pernicious when either approach is pushed to its logical (or illogical) extreme. It has been argued, for example, that free expression is subject to regulation if it adversely affects the normal functions of the university by creating outside hostility to the campus. It has also been argued that "normal functions" should be so narrowly construed that only direct physical interference with classroom activities is punishable.

The resulting debate has released a flood of rhetoric which sometimes has been merely useless and more often exacerbating. Appeals for a return to law and order for a pledge of allegiance to the principles of December 8 evade the critical question of apportioning the relative weight between the planned order epitomized by "law enforcement" and the tolerance of disorder implicit to at least some degree in any system that assigns the highest value to freedom of speech.

Many of the rules controversies demonstrate the trouble created by the failure to resolve the question of priorities between these two approaches. For example, what is intrinsically the relatively simple and unimportant issue of voice amplification has repeatedly been catapulted to stages that precipitate major crises. The narrow scope of the rules permitting amplification, the ways in which the ambiguities in those rules have been resolved, the controversy engendered by proposals to move the location of amplified rallies, and the penalties imposed for sound amplification offenses form a pattern of enforcement that we find inexplicable if judged solely by the standard of preventing unnecessary interference with other university activities. It is worth recalling, therefore, what is actually at issue.

On the one hand, within any reasonable definition of a university's "normal functions," noise control is an appropriate subject for regulation. The fact that too much noise is an unavoidable fact of life on many parts of the campus or that some kinds of noise are not regulated by rule[10] should not preclude a rule-making agency from taking such steps as it thinks wise in order to reduce the distractions caused by unnecessary sound. Total prohibition of voice amplification by students, however, would appear to be inconsistent with any reasonable reading of the resolution of December 8, would probably be an unconstitutional restraint on free speech, and would certainly unnecessarily inhibit the kind of free speech and open inquiry which, regardless of the scope of the First Amendment, should be protected by principles of student academic freedom. If one wishes to facilitate student meetings and communication on whatever subjects concern them, then open-air meetings at places that students frequent are among the most obviously useful means to accomplish that end, and to the extent that such meetings attract the attention of more than a few listeners, some form of voice amplification becomes a necessity. We have already indicated our belief that the student "free forum" often has substantial educational value, and it is important to recognize that it, too, has become an important "normal function" of the university.

---

[10] The rules do not, for example, regulate the University Band, which practices on numerous fall afternoons in an area adjacent to many university offices and classrooms.

We are witnessing an unresolved struggle in which the campus is trying simultaneously to achieve and to resist the integration of new norms that flow from concepts of free speech and advocacy. Our official policy, stemming from the resolution of December 8, calls for such an integration. But before that policy can be truly built into our institutional life, the element of ambiguity must be resolved by an increased recognition that free speech has some costs, including toleration of new sounds and combinations of sounds, as well as some reconstruction of what we mean by "order."[11]

In 1949 the Supreme Court said that speech "may indeed best serve its high purpose when it induces a condition of unrest, creates dissatisfaction with conditions as they are, or even stirs people to anger."[12] In its doctrines on picketing and demonstrations, the Court has recognized that communication of ideas in nonviolent but militant demonstrative forms may be regarded as necessary and protected in a free society. This abrasive quality of free speech results from certain characteristics of those who are strongly motivated to radical political action: a heightened sensitivity to conditions they regard as abhorrent, a surer grasp of opportunities for change, and a greater disposition to act with passion, to speak in anger, and to be scornful of pleas for deferred gratification. If the constitutional concept of free speech counsels restraint in dealing with these aspects of free speech in ordinary civic life, in a campus context still greater restraint is appropriate. Law enforcement must be infused with a lively appreciation of the protester's sense of urgency and the special circumstances that induce a particular protest. Nothing could be more destructive of genuine educational regeneration than to encourage the view already held by some that campus morality equates respect for time, place, and manner rules and the goals of peace and racial justice.

When free speech is genuinely made part of our campus life,

[11] The problem is illustrated by the language in our charge which refers to "increasing civility" in connection with the amplified free forum. We believe that there are far better methods for the discussion of problems than those that have sometimes been evident at our noon rallies. To the extent, however, that "encouraging civility" means to encourage students to talk politely to their opponents or not engage in radical or aggressive rhetoric, we do not believe that such matters can in practice be controlled by rule. More importantly, they would not appear to be appropriate subjects of regulation at all under the resolution of December 8. The problem of civility is an important one for our educational system generally; we do not see how coercion can be applied in its solution.

[12] *Terminiello* v. *Chicago*, 337 U.S. 1, 4 (1949).

the strident sounds of a political assembly will be as readily tolerated as the discordant notes of a practicing University Band; and violations of rules governing political conduct will be as coolly handled, with as much concern for the student as a person, as more traditional student offenses. We must take care lest preconceptions regarding the serenity of campus life, as distinct from reasoned principles upholding "normal functions," become the operative criteria we apply when questions of conduct arise in the political area. If our responses are unthinking, we may find ourselves with no better justification for what we do than the comfort of habit and custom.

Obviously the concept of "law and order" is problematic. The December 8 resolution began but did not finish the inescapable task of determining the concepts of rule content and rule enforcement most congenial to our aspirations for the university. That task in turn requires that the aspirations be known and the priorities among them determined. Rules and procedures are not likely to be neutral in their effect; they can either powerfully reinforce or subtly undermine the achievement of given conceptions about a university. This is why this discussion constitutes the last section of our report, for it would be foolhardy to draft either rules or procedures without some agreement about the purposes they are designed to serve.

In the proposals on rule-making and rule enforcement that we present later in this chapter, "law" seeks to embody the values to which we assign the highest priorities: educational regeneration, the fullest encouragement of intellectual inquiry, and a system of governance characterized by openness, mutual trust, and the progressive integration of students as responsible partners in community decision-making. "Order" describes the kind of social and intellectual climate that best promotes realization of these values, typified by the stimulation and excitement of intellectual involvement, the respect for self which stems from concern for the ends as well as the means of intellectual inquiry, and the respect for others which tempers the clash of ideas with human warmth.

≫ PRINCIPLES FOR DISCIPLINARY PROCEDURES ≪

Our recommendations for dealing with questions of law and order on the campus are embodied in a proposed code of "Basic Regulations Governing Enactment and Enforcement of Campus Rules,"

following as Chapter Eleven. As the chapter title suggests, these
proposals are not detailed campus rules, but rather specify the basic
structures and policies by which the rules would be enacted and enforced. In this attempted resolution of the very difficult problem of
defining and giving institutional shape to a concept of law and order
appropriate to this university, we have been guided by the following
principles.

 Redefinition of the Chancellor's Role. We have already discussed, in the context of his relationship with the Academic Senate,
the importance of achieving for the Chancellor that "distance" which
is a necessary prerequisite for a unified leadership role. It is equally
important that his relationship with the students be transformed so
that the present image of the role will no longer be one that concen-
trates on rule-making and rule adjudication. We believe that, in consultation with students and faculty, he should make provision for others
to carry out these duties instead of assuming direct personal responsibility for them himself. This would not only free time for the urgently
required tasks of educational leadership and reform, but, equally important, it would place his role in the eyes of students in a new and
far more constructive perspective. Our Basic Regulations embody
two fundamental changes whose objectives are to implement this role
transformation.

 First, we recommend the creation of a court system whose
faculty and student members would be appointed by an independent
tripartite Joint Appointments Commission and whose decisions would
be final, subject to the student's appeal to the Chancellor for mitigation
of penalty. Among its other duties, this court system would exercise
final power to review the alleged invalidity of a rule. Second, we recommend the reconstitution of the Rules Committee, most of whose
members would also be appointed by the Joint Appointments Commission, as a permanent body to formulate the campus rules subject
to the Chancellor's final power to promulgate a rule.

 These proposals rest on the pragmatic assumption that the
present structure of legal authority in the governance of the university
will remain unchanged in the immediate future. It is our position,
which we support below, that the Chancellor presently has the power
to delegate final judicial decision-making powers, while retaining the
ultimate authority to revoke that delegation. Our rule-making proposals give stature and permanence to the Rules Committee and impose

detailed procedures to ensure full public discussion of proposed rules. Though these provisions are designed to inhibit the administration's exercise of its rule-making power and to transfer the major responsibility for rules to the committee, in this instance the Chancellor's final rule-making authority remains intact. Similarly, we assume that the Chancellor alone has the power to promulgate the proposed Basic Regulations as campus law.

Although we felt the necessity of designing a system that would permit immediate and substantial improvements within the confines of the present legal system, we do not think this compromise should be regarded as necessarily permanent. As we have already noted in our discussion of the reform of the Academic Senate (at page 106), it is impossible at present to project what changes in campus governance might be appropriate after achievement of substantial decentralization, development of viable forms of representative student organization, and resolution of the problem of appropriate modes of governance participation for presently unrepresented segments of the campus community. If a legislative body in which faculty, administrators, students, research personnel, and nonacademic employees were represented should evolve, it would probably warrant substantial reallocation of legal authority for rule-making and rule-enforcement.

We appreciate the risks that our proposed changes must present when viewed from the perspective of the Chancellor's office. Despite the care with which the proposed court system has been designed, there is always the possibility that it will commit a serious mistake; under our proposal, the Chancellor could not correct past errors, although he could change the system for future cases. We urge, however, that risks of possible harm are inherent in any conceivable solution to our problems.

Policy must, therefore, be made on the basis of our best assessments of relative probabilities. We are convinced that there are much greater risks for this campus if the Chancellor continues to retain the power of final responsibility for every decision. As the Regents have exercised their ultimate responsibility for law and order on the campus by delegating it to the Chancellor, so we believe that he in turn can best carry out this duty by a subdelegation of as much of the rule-making burden as possible to a representative agency and by delegation of final judicial responsibility to an independent court system. In the long run, such delegations will improve the Chancellor's position in dealing with society beyond the campus. In the short run, these actions seem to us an essential first step in rebuilding the necessary bases of mutual trust and confidence on which the future of this campus depends.

An Independent Judiciary. The absence of adequate provisions for the independence of the judicial system is the major defect of present disciplinary procedures on this campus. The Chancellor, as the chief executive of the campus, has responsibility for the maintenance of order on the campus, which requires that he ultimately determines the formulation of its law enforcement policy. During the recent crises surrounding Stop the Draft Week and recruiting at the Placement Center, the Chancellor twice issued warnings of serious disciplinary consequences for rules violations, statements that he later quite accurately referred to as "deterrents."[13] A necessary consequence of this executive function is that it cast the administration as a partisan with a stake in the success of its chosen enforcement policy.

The serious problem arises from the fact that an office that so openly takes an adversary role is also cast in the role of final judge in its own cause. In minor cases, members of the administration have final power of decision without right of appeal in many instances. In all cases of any substance, the decisions of the Dean, committee, or hearing officer are advisory only, the Chancellor retaining final power of decision. Below the Chancellor, the judicial function is exercised by the deans, directly in many cases or often indirectly through their relationship with the self-perpetuating Men's and Women's Judicial Committees. Many other cases are heard by the Student Conduct Committee or occasionally by a hearing officer; the Chancellor retains final power to name these judges. Thus the structure is one in which the administration can both control the selection of judges and change their advisory verdicts without any stated limitation.

No matter how much goodwill may be invested in a structure of this sort, it is basically wrong in principle. The tradition of separation of powers is deeply rooted in the United States, and the separation of prosecutorial and judicial functions is an elementary concept of due process. It was argued in testimony before the Commission that the administration's retention of this sweeping authority in disciplinary cases has been a mere formality. In practice the Chancellor has del-

[13] *Daily Californian,* October 18, 1967, p. 20; *ibid.,* November 2, 1967, p. 9; Speech to the Academic Senate, *Campus Report,* November 8, 1967, p. 2.

egated much of the process by which Student Conduct Committee members and hearing officers are selected to the Academic Senate. Moreover, we have encountered only one case (which may well have been inadvertent) in which the Chancellor increased a penalty assessed by the Student Conduct Committee, and we regard it as highly unlikely that he would substitute his own judgment of guilt for a committee finding of innocence, a situation that at least in recent times appears never to have arisen.

Formal transfer of the power to select judges from the Chancellor to an agency substantially independent of the administration and delegation of final power of decision to the judiciary would not substantially change the actuality of present practice.[14] From the student perspective, however, the fact that "advisory" recommendations are in fact final is not self-evident, and to accord formal recognition to the practical actuality would effect an important change in campus attitudes toward the fairness of our disciplinary procedures. It seems to us self-evident that the policy advantage that would result from making this merely formal change would be overwhelming and would bring us into line with the standards recommended by national bodies such as the A.A.U.P.

We believe that the Chancellor has the authority to make the delegations of judicial finality and appointment that would be required to implement our proposals. The only relevant Regental declaration arose in the immediate aftermath of the Free Speech controversy on December 18, 1964:

> The Regents reconfirm that ultimate authority for student discipline within the University is constitutionally vested in the Regents, and is a matter not subject to negotiation. Implementation of disciplinary policies will continue to be delegated, as provided in the By-Laws and Standing Orders of the Regents, to the President and Chancellors, who will seek advice of appropriate faculty committees in individual cases.

This declaration, however, was a response to one clause of the resolution of December 8, which incidentally put the Academic Senate on record in favor of administrative abstention from the exercise of judi-

---

[14] The major difference involves the role of the Dean of Students. Our principal rationale for this change is discussed in the two immediately following subsections. It is important to add, however, that the confusion of the Dean's present role as both prosecutor and sometimes judge illustrates the kinds of problems with which we are concerned.

cial authority in the political field, and which provided that "Future disciplinary measures in the area of political activity shall [sic] be determined by a committee appointed by and responsible to the Berkeley Division of the Academic Senate." It is clear that the Regents regarded this bluntly assertive Senate action as a challenge to their ultimate authority and responded in kind. In such a context, the Regents' declaration has little weight in a determination of chancellorial powers of subdelegation, a subject not raised by the Senate resolution.

Subsequently, the Policies Relating to Student Conduct, issued on July 1, 1966, merely require the chancellors to "establish campus regulations *providing for* the handling of student conduct cases in accordance with basic standards of fairness" (emphasis added). This implies the power to delegate and adopts the precise approach that we recommend. All doubt on this question is resolved, in our opinion, by the subsequent directive of President Kerr to chancellors dealing with redelegation of authority, which was dated December 13, 1966, and which explicitly states that "This memorandum supersedes the provisions of any previously issued regulations and procedures which restrict your authority to redelegate." This directive explicitly provides that "you are hereby given full discretion to redelegate all authority delegated to you with the following exceptions. . . ." The only exception specified that relates to student conduct is the determination to dismiss a student. Our proposals are in conformity with this requirement; they allow the student to appeal to the Chancellor for mitigation of penalty in any case and provide that an appeal is automatic in the event of a judgment of dismissal by the court system.[15]

"Discipline" and Education. Our discussion has been permeated with the conventional terminology which refers to "academic discipline," but the fact that discipline occurs in a university setting means that it should be regarded as but one segment of an overall educational program. Academic sanctions can have very serious consequences for

---

[15] Considerable redelegation already exists on the campus. The Berkeley Campus Regulations Implementing University Wide Policies, IV-2-a, grant the Dean of Students final authority in the adjudication of any case, provided that only a relatively minor penalty had been imposed by the Dean. Similarly, campus practice regarding student discipline in cheating cases apparently extends substantial authority to the instructor concerned in making a final disposition of the offense, again subject to the limitations on penalty that can be imposed.

the individual concerned,[16] but only a tiny proportion of university disciplinary proceedings result in such severity. In most situations we can give full scope to procedures that reflect an informality and concern which allows problems to be resolved on a face-to-face basis. The reintegration of the student into the educational community and the provision of the help or counseling he may require, which are the essence of normal academic discipline, are best achieved through a flexible and informal process.

But the fact that the majority of cases can be handled informally does not obviate the necessity for providing the agencies and procedures necessary to ensure fairness and deliberation in adversary cases. The fact that formal due process protections will be required in only a statistically insignificant proportion of cases no more excuses failure to provide them than a hospital would be justified in not bothering to obtain an iron lung because most patients do not require one. When the occasion arises, the remedy is indispensable and will only be available if provision for it has been made in advance.

The criterion that should distinguish whether a case is to be handled formally or informally is whether it can honestly be described as a mutual attempt to solve a problem or is instead essentially adversary in nature. Three kinds of cases appear to require formality. The first is the rare instance in which the student denies the charge against him. The second, perhaps equally rare, is where the university is convinced that either its welfare, or the welfare of the student as the university conceives that welfare, requires the student's separation from the university, but the student may not agree. Third, unfortunately less rare in our recent history, are the cases in which the educational problem-solving approach must operate in an atmosphere contaminated by outside pressure for disciplinary action or internal temptation to use disciplinary action as a warning to the rest of the student body.[17] In

[16] Exclusion from the university in a world where higher education is increasingly a necessity will seriously disadvantage the student and imports a moral turpitude comparable to that of conviction of many crimes. Under present political circumstances, moreover, the suspended or excluded student loses his student Selective Service deferment and is subject to immediate induction. Even proceedings that result only in minor sanctions can have a serious cumulative impact if a "prior record" can have substantial impact in the event of a later rules violation.

[17] See the preceding discussion on an independent judiciary. In his warning on the pending Dow Chemical protests in which he tried to head off an

any of these situations, we can no longer be confident that the welfare of the individual student is the sole or even the dominant end of the disciplinary process.

Like many such distinctions, it is unfortunate that this criterion works best by hindsight; when a case is initiated, it is often not clear whether informal or formal proceedings will prove most appropriate. What begins as a routine informal case may develop adversary aspects as it goes along, while a political case that appears to be adamantly adversary may prove amenable to an informal adjustment. Thus the nub of the structural problem results from three related difficulties: formal procedure inhibits the flexibility required by informality; initial informality can seriously prejudice due process protection in cases where formality is ultimately required; we cannot be certain at the outset which category is most appropriate for a given case.

The solution for this problem, incorporated in our proposals, is in two parts: to protect the integrity of the informal, helping process by preventing any material developed in what should be an essentially confidential relationship of student and counselor from being used for disciplinary purposes without the student's consent; and to achieve realistic due process protection by as complete segregation as is practicable of the formal from the informal processes. This is accomplished in our recommended Basic Regulations by providing that each case is initiated by informal procedures before a panel (called the Preliminary Hearing Division) of the proposed Student Conduct Court. If this attempt to work out a mutually acceptable solution to the problem is successful, the case goes no further. If, however, the case develops adversary aspects, the Trial Division to which it is referred and which conducts the formal proceedings is composed of different judges who know nothing about the case's prior history, and evidence brought out

---

anticipated disruption, the Chancellor stated: "Any student who participates in action which interferes with the safety or freedom of students or of the interviewers, or with the normal functioning of University facilities, and any student who organizes an action for that purpose, will be placed on interim suspension and will thereafter be subject to dismissal from the University." *Daily Californian,* November 2, 1967, p. 9. In this sort of situation, where a threat of discipline is used for deterrent purposes, it is idle to suppose that a resulting case will be anything other than entirely adversary. Indeed, the unqualified warning that "any" student who violates rules "will be placed on interim suspension," apparently without regard to individual circumstances, indicates the extent to which deterrent policy has superseded policy centered upon the individual student's welfare.

in the informal stage before the Preliminary Hearing Division cannot be used against the student without his consent.

Discipline and Confidentiality. Closely related to the foregoing discussion is the conflict between the counseling of a student for the purpose of helping him, and the imposition of discipline upon him. We regard it as wrong in principle to mix the helping and disciplinary roles, and from the student's viewpoint we think it imperative that they be seen to be entirely separated.[18] It is a generally accepted principle of the counseling and helping professions that confidentiality is of the essence of the relationship, so that a person who goes for help can do so with full confidence that what he reveals will not lead without his consent to any punitive or other consequences with which he may disagree. A student can now go to the psychiatric clinic at Cowell Hospital with this assurance. The bifurcated court procedure described above represents our attempt to provide as comparable assurance as possible in disciplinary cases.

The principle that counseling should be confidential and without potential disciplinary repercussions has another important consequence that we have incorporated in our proposals: the divorce of the office of the Dean of Students from any major role in discipline. We have already made reference (at page 152 above) to the conflicts in the Dean's present role. Our recommendations would resolve these conflicts by a transfer of all of the Dean's present judicial functions to the proposed Student Conduct Court and by transfer of his present disciplinary role as an initiator of cases to a proposed agency, called the Legal Services Board, discussed below, which would, when necessary, service the court system by assuming the functions that in criminal cases are served by prosecutor and defense counsel.

The most important function we see for a dean is that of helping a student make the most of his educational experience. He is in the best position to assist the student to overcome personal, financial, or bureaucratic obstacles to the best utilization of the student's educa-

---

[18] When Professor Leon Henkin of the Committee on Academic Freedom testified before us, he described a case raised before the committee by students who alleged, among other complaints, that the Dean's role "puts the Dean in an untenable position as it prevents an open and candid exchange between the Dean and the students." Professor Henkin commented: ". . . we felt this had very great merit but that it did not involve any issue of academic freedom" and therefore "we recommended that the petitioners seek a change in the procedures."

tional opportunities, and he is in a key position to guide students to specialized counseling facilities when such referrals are appropriate. The deans who testified before the Commission at our hearings shared this conception of their professional role and stressed that the vast majority of cases coming before them did not involve disciplinary problems.

In testifying before the Commission, Dean of Students Arleigh Williams minimized the conflict between counseling and discipline. He told us:

> . . . I believe that there is more myth than fact attached to the theory that conflict is inevitable because one individual performs this dual function. Of course, conflict will arise occasionally, but I argue that it will be negligible if the "counselor-disciplinarian" respects the student as an individual, exercises a sensitivity in his treatment of the student, and is fair in his responses or judgments.

We have no reason to question the sincerity of Dean Williams' testimony; we think, however, that his statement misses the central importance of the principle that counseling should be confidential and therefore completely divorced from discipline. It is not the ability of the "counselor-disciplinarian" to be fair that is primarily at issue, but how the relationship appears to those who are to be counseled. In any counseling relationship, whether of lawyer and client, doctor and patient, or dean and student, the professional integrity of the counselor can usually be assumed. Confidentiality is nonetheless regarded as essential in order to encourage the fullest possible disclosure by the person seeking help.

We noted above the present availability of such confidential counseling in the services provided at Cowell Hospital. We think it critically important that the student be able to take his nonpsychiatric problems to a dean with similar confidence; we fear that the presently ambiguous position of the dean, because of the disciplinary aspects of his role, may seriously inhibit this end. We recognize, of course, that this is an assumption that is not susceptible of proof one way or the other. There is no way to determine how many students are plagued by problems that they do not fully reveal to a dean or do not take to him at all, or how much this situation would be improved if the dean's student-oriented confidentiality were fully assured. In this state of necessary uncertainty, we think it best to rely on the considerable experience of the traditional counseling professions, which reinforces the desirability of separating counseling from discipline.

The Non-Adversary Principle. Under present practices, most disciplinary cases are initiated by the Dean's office, and the Dean is usually responsible for preparation of the case. Under our recommendations, these functions would be redirected. As we have indicated, we purpose the creation of a new agency (the Legal Services Board) which would assume them. This agency, consisting of law professors, law students, and other students, would also fill several other needs of a campus judicial structure. Under our recommendations, it would provide advisers for students charged with violations, and it would render professional legal advice to the courts in those rare instances in which complicated legal problems were encountered. With this safe-guard, the present hearing officer procedure, which has only been utilized in two instances, is rendered obsolete and can be abolished.[19] We have combined all these functions in one agency to reinforce the dominance of an educational problem-solving approach to discipline. We considered creating the offices of student prosecutor and student defender. We believe, however, that this would put unnecessary emphasis on the system as a whole on an adversariness which in practice is rarely required.

URGENT NEED FOR REFORM

The recommendations embodied in the proposed Basic Regulations which follow will on first reading offend many readers because of their intricate detail and technical complexity. They appear as a demeaning contrast to the simplicity and candor associated with ideal educational settings. We, too, share the nostalgia for a community whose limited size and shared purposes permit it to dispense with rules

---

[19] In the rare instances in which formal trials posing complicated legal issues might occur, our recommendations provide that the chairman of the trial panel of the Student Conduct Court will be the law professor who heads that court. If the court wishes, it may ask the Legal Services Board to appoint a lawyer to supersede the Student Counsel in handling the case, or to appoint a legal adviser to the court. Thus these cases can be handled as part of the court's regular routine, whereas the separate hearing officer procedure currently in force by its very rarity emphasizes the spectacular aspects of the cases in which it is employed.

and procedure. Reality compels the admission that such a community does not resemble the Berkeley of 1968.

We would like to assume, moreover, that if we were to concentrate on intensified efforts for educational reform and the creation of new roles for students in educational policy-making, then the pettifoggery of rules and discipline would somehow be transmuted by new modes of cooperation and trust. We see no indication, however, that such a transmutation can occur, at least in the short run. Nor is abandonment of the struggle likely to occur spontaneously. There are disturbing signs that we are already caught in a cyclic process that generates its own perverse satisfactions. Too often we have witnessed the sudden surge of student emotion, soaring attendance at the Academic Senate, increasingly frenzied activity of administrators and faculty leaders. Like some other noxious customs, brinksmanship provides temporary relief for frustration, substitutes the exhilaration of crisis for routine, and nurtures illusions that a "final solution" is both possible and imminent. Such habits are hard to kick.

The blunt fact is, however, that the breaking of this cycle has become a prerequisite for the regeneration of the educational processes with which much of this report has been concerned. To this imperative has been added another that, at least in the short run, is even more compelling. It is now evident that we are on the threshold of what threatens to become the most dangerous assault on academic autonomy and integrity in the history of the modern public university. We simply cannot afford many repetitions of the events of mid-October, 1967, when an outside attack that should have united the campus instead became the occasion of a near-civil war.

There is no foreseeable solution of this impasse that does not entail substantial risk. One hypothesis is that the elimination of a coterie of activist leaders coupled with the stern reaffirmation of administrative authority would bring peace in our time. It is far from clear, however, how such "peace" could be achieved by these methods without doing irreparable damage to the culture in which the true university must be nurtured. There is perhaps at least symbolic significance in the suggestion, already advanced, that the campus be fenced and its personnel identified with badges as a means of eliminating unauthorized entry. Nor is it clear that even this kind of peace is obtainable. We do not equate student with Negro protest, but the rejection of the integration perspective by parts of Negro communities demonstrates the tenuousness of the line that separates protest as total rejection from protest as an assertion of the protester's desire to change a community to which he still feels meaningful ties. We believe that student protest is still predominantly of the second order and that it provides a base upon which we can build. The opportunity, however, may in retrospect prove to have been a fleeting one, as it was in the case of Negro protest.

The Commission believes that significant institutional reform is a method which offers far greater prospects for holding turbulence within manageable limits while at the same time reaffirming rather than weakening our underlying educational principles. Such reform, if executed with conviction and dispatch, could break the ominous circle of distrust in which we have all become trapped. We have therefore devoted major effort to an exploration of the direction and substance of possible reform.

One striking characteristic of the Berkeley scene repeatedly encountered in our study has been its inhospitality to the reform of its methods of law-making and the administration of campus justice. As is perhaps true with most institutions, there has been an unfortunate tendency on this campus to couple a refusal to carry out reform under threats of coercion during periods of crisis with a failure to get reform accomplished under the soporific influence of periods of calm. We have encountered numerous instances of prolonged delay in implementing even the simplest and most obvious reforms that have been recommended for campus disciplinary procedures. There have been interminable delays in implementing rules changes recommended by the Academic Freedom Committee[20] or even starting the "compilation

---

[20] The Provisional Campus Rules issued in September 1965 included in the procedures governing disciplinary hearings a clause reading: "An adequate summary of the proceedings will be kept." The Academic Freedom Committee requested that this be amended by adding: "The student shall be furnished a draft of the summary and shall have the opportunity to submit written comment which will be incorporated as a part of the record." This recommendation expressed a minimum demand of due process and is presumably noncontroversial. When the revised rules were issued in September 1966, the recommendation was not incorporated; Professor Leon Henkin, chairman of the committee, said in his testimony before the Commission that no objection to the recommendation had been expressed by the Chancellor and that "I think he forgot to look at our recommendations." The committee again requested that the change be incorporated and was informed, prior to Professor Henkin's testimony before us on March 2, 1967, that the change was in

and codification of all administrative regulations which concern students," requested by a 9–0 vote of the Rules Committee in April 1967.[21]

We believe part of the reason for these delays stems from the paralysis of the Rules Committee, the harassment of an overworked administration, and the failure to lodge responsibility for getting on with the task of reform in any one agency. There are two other factors, however, that appear to have been major influences in impeding change. The first can be illustrated by one aspect of our own institutional life as a Commission. We have enjoyed a luxury denied to the administration and the Rules Committee: relative detachment from daily problems. We have had no administrative or political responsibility for solving today's crisis and have assiduously avoided becoming involved in the many immediate problems which, after our establishment, various campus groups asked us to consider. This has given us breathing space for the development of the reforms in disciplinary structures and procedures presented in this report, reforms which, in our opinion, provide a sound basis for the breakthrough that is so badly needed in this area.

The second factor is manifested by the complexity of our proposed Basic Regulations. We soon found that the task on which we embarked was an arduous one. Any document that merely brought together all the procedures currently in use in dealing with student discipline would be of comparable length and complexity to our Regulations. The difficulty is compounded, moreover, in any forthright attempt to accommodate both informal help and formal protection

---

process. The rules currently being distributed to students still do not incorporate it.

[21] Minutes, Campus Rules Committee, April 21, 1967. The request was formally communicated to the Chancellor on May 3 and apparently accepted by the Chancellor in his letter to the committee of June 2, 1967. An administration memorandum dated December 28, 1967, refers to a proposed redraft of the university-wide rule on the standard of conduct for students as "the most reasonable starting point for such an effort" at codification. In general the responses of the administration to the 1967 Rules Committee illustrate the great difficulties of accomplishing anything in "normal" times. Even so apparently innocuous a request as that the committee be allowed to have cochairmen was submitted on March 6 and not approved until April 10. To understand student reaction, this sort of delay must be considered with the fact that the faculty members of the committee were not appointed by the Chancellor until February 17, when the academic year was more than half over.

in a single system without compromising the integrity of either approach.

The detail, therefore, is first and foremost a reflection of the difficulty of the problems with which the Regulations deal and of the fact that the commitment demanded of us and the detachment permitted us proved to be prerequisites for reaching accord on such a wide range of controversial topics. None of the detail is superfluous, for every provision is a response to a problem that has arisen or is likely to arise. Failure to accord complex problems the detailed attention they deserve at the time such legislation is drafted does not cause the problems to vanish; it simply means that attempts to find solutions are postponed, often to times of stress when calm and unhurried consideration of their intricacy is impossible.

Accordingly we recommend that each Senate adopt a resolution along the following lines:

1. Subject to the review provided for in pars. 2 and 3 of this resolution, the Senate approves the Basic Regulations as sound in principle and recommends their prompt promulgation by the Chancellor.

2. Before transmitting this recommendation to the Chancellor, the Senate instructs its Committee on Academic Freedom[22] to review the Basic Regulations and append any comments or alternative provisions which it may wish to add.

3. Upon completion of its review the committee shall forward this resolution to the Chancellor unless it is of the opinion that serious objections require that the whole matter be returned to the Senate for further Senate action.

4. In carrying out its duties under this resolution, the Committee on Academic Freedom is instructed to consult fully with the parallel committee of the other Senate and to attempt to resolve any differences between them in the interest of prompt implementation of this recommendation.

This recommendation is not intended to inhibit full debate in each Senate on the principles that would be implemented by the rules. On the two previous occasions at which the Academic Senate considered the existing rules, there was no attempt for the whole body to

---

[22] The student Senate currently does not have an Academic Freedom Committee. We hope that it will promptly appoint one, at least on a temporary basis, to serve this review function. See our recommendation, p. 145.

consider them in detail; rather, only the general principles involved were posed as issues.[23] We urge a similar procedure in this instance. We see possibilities of endless delay and serious divisions between the two Senates if each Senate starts to debate and amend the Basic Regulation section by section. The campus cannot afford such delay.

[23] The most recent occasion resulted in a voice vote which approved the rules as "sound in principle." The resolution was put to the Senate by the chairman of the Academic Freedom Committee, acting as an individual, at a meeting which took place just before Charter Day, 1966, when serious disruption and rules violations were threatened. There was no advance notice in the call to the meeting that the question would be raised. Minutes, March 22, 1966, p. i. Moreover, the Academic Freedom Committee has frequently acted without consulting the whole Senate in commenting on and suggesting changes in the existing rules. The Senate has never objected, and it would seem appropriate to repose the same responsibility in the committee in connection with these proposals. See also Minutes, October 11, 1965.

Chapter XI

⚹⚹⚹⚹⚹⚹

Basic Regulations Governing Enactment and Enforcement of Campus Rules

The regulations that follow distinguish what we regard as "basic" legislation from the actual content of the rules that govern student conduct. The former include the composition and functions of the agencies involved in rule-making and rule adjudication (Sec. 106); the provisions of the maximum practicable number of channels by which student grievances can be adjudicated in an orderly fashion before they generate major crises (for example, Secs. 107, 306, and 602–603); the means by which diverse demands for formality and informality can best be compromised (Secs. 507–510); and the clear statement of the procedural protections and fundamental rights of students (for example, Secs. 400–407, 508–509).

The campus rules, on the other hand, deal with the implementation of these principles in an immediate and, to some extent, inevitably political context. As we conceive the role of the Rules Committee, it will regulate student organizations, and the use of campus facilities by students and student political activities; and it will define the conduct subject to academic discipline and determine what sanctions to apply (Sec. 303). Other than to specify what we consider to be the appropriate limits for the imposition of academic discipline (Sec. 104), the Commission has not concerned itself with the content of the rules.

Our structural innovations stem from a proposed Joint Appointments Commission, composed of two students, two faculty members, and one administration representative, which would have the duty of appointing or nominating for appointment the members of all our other agencies (Secs. 200–204). Such a commission is the best method we have been able to develop under present circumstances to deal with the very difficult problem of getting adequate representation of qualified students to serve in important campus-wide capacities. It should not be regarded as permanent; once viable methods of central student organization based on strong local constituencies have been developed, direct appointment of student agency members by a Student Senate might well prove a more appropriate form of selection. At the present time, however, there is no organization that adequately represents all students or even a substantial proportion of them. We hope the Joint Appointments Commission will provide a workable substitute and at the same time strengthen faculty selection.

Under our recommendation, the central adjudicatory function would be served by a faculty-student Student Conduct Court (Secs. 500–512). This court is divided into a Preliminary Hearing Division, for initial investigation of all cases and the informal final resolution of most cases, and a Trial Division, for the formal adjudication of those cases where such procedure is required. The total membership of the court is divided equally between faculty and students; it will do its informal work in units of one student and one faculty member and its trial work in panels of three or five with a student majority. The two divisions would be segregated in order to permit the fullest exploration of a case at the informal level without prejudicing the rights of a defendant in those cases where informal negotiations break down and a full trial is required. The chairman of the Student Conduct Court would be a law faculty member to provide the court with legal expertise where that is needed and thus to obviate the need for the hearing officer procedure.

Although the low volume of cases reported to us by the Deans apparently would not necessitate an elaborate structure of lower courts, the Student Conduct Court may delegate some of its minor functions to local bodies such as a living unit tribunal or an honor committee in a particular school (Sec. 512). We do not recommend that the Men's and Women's Judicial Committees be continued; the method by which their members are selected is inappropriate, their procedures fail to meet necessary standards and achieve neither the benefits of informality nor the protection of formality, and their relationships with the Deans are ambiguous and compromise their independence. We prefer to give the Student Conduct Court a free hand to encourage decentralization where it is appropriate while retaining close working relationships with the lower courts.

A student who is disciplined in the Student Conduct Court can appeal to the Chancellor for mitigation of the penalty. For the rare cases where appellate review is required or the validity or construction of campus rules is at issue, we have also made provision for a Campus Review Court consisting of five faculty members and two students (Secs. 600–605). The most important function of the Campus Review Court is its final authority to determine the legality of rules, administrative policies for the enforcement of rules, or administrative decisions interpreting a rule (Secs. 602–603). Determination of the validity of a campus rule may be raised either by an original petition filed before the Court by anyone who wishes to challenge a rule or by reviewing of a judgment on rule validity of the Student Conduct Court. We expect that few cases will come to the Campus Review Court, which is conceived of as largely a stand-by, safety-valve institution.

General criteria by which to determine whether a rule is "valid" are suggested in Sec. 107. In matters affecting the interpretation of constitutional, federal, or state law, or of university-wide law, we would expect the Campus Review Court to follow the precedents of the civil courts. Provision is made for the court to obtain legal advice (Sec. 602, discussed below) to assist it in reaching these determinations. In other cases, the alleged grounds for invalidity will raise questions of Academic Senate policy or student academic freedom. In such instances, the court will doubtless wish to obtain the advice of the Senate Policy Committee or the student or faculty Committees on Academic Freedom before reaching its decision.

Of course we recognize that "student academic freedom" is an ill-defined and open-ended concept. We have already indicated, moreover, that Academic Senate policy, at least as represented by the resolution of December 8, 1964, poses difficult problems of interpretation. As concepts, they resemble both academic freedom as applied to faculty and the protections gathered together under the caption of due process. In both of these areas, law slowly achieves specificity through the trial and error process of litigation. We see no alternative to providing similar flexibility for the implementation of rapidly developing concepts about students' rights.

From a theoretical standpoint, the Campus Review Court is both our most important and most difficult innovation. It seems clear that there must be some final source of authority on the Berkeley campus for adjudicating rule validity and rule interpretation. We reject the use of Regents' Counsel for this purpose, both because the subject matter is one in which Berkeley should have full autonomy and because the procedures followed in obtaining his opinion deny litigants reasonable opportunity to be heard. We have rejected the Committee on Academic Freedom as a final arbiter because its jurisdiction is too restricted, being limited to questions of academic freedom. We have rejected the Senate Policy Committee because its jurisdiction is too broad, going beyond the purely juridical matters; the Policy Committee is inevitably and properly involved in political and executive problems from which a review court should be insulated. Finally, utilization of any of the foregoing methods of review would have the very serious defect of excluding student participation from an area where significant student involvement is appropriate. Accordingly, we see no alternative to the creation of a new body.

The courts would be assisted by the Legal Services Board, an agency composed of law-trained faculty, law students, and certain other student members. This Board would handle the preparation of cases for presentation to the courts, supply advisers or lawyers as needed to students brought before the courts, and assist the courts in resolving legal issues that may come before them. We have combined these services in one agency because of our emphasis on discipline as a non-adversary, educational function, and we would assume that student members, during their term of service on the Board, would function in varying capacities at different times. We also assume that the student members, many of whom will have had substantial legal training, would handle most of the work. We have been generally concerned with the burden our various proposals place on faculty members; in particular, our Basic Regulations involve substantial participation of a few members of the law faculty. We think it is important to minimize this workload insofar as possible, and we do not anticipate any large number of cases in which faculty members of the Board would be directly involved.

The final agency whose existence and functions are codified by our proposed regulations is the faculty-student Rules Committee. While a representative of the administration would meet with the Rules Committee, he would not have a vote because our proposal leaves final authority in rules matters to the Chancellor. We have attempted to remedy the defects that have been evident during the last two years within the operation of the experimental Rules Committee, which functioned without notable success during parts of the last two academic years.

ᔥ CONTENTS ᔊ

⫸ *GENERAL PROVISIONS* ⫷

Sec. 100. These Regulations govern the methods of enactment and enforcement of the Campus Rules and provide for courts and agencies to carry out these objectives.

Sec. 101. The objectives sought by the adoption of these Regulations are:

(1) to provide for a judiciary that is independent of executive or prosecutorial functions;

(2) to create rule-making machinery that is broadly representative of all campus interests concerned with the rules;

(3) to devise procedures for the selection of judges and rule-makers which, given the size, complexity, and diversity of the campus community, are best calculated to create enacting and adjudicative bodies that are of high quality and representative of the diversity of interests characteristic of this campus; and

(4) to protect the academic freedom of students by the codification of procedures that are fair and consistent with widely held concepts of due process of law.

Sec. 102. The objectives sought by the Campus Rules whose enactment and enforcement is provided for in these Regulations are:

(1) to adapt University-wide policies to the particular needs of the Berkeley campus;

(2) to provide for a body of substantive campus law that reflects and promotes the University's commitment to an educational atmosphere hospitable to innovation and exploration;

(3) to adjust the concept of law and order to the unique context of a community dedicated to the protection and encouragement of intellectual inquiry, including the full examination of unorthodox or controversial ideas;

(4) to define prohibited conduct with the precision necessary to give adequate warning of the line between what is and what is not proscribed;

(5) to employ those sanctions best calculated to educate violators and strengthen their ties to an educational community rather than to punish, to graduate sanctions according to the seriousness of the violator's threat to the University community and its essential functions, and to provide standards which give fair warning of the manner in which aggravating or mitigating circumstances will be considered in the assessment of sanctions;

(6) to carry out the philosophy that University authority is limited in scope, that the University does not stand *in loco parentis,* and that discipline is imposed only for offenses that impair the orderly functioning of the University, not for enforcement of civil law.

Sec. 103. "Academic discipline" consists of sanctions imposed for violations of the standards of conduct prescribed in these Regulations and the Campus Rules.

Sec. 104. The following standards define conduct that is subject to academic discipline:

(1) "Academic Standards" are those that directly affect the evaluation of the academic quality of a student's work in a course or academic program and the estimation of his scholarly potential. Violations of academic standards include failure to complete required work, plagiarism, and cheating.

(a) Discipline imposed for violations of academic standards is subject to the rules and practices of the Academic Senate and are not governed by Regulations and the Campus Rules, provided that the sanctions thereby invoked are reasonably related to academic evaluation of the student's work and are within the traditional prerogatives of an instructor or academic unit, e.g., exclusion from a course or program or the assignment of a lower grade for the work involved. Such academic sanctions are not included in a student's disciplinary record.

(b) If in a particular case an instructor or academic unit is of the opinion that traditional academic sanctions pursuant to par. (a) above constitute inappropriate or insufficient discipline for a violation such as cheating, the case may be referred to the Student Conduct Court for further action. In this event these Regulations and the relevant provisions of the Campus Rules are applicable.

(2) "Regulatory standards" are those embodied in the provisions of the Campus Rules that regulate the free exercise of political and other forms of student expression, the right of students to associate together in organizations, and their use of university facilities to hold meetings or organize or plan activities. The purpose of the regulatory standards is to facilitate the freest exercise of these rights consistent with reasonable protection of the normal educational functions of the University. These Regulations and the Campus Rules are applicable to proceedings which result from violations of regulatory standards.

(3) "Criminal law" refers to that body of law that defines the minimum standards of conduct imposed on all persons, including students whether on or off campus, whose violation may render the violator subject to prosecution and punishment in the criminal courts.

(a) Violations of the criminal law by students are subject to academic discipline pursuant to these Regulations and the Campus Rules only when the conduct:

(i) physically harms, or imminently threatens physical harm to a member of the University community; or

(ii) directly affects the property of the University or of members or guests of the University community, e.g., by theft or malicious damage.

(4) Violations of the criminal law by students are not subject to academic discipline, but are the exclusive concern of the state or federal courts, if the conduct, whether or not it happens to occur on campus, is not also a violation of one of the University standards enumerated in pars. (1), (2), or (3) above.

(5) If an act simultaneously violates both the University's standards defined in pars. (1), (2), or (3) above and state or federal criminal law and is prosecuted in the criminal courts, the University will normally accept the court's judgment as the full disposition for the offense.

Sec. 105. To the extent specified below, the following classes of persons are subject to academic discipline pursuant to these Regulations and the Campus Rules:

(1) (a) A "student" is a person currently registered on this campus as a student or who was so registered in the immediately preceding quarter.

(b) A student is subject to any discipline or sanction provided for in the Campus Rules.

(2) (a) An "employee" is a person who is employed in any capacity by the University, including a part-time employee.

(b) These Regulations and the Campus Rules are not applicable to an employee, except that if a person is both an employee and a student, e.g., a teaching assistant, his employee status may be indirectly affected if it is conditioned on continued student status.

(3) (a) A "nonstudent" is any person who is not a student or employee as those terms are defined in this section.

(b) A nonstudent is subject to either of the following forms of academic discipline:

(i) sanctions analogous to those provided for the violation if he were a student, which shall be applicable to any future status as a student on this campus and which shall include conditions such as probation to take effect upon his admission or readmission or the suspension or denial of the possibility of his readmission;

(ii) denial of access to some or all campus facilities for a specified period of time.

Sec. 106. (1) These Regulations provide for the creation, composition, and duties of the following:

(a) The Joint Appointments Commission (Secs. 200–204);

(b) The Rules Committee (Secs. 300–309);

(c) The Student Conduct Court (Secs. 500–512);

(d) The Campus Review Court (Secs. 600–605);

(e) The Legal Services Board (Secs. 700–703).

(2) Members of the courts and agencies specified in par. (1) above shall serve the following terms of office:

(a) To provide continuity of functions, faculty members appointed to the various bodies provided for by these Regulations shall serve two-year staggered terms, after which they are ineligible for reappointment for an interval of at least one year. Some initial appointments shall be for one year as required to establish a rotation of staggered terms.

(b) Student members shall be appointed for one-year terms. They are eligible for reappointment to a second but not any subsequent terms. Where feasible, sufficient reappointments to provide continuity shall be given favorable consideration.

(c) Members appointed to represent the Chancellor shall serve such terms as are designated by the Chancellor.

(d) A member designated as chairman shall serve in that capacity for a one-year term.

(3) At the time members are appointed to these courts and agencies, the appointing body shall name an alternate for each person appointed so that any vacancies that occur can be filled immediately.

(4) These courts and agencies should be provided with administrative and secretarial assistance, office space, and the budget required for the adequate performance of their duties. Upon the recommendation of the Joint Appointments Commission with the approval of the administration, students carrying heavy responsibilities in the execution of their duties on these courts or agencies may be provided with financial assistance to compensate them for the loss of opportunity for other employment.

Sec. 107. (1) A rule is invalid if it violates federal or state law, the rules and policies of the Board of Regents or the President of the University, the prerogatives of the Chancellor, these Regulations, or the traditions of campus academic freedom as these are determined by the Campus Review Court.

(2) The alleged invalidity of a rule may be determined in a declaratory judgment action brought before the Campus Review Court pursuant to Secs. 602–603 of these Regulations.

(3) The invalidity of a rule is a defense and may be alleged in proceedings before the Student Conduct Court pursuant to Secs. 509 (2) (b) and 509 (4) of these Regulations.

(4) If a student advances the invalidity of a rule as a defense before the Student Conduct Court and it is ultimately determined that the rule is valid, the student's failure to avail himself of a reasonable opportunity to bring a declaratory judgment action pursuant to Secs. 602–603 to test the rule's validity before he violated it shall be considered as an aggravating circumstance in assessing the discipline to be imposed upon him.

Sec. 108. No academic discipline shall be imposed unless

(1) the conduct has been previously proscribed by a rule promulgated and published in accordance with these Regulations; and

(2) it has been finally determined in accordance with the pro-

cedures prescribed in these Regulations that the charged student has violated the rule.

Sec. 109. At the time that these Regulations become effective, all rules currently in effect shall be published in the form provided by these Regulations and shall remain in force, subject to amendment or repeal pursuant to Secs. 306–307 of these Regulations. Rules not published pursuant to this paragraph are deemed to be repealed as of the date that these Regulations are made effective.

Sec. 110. These Regulations shall be enacted by promulgation of the Chancellor after consultation with the Academic Senate and the Student Senate. The promulgation shall state the date on which they become effective.

⇘ *JOINT APPOINTMENTS COMMISSION* ⇙

Sec. 200. The Joint Appointments Commission shall have the duties of appointing the members of the Student Conduct Court and the Legal Services Board, and of nominating the members of the Campus Review Court and the Rules Committee.

Sec. 201. (1) The Joint Appointments Commission shall consist of five members, as follows:

(a) two faculty members appointed by the Academic Senate Committee on Committees, at least one of whom should be a member of that committee;

(b) two student members, one undergraduate and one graduate, appointed by the Student Senate, at least one whom should be a member of that Senate's Committee on Committees;

(c) one member appointed by the Chancellor.

(2) Appointments to the Commission shall be made at the beginning of the Fall Quarter.

(3) The Commission shall select its own Chairman.

Sec. 202. The Joint Appointments Commission is charged with making a thorough canvas of the faculty and of the graduate and undergraduate student body in seeking those best qualified for appointment. It shall invite all registered student groups and the respective faculties to submit names for its consideration, both kinds of groups being invited to submit both faculty and student names. It shall make its files of student nominees available to the Student Senate's Committee on Committees, and its files of faculty nominees to the

Academic Senate's Committee on Committees, for their use in the selection of other committees. In making its appointments and nominations the Commission shall give appropriate consideration to the representation of both graduate and undergraduate students. Not later than the end of March the Commission shall make its appointments and submit its nominations for the next ensuing academic year.

Sec. 203. (1) Appointments by the Joint Appointments Commission of members of the Student Conduct Court and of the Legal Services Board shall be final.

(2) Nominations of faculty members of the Campus Review Court and of the Rules Committee shall be submitted to the Academic Senate, and nominations of student members of the Campus Review Court and the Rules Committee shall be submitted to the Student Senate. Such a nomination shall become a final appointment unless it is rejected by the Senate to which it is submitted at the next scheduled meeting of that Senate which occurs at least fifteen days following the date of submission. In event of such a rejection, the Joint Appointments Commission shall submit a new nomination.

Sec. 204. The Joint Appointments Commission is also charged with:

(1) the implementation, through its recommendations to the administration, of the provisions of Sec. 106 (4); and

(2) the continuing evaluation of the governance structures created by those regulations. Not later than the first of May each year the Commission shall submit a report to the two Senates and to the Chancellor. This report shall include an evaluation of the Commission's own selection procedures, the functioning of the court system and of the Rules Committee, and the adequacy of these Regulations. The report shall propose any changes which the Commission believes to be desirable.

⊁ THE RULES COMMITTEE ⊱

Sec. 300. The Rules Committee shall have the duties of reviewing, enacting, amending, and publishing the Campus Rules, subject to the consent of the Chancellor as specified in these Regulations.

Sec. 301. (1) The Rules Committee shall consist of:

(a) four faculty members, who with two alternates shall be

appointed by the Joint Appointments Commission with the consent of the Academic Senate;

(b) four students, one of whom shall be the vice-president of the student body and the other three, with two alternates, appointed by the Joint Appointments Commission with the consent of the Student Senate; and

(c) one nonvoting representative of the administration appointed by the Chancellor.

(2) The administration representative may designate an alternate to act for him at any meeting.

(3) The Joint Appointments Commission shall designate one of the faculty members and one of the student members to act as cochairmen.

(4) The committee may request the Legal Services Board to provide it with a consultant to advise it on questions of constitutional law or other legal matters.

Sec. 302. The Rules Committee shall determine and publish its own rules of procedure, which shall make provision for:

(1) the quorum required to transact business;

(2) procedures whereby members of the campus community can submit written comments on proposed legislation or petitions requesting specific action by the committee;

(3) adequate notice to the campus community of the agenda of its meetings and the text of any proposed rules that are to be considered;

(4) specific notice of a proposed rule to a petitioner of that rule; to any person or group known to the committee that would be affected by that rule; and to any group that has requested regular notice of the committee's meetings.

Sec. 303. The Campus Rules shall be enacted and amended pursuant to Secs. 306–308 of these Regulations and shall provide for:

(1) rules defining and providing sanctions for violations of academic standards that may be referred to the Student Conduct Court pursuant to Sec. 104 (1) above;

(2) rules establishing regulatory standards as defined in sec. 104 (2) and providing sanctions for their violation;

(3) rules which provide, consistently with Sec. 104 (3), those violations of criminal law that are subject to academic discipline and that provide academic sanctions for their violation;

(4) regulations governing the registration of and use of campus facilities by student organizations;

(5) regulations specifying which violations of academic standards shall be entered on the student's record and the effect of a prior record in the event of subsequent violations;

(6) regulations which ensure the confidentiality of student records and minimize the risk of improper disclosure or subpoena of those records.

Sec. 304. In the discharge of its duties pursuant to par. (4) of Sec. 303 above, the committee may delegate to appropriate groups its functions of detailed rule-making or rule-administration, subject to general standards established in the Campus Rules.

Sec. 305. The committee shall assume responsibility for the publication of the Campus Rules and for facilitating their distribution to the campus community. Between periodic updated revisions of the Rules, the committee shall adopt a method such as a loose-leaf format or the use of supplements to ensure that the published version of the Rules is promptly updated. The committee shall also maintain a file, which shall be open to inspection, of all court opinions delivered to it pursuant to Secs. 510 and 605 (4).

Sec. 306. The following procedure shall be followed in ordinary situations when a proposal for enactment, amendment, or repeal of a rule is initiated by the committee or by petition:

(1) The committee shall act only after it has complied with its procedures consistently with Sec. 302.

(2) The action taken by the majority of the committee shall be promptly published by the committee, released to the *Daily Californian,* and transmitted to the Chancellor. The committee is encouraged to append to the text of its proposal a statement of the reasons which prompted its action.

(3) The proposal shall become effective 30 days after it has been transmitted to the Chancellor unless prior to the expiration of that time the Chancellor acts in accordance with par. (4) below.

(4) If the Chancellor wishes to change the proposal, to have it reconsidered or tentatively to reject it, he shall return it to the Committee with a statement indicating his recommendation and the reasons therefor.

(5) If the committee wishes to pursue the matter further, it shall act again on the proposal at a meeting at which the Chancellor

or his representative and any other interested person shall be given the opportunity to be heard.

(6) If the proposal is again approved by a majority of the committee, the procedure specified in par. (2) above shall again be followed. At the expiration of 30 days after transmission to the Chancellor the proposal shall become effective unless during this period it has been disapproved by the Chancellor, in which event it shall not be effective.

Sec. 307.   The following procedures shall be followed in ordinary situations when a proposal for enactment, amendment, or repeal of a rule is initiated by the Chancellor or his representative.

(1) The Chancellor shall submit his proposal informally, with the request that the committee discuss it. The committee shall consider the request promptly in an informal session which may be without public notice and closed to the public.

(2) If the committee tentatively agrees with the proposal, it shall initiate the proposal formally and institute procedures under Secs. 302 and 306.

(3) If the committee tentatively opposes the proposal or wishes to amend it, it shall so inform the Chancellor with a statement of its reasons. The Chancellor may then withdraw the proposal, resubmit it after accepting any amendments suggested by the committee, or resubmit it with his reasons to the committee with a formal request that it be enacted.

(4) The committee shall act on any such resubmission promptly, either enacting the proposal after complying with the procedures specified in Sec. 302 or informing the Chancellor that it refuses to act.

(5) In the event that the committee pursuant to par. (4) above refuses to enact the Chancellor's proposal, the Chancellor may within 30 days of receiving notice of the committee's action enact his proposal by promulgation, specifying the date on which it will become effective. In this event, the committee shall promptly publish it pursuant to Sec. 305.

Sec. 308.   The following procedures are applicable in special circumstances that preclude use of the ordinary procedures stipulated in Secs. 306 and 307.

(1) In the event of an emergency because one or more campus rules are superseded by Regent or court decree or because of other circumstances that urgently require immediate rule-making action,

either the Chancellor or a cochairman of the committee can initiate informal procedures for the enactment of temporary rules. This action shall be taken by a written statement summoning the committee to an emergency meeting which shall specify the reasons why emergency action is required and the general nature of the temporary rules that are to be proposed.

(2) Under these emergency procedures the notice, quorum, and other procedural requirements of Secs. 302, 306, and 307 are suspended, but every effort shall be made to

(a) convene as many members of the committee as possible for the emergency meeting;

(b) to the extent feasible, give public notice to the statement invoking the emergency procedures;

(c) give as full public notice as possible to any temporary rules that are adopted pursuant to this section.

(3) After the emergency meeting or meetings of the committee, the committee with the concurrence of the Chancellor, or the Chancellor after consultation with the committee, may promulgate a temporary rule to take effect immediately or at such time as the rule may specify.

(4) The temporary rule may state a time or the occurrence of a contingency, such as the termination of the emergency, after which it will cease to be effective. In any event no temporary rule enacted under this section shall be effective for more than 60 days unless before the expiration of that time period it shall have been reenacted pursuant to the ordinary procedures of Secs. 302 and 306 or 307.

(5) A temporary rule can be challenged under Sec. 602 of these Regulations in the same manner as any other rule.

Sec. 309. (1) The committee may establish a local Regulatory Unit in a school or college or in a geographical area such as a living unit which is used predominantly for a special nonacademic purpose by a definable group of students. The committee may create such a unit on its own initiative or on petition and shall, if the group meets the definition of a unit, create one if in a referendum a majority of the students concerned requests such action. Authorization for a Regulatory Unit shall be effective for two years, after which it must be renewed.

(2) A Regulatory Unit may enact rules applicable to its internal affairs provided such rules are not inconsistent with the Campus

Rules or the standards of these Regulations. The maximum sanction which can be provided for violation of a unit's rules is exclusion from the facility being regulated, and no academic sanctions can be imposed. A unit may also provide for the local enforcement of its rules consistent with Sec. 512.

(3) Rules enacted or amended by a Regulatory Unit shall be promptly forwarded to the committee for its information.

(4) Any member of the committee or any student in the Regulatory Unit may initiate proceedings to have a unit rule declared invalid. After a hearing of which the members of the Regulatory Unit shall be given notice and at which they shall be heard, the committee may declare the challenged rule invalid if it finds that it is inconsistent with Campus Rules or with these Regulations.

☙ GENERAL STANDARDS IN FORMAL DISCIPLINARY PROCEEDINGS ❧

Sec. 400. (1) Except under emergency circumstances, University premises occupied by students and the personal possessions of students shall not be searched unless authorization has been obtained from the Student Conduct Court. An application for a search shall specify the reasons for the search and the objects and information sought. The student should be present, if possible, during the search. For premises not controlled by the University, the ordinary requirements for lawful search shall be followed.

(2) Students arrested or detected by University officials in the course of serious violations of University regulations or infractions of ordinary law shall be informed of their rights. No form of harassment shall be used by University representatives to coerce admissions of guilt or information about the conduct of other suspected persons.

Sec. 401. Pending action on disciplinary charges, the status of a student shall not be altered, or his right to be present on the campus and to attend classes suspended, unless the Student Conduct Court determines that his suspension is required for compelling reasons related to the student's physical or emotional safety or health or to the protection of other members of the University community.

Sec. 402. (1) The student shall be informed, in writing, of the reasons for the proposed disciplinary action with sufficient particularity, and in sufficient time, to ensure opportunity to prepare for any proceedings.

(2) The notice to the student shall include statements of:

(a) the text of any legislation or regulations alleged to have been violated; and

(b) the charges in the particular case; and

(c) a detailed summary of the evidence upon which the charges are based; and

(d) a first list of witnesses to be called, with the names of additional witnesses to be communicated when they become known; and

(e) a statement of the Court's procedures; and

(f) a statement that the student may be advised by counsel and/or advisers of his own choice, and that the Court upon his request will appoint a legal adviser to assist him.

Sec. 403. The student has the right to be assisted at all stages of the proceedings by advisers or counsel of his choice. He has the right to have legal assistance provided for him by the Court from the panel of legal advisers upon his request, and he must be notified of this right at his first appearance before the Court.

Sec. 404. All hearings shall be private unless the student elects in writing to have proceedings in the Trial Division at a public hearing.

Sec. 405. The burden of proving the charge by a preponderance of the evidence shall be upon the officials or counsel bringing the charge.

Sec. 406. (1) Unless otherwise determined by the Court, evidence shall be submitted in the following order: evidence submitted in support of the charges, evidence submitted by the student, rebuttal evidence in support of the charges, rebuttal evidence submitted by the student, and closing arguments.

(2) The University shall make available to the student all assistance which is within its authority under law to require the presence of witnesses and the production of other evidence.

(3) Normally no testimony shall be received where the opposing party has not been afforded the right of confrontation and a reasonable opportunity for cross-examination. If a witness is unavailable, the Court shall determine whether or not in the interest of fairness the evidence of such witness shall be admitted.

(4) The rules of evidence of law courts shall not be binding but may be consulted by the Court at its discretion. In no case shall the Court consider evidence unless the student has been advised of its source and content, and unless he has been given an opportunity to rebut unfavorable inferences that might otherwise be drawn.

(5) Improperly acquired evidence shall not be admitted. All matters upon which the decision may be based must be introduced into evidence at the proceeding before the Court. No person shall attempt to influence the Court except through argument presented openly at the hearings.

Sec. 407. (1) The Court shall provide for a verbatim record, such as a tape recording, of all proceedings. As part of its decision, the Court shall prepare a digest of evidence presented at the hearing and its findings of fact on any disputed issues. A copy of the digest shall be submitted to the student, and if he challenges its accuracy the Court shall attempt informally to reach a mutually satisfactory text; if necessary, a formal hearing shall be held to resolve disputed questions concerning the digest.

(2) Upon at least 48 hours advance notice to the Court by the student, the Court shall provide a legal transcript of any proceedings before the Trial Division, the expense to be allocated by the Court between the University and the student.

⊱ THE STUDENT CONDUCT COURT ⊰

Sec. 500. The Student Conduct Court shall have exclusive jurisdiction over all disciplinary cases involving students, with the powers enumerated in Sec. 512 below to delegate some of its functions to inferior courts.

Sec. 501. (1) The members and alternate members of the Court shall be appointed by the Joint Appointments Commission.

(2) The Court shall consist of:

(a) four faculty members, one of whom shall be a member of the law faculty who shall serve as Administrative Chairman; and

(b) four student members.

(3) At the time the Court is appointed, two students and one faculty member shall be named as alternate members of the Court. Vacancies occurring on the Court shall be filled from the list of alternates, and, in the event that the Court's volume of business requires it,

the Commission may at the Court's request, appoint the entire alternate panel as full members of the Court.

Sec. 502. (1) The Court shall consist of two Divisions, a Preliminary Hearing Division and a Trial Division. The Administrative Chairman shall assign each member of the Court to one of these divisions and the assignments shall be rotated monthly or in some other appropriate sequence, except that the Administrative Chairman shall not serve as a member of the Preliminary Hearing Division.

(2) The Preliminary Hearing Division shall consist of one faculty member and one student member of the Court. It shall informally consider any case submitted to the Court for the purpose of attempting to reach a mutually satisfactory resolution of the problem and thus avoid the necessity of formal proceedings. The duties of the Preliminary Hearing Division are specified in Sec. 508 below.

(3) The Trial Division shall consist of all members of the Court who are not serving on the Preliminary Hearing Division. It shall hear and decide all cases referred to it by the Preliminary Hearing Division for formal adjudication. The duties of the Trial Division and the method of assigning judges to hearing panels are specified in Sec. 509 below.

Sec. 503. (1) The Court shall have exclusive jurisdiction over the following preliminary matters:

(a) to authorize and regulate, consistently with the provisions of Sec. 400 (1) and of constitutional law, search of students, their possessions or the premises occupied by them; and

(b) to suspend a student pursuant to Sec. 401 pending adjudication of charges against him.

(2) The Court shall determine and publish the procedures it will apply in proceedings arising pursuant to this section. These procedures shall specify the circumstances under which, in the event of an emergency, the Administrative Chairman and other designated members of the Court are authorized to act for the Court.

Sec. 504. Disciplinary cases shall be initiated by complaint and petition.

(1) A complaint shall be in writing, shall be signed by the complainant, and shall state the name, address, and telephone number of the complainant; the name, and if known, address, and telephone number of the suspected student; the time and place of the alleged violation; a brief description of the facts believed to amount to a vio-

lation of a rule; the source of the complainant's knowledge of these facts; and the names of any other persons who may have knowledge concerning the alleged violation.

(2) The complaint shall be submitted to the office of the Legal Services Board which, pursuant to Sec. 702, shall designate a Student Counsel to process the case. On the basis of this complaint and on such other evidence as may be available, the Student Counsel shall promptly determine whether or not there is reasonable cause to believe that the student has committed a violation of the rules. If he finds such reasonable cause, he shall promptly file a petition with the Court pursuant to Sec. 505. If he concludes that there is not reasonable cause, he shall inform the complainant of his decision.

(3) A complainant may appeal a decision of the Student Counsel not to file a petition by submitting his complaint directly to the Court, asking it to overrule the Student Counsel's determination of lack of reasonable cause.

(4) When a complaint is submitted to the Court pursuant to par. (3), the Administrative Chairman shall, after consultation with the Student Counsel if appropriate,

(a) direct the Student Counsel to file a petition and proceed with the case; or

(b) make a final determination that no petition shall be filed.

(5) The Administrative Chairman on his own initiative or on request of the complainant may, if the circumstances make such action advisable, instruct the Legal Services Board to appoint another Student Counsel or to name a faculty member of the Board to supersede the Student Counsel.

Sec. 505. The petition shall be prepared by the Student Counsel or his substitute for submission to the Court. It shall be in a form to be prescribed by the Court, shall state the basis of the Student Counsel's conclusion that there is reasonable cause to believe that the student committed the violation, and shall include all the information which pursuant to Sec. 402 (2) is required when giving the student notice of the charge. The complaint shall be attached to the petition.

Sec. 506. (1) Promptly after submission of the petition to the Court, the Court shall mail or otherwise serve upon the student a written notice of the charge. The notice shall comply with Sec. 402 and shall direct the student to report for a hearing.

(2) In normal cases the notice shall give the student the op-

tion of reporting initially either to the Dean's Office pursuant to Sec. 507 or to the Court's Preliminary Hearing Division pursuant to Sec. 508. In such cases, the student shall be directed promptly to contact the office of his choice to make an appointment for a preliminary conference.

(3) If on the basis of the petition it appears that the charge is a serious one which, if established, is likely to result in a severe sanction, the Administrative Chairman, after consultation with the Student Counsel, may direct that the notice require the student to report directly to the Preliminary Hearing Division.

Sec. 507. (1) If the student elects to report to the Dean's Office, the Court shall transfer its file in the case to the Dean. After an initial conference with the student, the Dean shall either

(a) with the consent of the student, make an informal but final disposition of the case, which may not include any disciplinary sanction more severe than a warning or an order to make restitution; or

(b) return the case to the Court for proceedings in accordance with Sec. 508.

(2) In a conference with the Dean, the student has the same rights as those specified in the last sentence of Sec. 508 (2). Any statements made by the student at the conference are confidential and may not be used without the student's consent in any formal proceedings before the Court. If a student not subject to a pending disciplinary proceeding comes voluntarily to the Dean's Office for counseling or assistance, any disclosures he makes in the course of counseling cannot be made the basis of a disciplinary proceedings.

Sec. 508. (1) A case submitted to the Preliminary Hearing Division directly by the Administrative Chairman, by the Dean pursuant to Sec. 507 (1) (b), or by the student's exercise of his option to report directly to the Division, shall be heard informally by the Division.

(2) Except as provided in this section, the rules of procedure applicable in student disciplinary cases are not mandatory in the informal proceedings before the Division. The Student Counsel or his substitute shall participate in the hearing. The Division may examine any witnesses it desires or receive evidence of any kind; solicit a statement or recommendation from the appropriate Dean; and, with the student's consent, obtain a psychiatric consultation and recommendation. The student cannot be compelled to make a statement or answer

questions, but he has the right to be heard by the Division if he so desires and may appear with an adviser or counsel.

(3) At the conclusion of its investigation, the Preliminary Hearing Panel shall refer the case to the Trial Panel for formal hearing and decision unless both the Division members agree:

(a) that the case shall be dismissed because there is insufficient evidence of any violation, or

(b) with the consent of the Student Counsel and the student, that the case shall be referred for disposition to an inferior court established pursuant to Sec. 512 or

(c) with the consent of the Student Counsel and the student, that the case should be concluded by an informal disposition, which may include a warning or any other authorized penalty less severe than suspension or dismissal; or referral for counseling or other assistance to the Dean's Office, Cowell, or any other appropriate agency or person. Any disposition that is reached pursuant to this clause shall constitute a final settlement of the case.

(4) The Student Counsel can appeal a dismissal of the case under par. (3) (a) to the Trial Division.

(5) No member of the Court shall sit as a member of the Trial Panel in any case that he has considered as a member of a Preliminary Hearing Division, nor shall any statement or admission of a student to the Preliminary Hearing Division be admissible in a proceeding before the Trial Division without the student's consent. Members of a Preliminary Hearing Division shall not discuss with other members of the Court cases they have heard in preliminary hearing which are still pending before the Trial Division.

Sec. 509. (1) The Trial Division shall hear all cases referred to it for formal adjudication by the Preliminary Hearing Division. It shall consist of a panel of either three or five members appointed by the Administrative Chairman from the members of the Court, subject to the restriction in Sec. 508 (5).

(2) A five-member panel consisting of the Administrative Chairman sitting as chairman, one other faculty member, and three student members shall hear cases in which:

(a) novel or important questions of rule interpretation are presented;

(b) it is alleged that a rule which the student is charged with violating is invalid;

(c) complicated legal issues are likely to arise; or

(d) in the opinion of the Administrative Chairman a five-member panel is appropriate.

(3) All other cases shall be heard by a three-member panel consisting of one faculty member and two students appointed by the Administrative Chairman on a rotating basis. One member of the panel shall be designated as its chairman.

(4) In referring cases to the Trial Division the Preliminary Hearing Division shall indicate those cases that fall within par. (2) above and therefore require a five-member panel. A student who expects to challenge the validity of a rule or to be represented by counsel must give notice of such fact to the Court at least 48 hours before the scheduled hearing date. In a case being heard by a three-member panel, if it develops that the case is one appropriate for a five-member panel, the panel may at any time adjourn the hearing so that it can be transferred for a new hearing before a five-member panel.

(5) The Administrative Chairman on his own initiative or at the request of the Student Counsel may appoint a member of the Legal Services Board to assist the Student Counsel. In a complicated case in which the student is to be represented by counsel, the Administrative Chairman may instruct the Legal Services Board to designate a faculty member of the Legal Services Board to supersede the Student Counsel in the presentation of the case to the Trial Division.

(6) All proceedings before the Trial Division shall be conducted consistently with Secs. 403 through 407 of these Regulations.

Sec. 510. In preparing its disposition of a case, the Trial Division shall comply with the requirements of Sec. 407 (1). The final decision of the Court shall be embodied in a written opinion which, without identifying the student, summarizes the facts, the disposition, and the reasons for the disposition. A copy of the opinion shall be delivered to the student, the Student Counsel or his substitute, the Rules Committee, and the Joint Appointment Commission.

Sec. 511. (1) Within ten days of the delivery of the Court's decision and opinion to him, the student may:

(a) appeal to the Chancellor solely on the ground that the penalty is excessive, and the Chancellor in his discretion may mitigate the penalty; or

(b) appeal to the Campus Review Court in those cases in which that Court is authorized to hear an appeal.

(2) If the decision of the Court involves the construction or validity of a rule or regulation, the Student Counsel may appeal the Court's disposition of that issue to the Campus Review Court. In the event that the Student Conduct Court has found a rule or regulation invalid, an appeal must be taken.

(3) If the decision of the Court imposes the penalty of dismissal, an appeal to the Chancellor for mitigation of penalty is required.

(4) Except as provided above in this section, the disposition of the Student Conduct Court shall be final.

Sec. 512.   (1) The Court may, pursuant to regulations which it may promulgate, delegate its functions to an inferior tribunal with jurisdiction over a particular segment of the campus, for example, a school, college, or Regulatory Unit. No such inferior tribunal shall operate without the approval of the Student Conduct Court, which in its discretion may revoke its approval at any time.

(2) No inferior tribunal shall be delegated jurisdiction to hear any case in which the penalty may be disciplinary probation, suspension, or dismissal.

(3) In any proceeding before an inferior tribunal, the student shall be informed that he may elect to have his case heard by the Student Conduct Court. If the student so elects, the case shall be referred to the office of the Legal Services Board pursuant to Sec. 504 (2).

(4) A student may appeal the decision of an inferior tribunal to the Student Conduct Court. The Student Conduct Court shall determine its own procedures for such appeals, which may include the option of giving the student a new trial before the Trial Division.

(5) The Administrative Chairman and the Legal Services Board are charged with responsibility for supervision of any approved inferior tribunals to ensure that their procedures conform to the standards laid down in these rules.

⊁ THE CAMPUS REVIEW COURT ⊱

Sec. 600.   The Campus Review Court shall have both original and appellate jurisdiction in cases which challenge the validity of a campus rule, original jurisdiction temporarily to enjoin the enforcement of a campus rule, and limited appellate jurisdiction in other cases.

Sec. 601. (1) The Campus Review Court shall consist of five members of the faculty and two students.

(2) The faculty members and two alternates shall be appointed by the Joint Appointments Commission with the consent of the Academic Senate. The student members and two alternates shall be appointed by the Joint Appointments Commission with the consent of the Student Senate. Any vacancy occurring on the Court shall be filled by an alternate selected by the Joint Appointments Commission.

(3) The Joint Appointments Commission shall designate one of the faculty members as chairman.

Sec. 602. (1) The Court shall have original jurisdiction to hear and to decide cases in which

(a) the invalidity of a campus rule is alleged; or

(b) an administrative policy is alleged to be inconsistent with the Campus Rules or these regulations; or

(c) an administrative decision interpreting a rule is alleged to be inconsistent with that rule.

(2) Any person may begin such a proceeding by filing with the Court a written petition which contains:

(a) a specification of the rule, policy, or decision alleged to be invalid; and

(b) the grounds of the alleged invalidity; and

(c) an argument in support of the petitioner's position.

(3) The Court shall deliver copies of the petition to the Rules Committee, the Chancellor and, if appropriate, to the faculty and student Committees on Academic Freedom.

(4) Upon request, the Court shall instruct the Legal Services Board to appoint a law student or faculty member of the Board to assist the petitioner in the presentation of his case.

(5) The Court shall instruct the Legal Services Board to appoint a faculty member of the Board to serve as Legal Adviser, to represent the public interest, and to present any grounds upon which the challenged rule or regulation could be upheld. The Legal Adviser shall file a written answer to the petition. A copy of the answer shall be delivered to the petitioner, who shall be given a reasonable time to file a written reply. The Court shall receive and may request written comments on the petition from any appropriate agency, e.g., the Rules Committee, the faculty and student Committees on Academic Freedom, the Committee on Privilege and Tenure, the Chancellor, or Re-

gents' Counsel. Copies of any such comments shall be delivered to the petitioner and the Legal Adviser.

Sec. 603. (1) A petition alleging the invalidity of a campus rule or policy regulation may be accompanied by a petition for a temporary injunction to restrain enforcement of the challenged rule or policy pending the decision of the Campus Review Court. The procedure to be followed shall be:

(a) The petition shall be in writing and shall specify the circumstances which allegedly would cause unjustifiable hardship upon the petitioner were the injunction not to be granted.

(b) The petition shall be delivered to the chairman of the Campus Review Court or, if he is unavailable, to any other member of the Court.

(c) Copies of the petition shall as soon as possible thereafter be delivered to the Chancellor and to the Rules Committee.

(d) The judge receiving the petition shall endeavor to convene as many members of the Court as possible and in any event not less than two judges in addition to himself to rule on the petition for the injunction, provided that a majority of those participating be faculty members.

(e) The participating judges may hold an informal hearing or hearings, or confer with the parties by telephone, or follow any other procedure that seems advisable to them under the circumstances.

(2) If a majority of the participating judges conclude that delay would impose unjustifiable hardship upon the petitioner, and that there is reasonable ground to believe that the full court might hold the challenged rule invalid, and that enjoining enforcement of the rule would not unduly impair the normal functions of the University, it shall grant the injunction for a period not to exceed seven days. Within this time the full Court shall be convened and shall either dissolve or continue the injunction pending final disposition of the case.

Sec. 604. (1) The Court shall have appellate jurisdiction to review a decision of the Student Conduct Court on any of the following questions:

(a) the Student Conduct Court's ruling on the construction or validity of a campus rule or regulation; or

(b) an allegation by the student that he was denied the procedural protections of these Regulations; or

(c) any other case in which the Court, on the basis of the

appeal presented to it, decides that manifest injustice may result unless it reviews the case.

(2) An appeal shall be in writing and shall be filed within ten days of the final decision of the Student Conduct Court. It shall specify the grounds of the appeal and, in the event of an allegation of manifest injustice pursuant to par. (1) (c) above, shall set out with particularity the nature of the alleged injustice and the reasons why the Court should intervene.

(3) The Court may request the Student Counsel or any other appropriate agency to file a written answer to an appeal. A copy of any such answer shall be delivered to the appellant, who shall be given a reasonable time to file a written reply.

(4) If this action has not already been taken pursuant to Sec. 501 (5), the Court may instruct the Legal Services Board to appoint a faculty member of the Board to assist the Student Counsel, or, at its discretion, to supersede him.

Sec. 605. (1) If the Court finds that a petition or appeal is without substantial merit, it may dismiss it without holding a hearing and without written opinion.

(2) In all other cases, the Court shall hold a hearing at which the petitioner or appellant and the representative of the public interest shall be given the right to oral argument and to present any relevant evidence.

(3) For the purposes of such a hearing the Court may appoint a faculty member of the Legal Services Board to assist it in resolving legal issues.

(4) Except as provided in par. (1) above, the Court shall write an opinion which in the case of an appeal shall not identify the student. Copies shall be delivered in the same manner specified in Sec. 510.

(5) The Court's decision shall be final, subject to an appeal to the Chancellor for mitigation of penalty pursuant to Sec. 511, in cases where that remedy is made available or is required.

THE LEGAL SERVICES BOARD

Sec. 700. The Legal Services Board shall have the duties of designating a Student Counsel in each case initiated in the Student Conduct Court and, upon request, of providing legal services for the

Rules Committee, individual students, and the courts in the performance of governance and adjudicatory functions pursuant to these Regulations.

Sec. 701. (1) The Legal Services Board shall be appointed by the Joint Appointments Commission and shall consist of:

(a) at least three faculty members who shall either be members of the law faculty or faculty members in other departments who are members of a bar; and

(b) at least three students who during their term of service will be in the second, third, or graduate years of study in the law school; and

(c) at least three other students.

(2) If required, the Joint Appointments Commission may appoint additional members to the Board at any time.

(3) The Joint Appointments Commission shall designate one of the law student members to serve as chairman.

Sec. 702. (1) The Board shall designate one or more student members to serve as Student Counsel. It shall devise procedures for the rotation of this position among the student members and for the assignment of each individual case to a Student Counsel.

(2) The Board shall maintain an office to receive complaints pursuant to Sec. 504 so that the cases can be promptly assigned to a Student Counsel.

(3) The Student Counsel assigned to a case shall have the following duties:

(a) he shall investigate the complaint and, if he determines that there is reasonable ground to believe that the student committed a violation, he shall file a petition in the Student Conduct Court pursuant to Sec. 505;

(b) he shall assist the Preliminary Hearing Division in bringing to its attention all evidence relevant to the case;

(c) if the case is referred to the Trial Division pursuant to Sec. 509, he shall represent the public interest in proceedings before that Division, presenting all evidence that is relevant in determining whether or not the alleged rule violation occurred or what should be the proper disposition of the case;

(d) after consultation with the Board, he shall appeal the case if an appeal is allowed or made mandatory, and in the event of an appeal by the student shall represent the public interest in appellate proceedings before the Campus Review Court or the Chancellor.

(4) Upon request or upon its own initiative, the Board shall assign a Student Counsel to advise or participate in proceedings before inferior tribunals pursuant to Sec. 512.

Sec. 703. (1) Members of the Board shall be assigned upon request to serve as advisers to students or to the courts, as required to perform the duties specified in Secs. 403, 504 (5), 509 (5), 602 (4), 602 (5), 604 (4), and 605 (3).

(2) The Board shall devise its own procedures for making these assignments, provided that the court making the request may specify that only a law student member, or only a faculty member, be assigned to a specific case. Only law student members or faculty members shall be assigned to assist the Rules Committee if such assistance is requested pursuant to Sec. 301 (4).

PART FOUR

☙☙☙☙☙☙☙☙☙☙☙☙☙❧❧❧❧❧❧❧❧❧❧❧❧

EPILOGUE

The simple and obvious question that emerges from our analysis and proposals is, have we produced a utopian version of the university that exceeds the limits of practicable reform and is therefore irrelevant? This question deserves a hearing, because we are persuaded that it foreshadows a type of criticism that will be raised many times during the coming months.

Since this question has been raised even in the course of our own deliberations, we may summarize briefly its main outlines: There are, it is claimed, certain irresistible tendencies in our society, and certain hard facts about contemporary public education, that place insurmountable obstacles in the path of serious university reforms, especially if those reforms are aimed at restoring the traditional characteristics of an intellectual community—the disinterested search for truth regardless of its practical uses, the creation of physical settings adapted to the exploration of individual possibilities—in short, the forging of true communities of scholars and students. This vision of a university, it is argued, harks back to a bygone era; it is no longer feasible in a modern and dynamic society, with scientific, technical, and organizational needs that compel the public university to "meet its responsibility to society" by "maximizing its output" of trained personnel and the kind of knowledge necessary to sustain that dynamic; this vision is believed no longer feasible under the pressure of a society in which mass education and limited resources compel the university to take efficiency as its touchstone.

We are prepared to accept the charge that we have adopted a utopian and perhaps arcadian vision of the nature of a true university, for it is our belief that the preservation of the conception is crucial if we are to keep alive some memory of what a university is supposed to be. That memory is worth preserving precisely because it was humanistic in inspiration. It is the humanistic assertion of individual dignity, freedom, and intellectual creativity that is most threatened in modern technological society, and if these values cannot be restored and preserved in the university it is doubtful that there is any other place where they can be.

What we do not accept, however, is the charge that our proposed adaptation of this utopian vision to existing reality is impracticable. Educational ideals have been our point of departure, but in attempting to apply those ideals to our particular setting, we have done our best to subject present arrangements to careful scrutiny, weighing the promise of the future against the claims of the present, building on present arrangements wherever possible, suggesting alternative structures where it was clear that past practices have not worked well and the need for change was compelling. It is in this sense that we believe our proposals to be feasible rather than utopian, unless it is utopian to believe that the main directions of education can still be influenced by humanistic ideals.

We do not wish to convey the impression that our proposals could be effected in a brief period of time, still less that they can be implemented without encountering serious practical obstacles. We recognize that such problems as the standardization and depersonalization of education have societal roots, and cannot be conjured away by the magic of goodwill and the rhetoric of community. We recognize as well that the existing system, if it has not worked well, has at least worked to someone's satisfaction. The fundamental and pressing question, in our view, is not, however, whether it is possible in theory to surmount these obstacles, but whether this campus—its students, faculty, and administration—are prepared to make the attempt, to seek a new direction from the one that has both produced and characterized the tragic battles of the recent past, a direction that we believe to be faithful to the best ideals of the university. The university cannot invite its students to respect inquiry and reflection as intrinsic goods and simultaneously continue to define its own excellence in the instrumental terms of training and efficiency laid down by society; it cannot strive for that intangible but crucial goal called the educated person while resting content with large classes, impersonal relationships, frenetic schedules, and a speedup system. Only our hope that the university community is now prepared to give these problems its urgent serious attention may, in the last analysis, prove to have been utopian. If so, the closing lines of More's *Utopia* may prove to be the final note of our own epilogue: "I needs confess and grant that many things be in the Utopian commonwealth which in our cities I may rather wish for than hope for."

PART FIVE

❧❧❧❧❧❧❧❧❧❧❧❧❧❧❧❧❧❧❧❧❧❧❧❧❧❧❧

THE DISSENTING REPORT

TO: The Academic Senate, Berkeley Division
    The ASUC Senate, Berkeley

Previous commitments made it impossible for us to participate in the meetings of the Commission after September 1. Consequently the bulk of the majority report was drafted in our absence. We are not able to endorse it. Our basic reasons are explained in Part I of this report. In Part II, we discuss some of the majority recommendations in detail. On August 26 [1967], we filed a memorandum explaining our recommendations. This is reproduced in Part III. Despite the differences between our position and that of the majority, there is considerable agreement on the issues of decentralization and lower division colleges. We are pleased to emphasize this agreement.

Rio de Janeiro   Albert Fishlow
Tel Aviv   David Freedman
February 27, 1968

The Challenge
to the University

ࣾࣾࣾࣾ

Agreed, the Commission was a direct product of the student strike of November, 1966; its goal was to identify and resolve some of the problems underlying that crisis. Chapter Two of the majority report isolates one such problem: the "interest group" conception of the university. This model describes the campus as made up of three conflicting pressure groups: the students, the faculty, and the administration. The majority rejects this description, and the corresponding view of politics as the art of reconciling conflicts of interest. But the students and administration accept this model, continues the majority, and as a result have been locked in a "sterile circle" of conflict since 1964. "When the campus has not been distracted by disputes over rules, it has been convulsed by the determination to defy them or obsessed by the determination to enforce them." (Page 18. The implication is clear: enforcing rules and defying them are equally disruptive.)

The majority does not identify more specific sources for these recurrent confrontations, and rejects as superficial the notion that they proceed from some basic political disagreement within the university. Instead, the conflict is seen as essentially self-generating, nurtured by an atmosphere of suspicion and moral failure. Strife is caused by the interest-group conception itself, due to the absence of "rational means of governance." "What is needed, in essence, are *settings* for productive argument and *processes* of reaching decisions which command the confidence and respect of the *community*" (page 21, emphasis supplied). Through student participation in governance, the campus is urged to transcend the interest group model, and reach a state of community, where the major decisions grow out of "open discussion in a spirit of mutual trust."

Parts II and III of the report work out, unwittingly but in great detail, precisely the trivial interest group model attacked so vigorously in Chapter Two. The students are treated as a political class, to which power must be transferred: it has to control the main disciplinary committee; it has to be represented on the committees of the departments and the Division. The numbers of representatives of the student, professorial, and administrative classes on these committees, and their internal structure, are specified in great detail. Students, for example, are to be included in the Academic Planning and the Admissions committees (page 142), but are to have only parallel committees on Academic Freedom and the Library (page 145). The reasoning behind such distinctions is obscure. But criteria like competence, interest, or responsibility have little influence in determining who has to be represented where: what counts is class membership.

Of course, no one really believes this nakedly simple interest group model, least of all the majority. Both the student body and the faculty are extremely complex. Both are marked by a large number of shifting coalitions of interest, professional and social and political and other. Many of these coalitions cut across the student-faculty line.

Both groups change over time, the student body changing rather quickly. Once this pluralism is incorporated into the abstract model, the model becomes both more plausible and less forbidding. But now the question underlying Chapter Two is unanswered: Is there a real political conflict, a contest over the allocation of power, on the campus? If so, it is difficult to believe that changed "settings and processes" will "command the confidence and respect of the community."

To us, the existence of this struggle is patent. The student activists are charmingly candid about their need to seize power within the university. And their methods are profoundly political. The point of much activist effort is to make the university either abandon rules altogether or enforce them massively. The activists indeed use and respect "coercion and pressure" rather than "persuasion based on reason and evidence." This pattern is by now so boringly familiar as not to require extended analysis here. The majority seems to accept many of these points. And this casts a long shadow over any "communitarian strategy."

For rhetoric about community is one of the few community activities on the campus. The word was introduced by the administration, appropriated by the activists, and is now embraced by the majority of the Commission. The report has many detailed and ingenious suggestions for achieving the form of community, but the substance is harder to construct. It depends on intangibles, on trust, on shared commitment and experience. Where this sharing does not exist, community structures are empty. Elaborating them merely widens the gap between reality and its official descriptions, and gives another lever to those who would further polarize the campus.

As we see them, the values of the university are reason, moderation, tolerance, detachment; the business of the university is education. The values of the activists are passion, subjectivity, openness, immediacy; the business of activists is social change. There is an obvious divergence here. The majority explicitly recognizes the difficulty of creating an atmosphere of trust, but is not responsive to the question of how to overcome the difficulty. Rhetoric is inadequate, and we do not believe that form creates substance.

✑ TWO CRUCIAL FAILURES

In Chapter One, the majority raises serious questions about the quality of education on the campus, and describes "two crucial failures" of the university. One lies in the large number of intellectually disengaged students on the campus. This is a problem of the first magnitude, which must be alleviated. The lower division colleges point in a hopeful direction. But the majority overstates its case. Doctoral candidates and freshmen, sociologists and engineers are all confounded. And the surprisingly high degree of educational satisfaction reported by most surveys of student opinion is simply ignored. It should be clear by now that Berkeley is an exciting and successful center for research and professional education. Very large numbers of students benefit from this excellence. It should be equally clear that Berkeley has failed to provide a reasonable education for too many students, notably in lower division humanities and social sciences. Nothing is gained by ignoring either half of this phenomenon.

But we do not share the majority's implicit assumption, that this intellectual disengagement is substantially connected with current forms of governance. The problem of student disaffection has been with universities for a long time, although the symptoms and apparent causes change. Many of these causes lie outside the control of the university: one example is social expectations about who is to be educated and why; another is the rapid development of knowledge and its consequent fragmentation; a third is present attitudes about the value of abstract thought. Finally, the disaffection as well as the goals of the student activists are plainly bound up with the politics of the nation.

The second crucial failure, continues the majority (page 14), is that the university has its priorities distorted: "the demands of external interests . . . have increasingly dominated the ethos of the university and shaped its educational activities." From the context, this presumably has the effect of diverting resources from "education" to "service." The majority returns to this theme on page 20: "The sources of our conflicts are very deep. They lie in the heterogeneity of values and concerns of a complex campus; in the numerous functions, over and beyond teaching and scholarly research, which the university has acquired or has had thrust upon it; . . . and in a concept of education which—tailored as it is to the demands of a society devoted to economic growth, technological advance, and increased international influence and dominion—has ceased to nourish the best aspirations of the contemporary student and faculty member."

We recognize this charge as an article of the student activist faith, but have no sympathy for it. What courses have been tailored to the demands of American foreign policy? What are these unnamed extraneous functions? We surmise that the external interests are foundations and government granting agencies. We cannot in good conscience describe most of the research supported by these interests as "service." There is no requirement to justify results in terms of immediate value. And we see little evidence that the pattern of research has been distorted by government grants. The majority may mean that outside subsidies to the Chemistry Department somehow rob the English Department of money. The opposite seems true: typical contracts pay 40 per cent overhead to general university funds, in addition to releasing university resources for use elsewhere. The majority could mean that grants divert effort from teaching to research. We believe that paying for time spent in research attracts many people to the university whose talents in research and in teaching would otherwise be unavailable here. Finally, again from context, the majority may simply mean that the university is serving the wrong social ends. That would be a bold claim. We agree there is real pressure to distort the values of the university, to divert university energies to immediate social ends. This comes from the student activists themselves, who insist on the irrelevance of disinterested, scholarly inquiry.

Our skepticism about the majority's diagnosis is matched by disappointment with its program, whose three main headings are decentralization, open discussion, and participation. In our August 1967 memorandum, reproduced as Part III of this report, we stressed the ideas of decentralization and lower division colleges. We saw these as means to improve the quality of decisions and strengthen the educational program of the university, taking for granted a severely classical view of education. We are pleased that the majority supports decentralization and lower division colleges. But we regret that these ideas are placed at the service of "community" and "participation." Thus, decentralization "is to serve the ends of participatory education" on page 61, while the proposal for lower division colleges "seeks to formulate new educational structures which would make possible a beginning toward the goals of participation and the development of genuine intellectual community" on page 71.

 OPENNESS

We substantially disagree with the majority on the issues of openness and participation. We consider first one train of argument that supports the case both for openness and for participation. University governance is by itself (page 46): "a vital experience in education or mis-education."[1] What can this mean? Plainly, administering a university is a demanding job, morally and intellectually. Men engaged in the profession affect the lives of others, and are themselves affected. A major part of the work lies in explaining the virtues of one course of action rather than another. These aspects can be described as educational. But they are also aspects of administering any important enterprise, and of many other professions. Being a university administrator or a mayor or a judge or a doctor is in a legitimate sense educational. In an equally valid sense, so is falling in love. Is the university obligated in consequence to provide these experiences for its students? The majority apparently leans in that direction. Our view is much more prosaic. Participating in administration is a good education for being an administrator. The main point of a university administration is not to educate; it is to provide the conditions under which members of the university can educate themselves. While the university has many conflicting uses, we are not ready to consider that a principal one is training future university administrators. By failing to keep track of such distinctions, the majority runs a real risk of doing for the university what the misinterpreters of Dewey did for the high school.

On page 48, the majority argues for openness on the grounds that governance must be educational: "It is vital that the university conduct its own decision-making process with equal devotion to the principles it applies in scholarly contexts: open inquiry, reasoned justification of conclusions, and the submission of findings to public evaluation and criticism." Plainly, administrators must be prepared to announce their decisions and justify them. Major and irreversible decisions are properly preceded by wide consultation. But the questions are: What is the relevant public? How much of the process leading up to the decisions should be open? The majority answers the first question by implication: the relevant public is the students, staff, and faculty of the campus. The majority answers the second question in

---

[1] As a consequence of this doctrine, "it would be desirable to incorporate analysis of university policies and problems directly into the academic program," on page 50. In a world of limited resources, this can be done only at the expense of more traditional academic pursuits. We view such a diversion with distaste.

apparent detail: administrators are to be questioned, hearings are to be held, and documents to be made public (page 51); students and occasionally staff are to be inserted in key committees (page 72, 102, 142–146); administrators are not to choose their own working committees (page 100); "public discussions [must take] place well before decisions are made; it must be clear to all parties that such discussions may in fact change the policies being proposed" (page 22). Various practical objections to these proposals come to mind, and there must be practical arguments in their favor.

Our first concern is the irrelevance of the analogy to scholarly inquiry. For the analogy produces different answers to the main questions. A scholar reports to a narrowly defined audience: his peers. A typical check on his work is through anonymous and expert referees, appointed quite bureaucratically by a self-perpetuating learned society. Membership in the relevant public is defined by the fundamental criterion of competence. Second, scholars rarely publish or defend the laborious process of trial and error that precedes a discovery. Only the greatest of men have their notebooks published, and then posthumously.

We are also troubled because the answer to the second question is really less specific than it may appear. Who is to question which administrators? What documents are to be available to whom? What guarantees are to be provided, so that all may know discussions have effect? What will be the forums for these discussions? Unlike the majority, we found that there exists abundant discussion of Berkeley's problems. At times, this seemed the favorite campus sport, both indoor and outdoor. Each reader can make his own evaluation of such discussions, and consider in what sense they will help the university resist external pressure (page 14) or restore its traditional values (page 206).

⊁ STUDENT PARTICIPATION

We next consider the case for student participation, which the majority makes in Chapter Six. "The preeminent argument for achieving student participation in the *shaping* of educational policy thus springs from our long-range educational ambitions and our apprehension about the wide gap presently separating our educational performance from the desirable goal of deeply involving students in the direction of their education" (page 82, emphasis supplied). The second half of this argument is circular: it is precisely the desirability of this goal which the majority must establish.[2] The first half of the argument is clarified in the next paragraph: the majority views student participation as a method for coping with the first failure they saw in the university—the intellectual disaffiliation of students. They come perilously close to asserting that if the university cannot involve its students in courses, let it at least involve them in administration.

On page 84, the majority's object is to create "an environment which values the student as an individual and demonstrates this respect by soliciting his participation in significant policy-makng for the community." We grant that trusting one student's judgment on admissions policy, say, very likely encourages him to think more deeply about who should go to university. We doubt that this affects his engagement with history or mathematics. And leaving aside the question of whether the university is obligated to offer proof of its respect for students as individuals, we cannot believe that including student representatives on committees would really prove the point. This is an exasperating application of the simple interest group model.

The principle that governance must be educational is applied to complete the rationale for student participation (page 85, emphasis supplied): "Learning should not be regarded as an isolated classroom experience, but rather as a sustained, continuous, *public* experience. Hopefully, so *communal* a venture would *blur the lines of authority* between dependent students and dominant professors. Intellectual exploration would become a common experience of developing understanding and would include sharing all the pain and triumph of intellectual creativity, instead of concealing that process and displaying to the student only the finely distilled result."

We do not think that vast amounts of intellectual creativity are concealed in committee. Nor do we visualize education and intellectual exploration as basically public experiences. The great advances in human knowledge do not come in the midst of searching public discussion. They are made by individual men, painfully alone with their

---

[2] This circularity appears at many other points. For example, on page 84: "Just as students must share with scholars the burdens and tensions of the intellectual life, so they should also share the genuinely difficult responsibility for posing sharp questions about the success and direction of policies and for making major decisions for their community." Again on page 111: "For this university and this society, a rebirth in education and the development of the student role in governance are closely dependent upon one another." The question is why.

thoughts. As for communal ventures blurring lines of authority, we find that a university is necessarily inegalitarian. It is an institution whose members adhere voluntarily, for limited purposes. These members differ widely in maturity, competence, attitude, and role. There are corresponding variations in authority. Unfortunately, this explicit inequality is intrinsic to most serious intellectual enterprise.

✒ POSSIBILITY OF COMMUNITY

The Epilogue anticipates a certain skepticism about the possibility of community. We share that skepticism, but disavow the argument put forward there on our behalf: that the university has "to take efficiency for its touchstone" and " 'meet its responsibilities to society' by 'maximizing its output' of trained personnel." These are not our ideas. The irresistible tendencies and hard facts that stand in the way of community building, and that the Epilogue dismisses, are manifest: size; budget; the professional attitudes of the faculty; the great range of ability, preparation, and interest among the students; the bewildering variety of activity, professional and other, on the campus. But the difficulty dismissed by Chapter Two, namely the existence of basic political strife on the campus, is an even more serious obstacle. Finally, in contrast with the implication of the majority, we insist that the disinterested search for truth thrives here, in the midst of these conflicts, as perhaps nowhere else.

We conclude that a policy aimed at legislating community has little chance of success, with or without reference to the bitter history of the past few years. Given that history, such a policy inevitably reduces to legislating a transfer of power, and risks exacerbating the conflict. Institutions like Antioch may embody many of the values held by the majority, and certainly have an honorable function. Berkeley has a rather different kind of excellence. We would think it foolish indeed to try to convert Berkeley into an Antioch. We would fear for the survival of Berkeley's excellence, and much doubt the possibility of attaining Antioch's.

✒ MAJORITY RECOMMENDATIONS ✒

We comment here on some of the more specific majority recommendations. Many of the proposals listed on pages 278–282 are not defined sharply enough for detailed criticism, but were considered in a more general context above. We point again to the agreement on specifics that developed on the questions of decentralization and lower division colleges.

⚛ THE ADMINISTRATION

The majority suggests that administrative committees be integrated into the Division's committee structure, and that faculty members of these committees be appointed by the Division's Committee on Committees. We do not see the virtue of preventing the Chancellor from choosing his advisers. Nor did we find evidence of duplication between administrative committees and Senate committees.

We are opposed to creating an Emergency Advisory Committee. This group would have no clear objectives or continuing responsibilities, for even crisis is a relative concept. Its pronouncements could easily confuse rather than clarify issues: particularly since it includes representatives of all segments of "the campus community," regardless of the nature of the problem. The Senate Policy Committee is available for consultation. It might be desirable to create a parallel student agency.

It is evident to us that these majority proposals will have the effect of isolating the Chancellor and substantially limiting his initiative. The majority denies such an intention, and maintains that their innovations will "improve communication and focus responsibility." But their elevation of the Chancellor (page 98) to the role of "spokesman for the whole community" is a prescription for unemployment, and differs from "titular monarchy" only in not being hereditary. By contrast, we think the administration should play an even more active role in providing educational leadership, planning and setting priorities, creating and revising the framework for local decision-making, and delegating authority within that framework. In our view, Berkeley cannot survive without a strong central executive.

⚛ STUDENT PARTICIPATION AT THE DEPARTMENTAL LEVEL

The majority proposes that students become members of regular departmental committees, attend departmental meetings, and evaluate faculty candidates for tenure. Student representatives are to be chosen through devices like the Council of Majors (Appendix D).

We object to these measures. We found little evidence[3] to support the idea that such participation will help Berkeley attain its educational objectives. We are not partial to the idea of redefining these objectives so participation by itself becomes a major goal.

In Part III, we argue that such measures may be detrimental to the quality of educational decisions. They may prevent candid discussion among members of the department on certain issues. They may prejudice the educational relationships between students and faculty. And student evaluations of faculty teaching ability are clearly harmful, unless the evaluators are both competent and objective. Compare the main obstacle seen by the majority (page 114): "Such innovations must withstand complaints of 'student apathy,' and overcome the risk that such participation will be kept token and peripheral." The majority shows an unseemly haste to introduce student representatives whenever possible, and not whenever appropriate.

The majority's departmental advising plan (Appendix D) is unrealistic. It will be very hard to secure the requisite continuity of advisers. In many departments, the advising groups will have no real purpose or substantive common activity, and will remain purely formal entities. The object of the Council of Majors, other than appointing representatives, is obscure. Finally, even a start on this plan will consume considerable amounts of faculty time, which could be much better spent elsewhere: teaching.

≫ STUDENT PARTICIPATION CAMPUS-WIDE

The majority proposes student membership on Academic Senate committees dealing with educational policy, including the proposed "Special Commission on Campus Decentralization";[4] and endorses the proposal to broadcast Academic Senate debates to student audiences.

We oppose these recommendations.[5] The first is precisely the

[3] The main items are anonymous faculty comments on page 114, and a quotation from the President of Wayne State University on page 144.

[4] Nonacademic staff are to be included in this committee and in the Emergency Advisory Committee. The majority does not present its reasoning. Does the argument that governance must be educational apply here too? If so, there are more obvious extensions.

[5] We regret that we also have to oppose the majority recommendations for a Student Services Policy Board to supervise university residences and the health service. Unfortunately, it is the university that will be held responsible for what happens, and not a student committee.

kind of tokenism condemned by the majority on page 116. It will do
nothing to satisfy the student activists. It is unlikely to interest the vast
majority of students. And it will do very little to help the Senate transact business. What is the value of student opinion on questions like
the proper relationship between deans and department chairmen? Indeed, these measures may have an adverse effect on the deliberations
of the Senate, for reasons explained above. And we reject the implicit
suggestion that the Senate is a legislative body responsible to the student public.

Students have a definite contribution to make, in their departments and on the campus level. We proposed a variety of methods to
extend consultation with students on the academic program and other
matters of interest. In particular, we proposed strong, parallel student
committees on educational policy and academic freedom. The majority
accepted the idea of parallel committees in some areas but not others.
We see no logic in their distinctions. We also proposed student representation on administrative committees dealing with the social and
cultural program. These committees are advisory, not legislative. Students have as much competence in these areas as anyone. Academic
Senate committees present complicated draft legislation to a large
body; *de facto,* their function is more than advisory. And these committees deal with areas in which the faculty has special competence
and responsibility.

☙ LAW IN THE CAMPUS COMMUNITY

We are deeply concerned by the section of the majority report
on disciplinary procedures. This massive labor was not undertaken out
of dissatisfaction with the way theft and cheating cases are handled. It
is clearly motivated by concern about the handling of time, place, and
manner rules. In our view, activists break these rules to score points
about the nature of the university, to force confrontations with the
administration, and to mobilize followers and enlist public sympathy.
In this context, the majority's "educational problem-solving approach"
to discipline on page 163 has a curious flavor: just what problems
should the university be solving for its activists? And it is idle to maintain that "the welfare of the individual student" who is being disciplined should be "the dominant end of the disciplinary process," as

the majority implies on the same page. Surely, a major and legitimate purpose of discipline is to protect the institution. In an ideal and communitarian world, there is no difference. This is Berkeley.

We cannot agree that enacting the majority's "basic regulations" is likely to "break the ominous circle of distrust" (page 169) in any useful sense. Our reasons should be obvious by now. Enacting the "basic regulations" means substantially shifting the authority for determining and enforcing the rules, and consequently for defining the boundaries of permissible behavior in the university. This includes the classroom as well as the Plaza. And this shift makes the next set of rules much harder to maintain, for all the painful lessons of the past few years will have to be learned again.

We therefore oppose the suggestion of the majority that the Division approve the "basic regulations" in principle, subject to review by the Academic Freedom Committee. We believe the Division has the responsibility of examining in detail each of the issues raised here, before approving anything. Our position will be described as precisely the kind of non-communitarian thinking that the Division must eschew. We ask only that the arguments and the record be considered.

THE BASIC REGULATIONS

We are against the proposal for a Student Counsel. Section 504 provides that discipline can be initiated only by complaint submitted to this officer. If a complaint is not accepted, the complainant can submit it again, directly to the Student Conduct Court (the basic disciplinary committee). But he is not entitled to representation before that committee; his case could very well be argued for him by the Student Counsel who initially rejected his complaint. In some cases, the accused student will deny the charges against him and retain professional counsel. Such cases are presented either by the Student Counsel, or by a member of the Legal Services Board, instructed by Section 702 (3) (c) to "represent the public interest." This system seems destined to produce cases tried by a panel of judges and two defense counsels. The complainant has absolutely no guarantee of a hearing.

The idea of a Joint Appointments Commission (Part 2 of the basic regulations) does not win our sympathy. We feel that appointments of faculty to the rules committee, the disciplinary committee, and other such committees, courts, and commissions (if there are to

be others) are best handled by the Division's Committee on Committees. We think the disciplinary committee should continue to have a
faculty majority: Section 501 provides nominal parity, and Section
509 provides a student majority on the panel hearing a case. We think
the rulings of the disciplinary committee have to remain advisory to
the Chancellor (compare page 159). We see no need for a Campus
Review Court. Its jurisdiction is carefully limited by Part 6 of the
Basic Regulations. There is no automatic right of appeal from decisions
of the Student Conduct Court, least of all for the complainant. If this
lower court avoids ruling directly on the merits of a campus regulation,
but simply refuses to punish a violation of it, the Campus Review
Court can intervene only if "manifest injustice may result" otherwise.

The basic regulations provide that the validity of a rule is open
to challenge through injunctive proceedings before the Campus Review Court (Section 603), declaratory actions before the Rules Committee (Section 306) and Campus Review Court (Section 602), and
as a defense for violations in disciplinary proceedings before the Student Conduct Court (Section 509) and the Campus Review Court
(Section 604). This will be construed as an invitation to violate the
rules serially. And the maze of overlapping jurisdictions is bound to
create confusion and instability. We believe that it should be possible
to argue the validity of a rule before the Rules Committee. And that
rules on the book should be enforced. Part III contains our reasoning
on these points and suggestions for change.

⇘ *OUR RECOMMENDATIONS* ⇙

On August 26, 1967, we filed a memorandum outlining our
views and proposals, on five topics: Decentralization, Lower Division
Colleges, Academic Senate, Student Participation, Disciplinary proceedings. This memorandum is reproduced here, with minor changes.
Question (1) and certain aspects of question (3) are probably outside
the competence of the Commission. We have become convinced, however, that they are of fundamental importance. We did not have the
time, staff, or experience to pursue these questions in depth. Nor have
we been able to take into account the events of the season. We are
persuaded, however, that our analysis and suggestions continue to afford a basis for constructive change.

⤢ DECENTRALIZATION

The pattern at Berkeley and at many other large institutions is to have most decisions made at least formally by the central administration, with relatively few people involved. It is then convenient to specialize: one man does personnel, one does space, another students, and so on. One reason for this centralization is the rather limited number of competent academic administrators. Another, peculiar to Berkeley, was the pervasive fear of relapsing into academic mediocrity with a consequent insistence on centralized quality control. Every department was afraid that its neighbor would make bad appointments or train incompetent Ph.D.'s and wanted the Budget Committee to supervise one process and the Graduate Council to supervise the other.

Still another Berkeley quirk is its situation in California, which implies supervision by the university-wide administration, the Regents, and the Legislature—supervision even over the expenditure by the university of money received from foundations and the federal government. This relationship imposes on the campus a serious imbalance between resources and responsibilities. In general, the campus is expected to educate a fixed and large number of students. The state provides funds for a barely adequate number of faculty. Ancillary funds, for administrative services and physical plant, are inadequate. The relationship also imposes a number of peculiar constraints on campus behavior. Many of these constraints derive from a desire to treat all campuses symmetrically, and from a past situation in which centralized control was needed to supervise the newer campuses.

One important example of this is admissions policy: the campus has surprisingly little to say about who is admitted here as a student. Another example is the very detailed budgetary control. In particular, the university-wide administration distinguishes money for physics from money for history. It distinguishes money for faculty from money for secretaries (the exchange rate leads to professors doing secretarial work). It even distinguishes assistant professor dollars from full professor dollars. For another example, nonacademic jobs must satisfy one of a series of job descriptions, set by university-wide. University-wide must approve of all pay raises above a certain level, both for academic and nonacademic positions. Even certain kinds of overtime payments require approval. A final example, astonishing in its triviality: Berkeley cannot decide for itself whether courses are to have letter grades or pass/not pass grades.

Many of these features are repeated on the campus, in the relationship between the departments and the campus administration. Part of the second control process is required by the first, part is indigenous. Departments cannot decide for themselves whether they need three assistant professors or two associate professors, nor can they choose between having an administrative assistant or a principal clerk in the front office. Unspent money and unfilled personnel slots do not keep well. Consequently, there is a real pressure on departments to spend all the money and fill all the slots, as projected in the budget, even when changing circumstances make these decisions less appropriate. Finally, specialization of administrative functions on the campus implies that certain agencies make decisions without resource constraints.

Another Berkeley problem is the diffusion of negative power. A great variety of people get to veto decisions. In particular, many procedures are extremely formalized, apparently so that decisions can readily be justified later on preset criteria. It follows automatically that many valuable proposals violate some rules, are therefore irregular, and can be turned down easily anywhere along the way. This accounts for the observed phenomenon of settlement among the relevant administrative assistants; another explanation is that only the administrative assistants have mastered the paper work. This excessive formality wastes everyone's time and frustrates useful energies. It may also frustrate other energies; as a set of precautions, it is very costly.

A final problem we wish to mention is information. Berkeley, like most universities but unlike any solvent corporation, is unbelievably ignorant about the details of its own operations, and does not really undertake much educational introspection. The current information-gathering apparatus consumes a great deal of time and often misses the interesting points. Elementary questions, like the size of Letters and Science, are research problems. Intermediate questions, like the amount of money being spent on lower division instruction, cannot be answered without the use of very imaginative back-of-the-envelope computations. Advanced questions, like the effect of educational policies on students, are being raised only now. Thus, the campus administration is required to spend time on routine problems without adequate information. This sometimes leads to mediocre decisions, or good decisions reached too late, or good decisions reached on time but not appreciated by those outside the decision-making apparatus. Irreplaceable administrative effort is wasted: effort that could be much better spent on planning, setting priorities, and external relations; effort that would be much better directed toward devising solutions for some of Berkeley's major problems.

Our general conclusion is that Berkeley should be administered as a large collection of relatively small and reasonably autonomous units. These units have to be compact enough so that their members have some common purpose and shared experience, and some awareness however dim of each other as people. Each of these units should have its responsibility and budget, derived by negotiation with its administrative supervisor. It should be fairly free to use the budget to carry out the responsibilities according to its best judgment. It has to be understood that units that perform badly over a period of time are going to lose their budget, or their independence, or both. Constraints on the units should be as much as possible in terms of total budget and minimum performance in various areas. Setting the proper performance levels, and devising methods to discover whether these levels are met, are the two main problems in this approach.

The natural existing units to work with are the departments (major and graduate instruction, research) and the research institutes. We think it is particularly important under this scheme to set up lower division colleges (p. 230) to look after the interests of the lower division. We do not think the present situation in the lower division is tenable. Either more resources should be expended on lower division instruction, or that section of the program should be given up completely.

One obvious exception of this set of generalities, and there are probably others, is allocation of money for construction. This should be done by the central campus administration; we do not want individual departments or other consortia of entrepreneurs putting up buildings. Parenthetically, it seems to us that more thinking has to be done about the physical plant, and that the Academic Senate should be involved in this.

The present proposal certainly requires bolder and tougher middle level administrators than have been exhibited up to now. They are going to have to restrain themselves from "improving" operations that are doing a satisfactory job, and they are going to have to say flatly on occasion that a unit is not doing a satisfactory job, and be willing to act on the statement. We recognize that nothing works out so neatly, especially at Berkeley. We do think it is very worth while to push on in the directions outlined. We hope that much can be done even within the present framework of university-wide policy, and improvements made in the past few years show that framework to be susceptible of change.

Here are some specific suggestions. These are interconnected; (1) and (2) are necessary conditions for many of the others.

1. Divide the College of Letters and Science into four colleges: humanities, life science, physical science, social science.
2. Set up lower division colleges, as described on page 230. These lower division colleges would have the primary responsibility for lower division instruction, and for breadth requirements.
3. The deans of the colleges arising from Letters and Science, the dean of the College of Chemistry, and the masters of the lower division colleges should report to one vice-chancellor. Deans of the professional colleges and schools should report to another vice-chancellor.
4. Chairmen of departments and directors of research institutes should report to the dean of the college in their area. The present advisory committees on institutes do not seem to function effectively and should be disbanded in favor of direct supervision by the dean.
5. The position of Graduate Dean would become superfluous and could be eliminated. The administration of grants and contracts should be under the supervision of the Vice-Chancellor for Research. Research institutes now reporting to the Graduate Dean should report to the dean of a college. The policy responsibilities should devolve to deans of colleges and department chairmen. A start has already been made in this direction.
6. The Admissions Office should take over the graduate admissions operation. It should also embark on a much more ambitious program of recruiting able undergraduates from the high schools. The campus should make every effort to secure more autonomy in setting its admissions policies. If this effort succeeds, it might be advantageous to have the various colleges on the campus substantially responsible for their own admissions standards, although there should be a minimum standard for the campus.

7. The faculty of each college arising from Letters and Science should determine its own form of organization. We suggest the election of a policy committee to act for the faculty. This committee would not have any administrative responsibility. The dean would be required to report his actions to it regularly, although not for confirmation. He would also be required to seek its advice on important policy questions. This committee should serve as the review committee for renewing the appointment of the dean (perhaps augmented by the chairmen of previous committees associated with that dean), and as the search committee for a new dean. This committee should also nominate candidates for Academic Senate committee positions, to the Committee on Committees. Most of the current Letters and Science faculty structure, which is now collapsing under its own weight, would become superfluous.

8. So far as possible, colleges should get block budgets from their vice-chancellor, and assign block budgets to the departments and institutes. In particular, departments should be able to spend their money relatively freely within their budget.

9. Departments should be able to hire non-Senate academic personnel and visitors without time-consuming and largely formal review. Tenure appointments, and promotions to tenure or overscale, should be made as now, except that we do not see the need for the university-wide administration to confirm over-scale promotions. Nontenure ladder appointments, and ladder promotions except to tenure and over-scale, should be made by the department with the consent of the dean.

10. Departments should be able to hire their own nonacademic personnel, and define their jobs. The Personnel Office should continue to provide centralized recruiting service and grievance procedures. It should ensure reasonable working conditions, and prevent grossly unequal compensation for similar work. Here as elsewhere, there is a familiar conflict between the demands of symmetry on one hand and flexibility on the other. At present, we feel that symmetry has won a lopsided victory, producing excessively rigid and standardized procedures.

11. Personnel decisions that do not require the consent of the dean should be reported regularly to him, with the documentation.

12. A committee of the Academic Senate (perhaps the Graduate Council or the Committee on Educational Policy) should decide

whether individual departments are authorized to offer Ph.D. programs. When a department has this authorization, it should set its own requirements for courses, languages, and examinations. Departments should allocate their own fellowship money. They should be permitted to institute new courses for a three-year trial period. Actions in these areas should be reported to the dean, but not for confirmation. The Academic Senate Committee on Courses should have jurisdiction only in case of conflict between departments, and in case a department wishes to continue a course past the trial period.

13. Departments should set their own major programs, with a minimum and maximum number of required courses specified by the college. We are skeptical of the educational value of more detailed breadth requirements. We do think it would be valuable for each college to suggest a number of coherent programs of courses, as models.

14. The college should conduct periodic reviews of the operation of each department, obtaining evaluations from the department and its members, from related departments in the university, and from outside experts. The appointment of a new chairman provides a natural occasion for such a review.

⇗ LOWER DIVISION COLLEGES[6]

The Structures. It is proposed to set up four new instructional units, the colleges, for lower division Letters and Science (or the colleges arising from it). Each college would have 250 freshmen (all numbers are tentative), 250 sophomores, and funds for 40 half-time teaching assistants and 10 FTE faculty (say 3 full-time, 14 half-time). Subject to this budgetary limitation, the composition of the staff should be decided by the individual college (some colleges might prefer more faculty, some might prefer more teaching assistants). By the second year of operation, two-fifths of the lower division population in Letters and Science would be in the college program, approximately, and the remainder would be in the regular program.

These colleges would be administratively responsible for the lower division education of their students; they would be small enough and might be competitive enough so this responsibility would be prop-

---

[6] This section is excerpted, with minor changes, from a Commission working paper published in the *Daily Californian*.

erly discharged. They would provide structures on a human scale, to which students and faculty could relate, and also furnish a clear locus of responsibility for the education of the lower division student.

Incoming freshmen would decide whether they wished to enter the regular program or the college program, and if the latter, which college. It should be moderately easy to transfer from one college to another, or from the college program to the regular departmental program. Students would therefore have the possibility of making informed choices among competitive and relatively coherent programs.

If the colleges succeed, six more should be created, to cover all of Letters and Science lower division. Furthermore, the college might go into upper division instruction on a small scale. For example, they might offer individual interdisciplinary majors under the supervision of the college faculty. Normally, after two years in the college, the student would declare a major and enter a department. Thus, departments would continue to be responsible for upper division and graduate work.

The academic program.   Colleges should be organized around a topic or set of disciplines. They should not be considered as junior departments or as miniatures of Letters and Science. The programs should be substantially different from college to college, and should change over time within each college. Students going through one college together would, however, follow relatively similar programs. This should facilitate the process of students learning from each other.

The college program should count as two courses each quarter in the freshman year and one or two courses each quarter in the sophomore year. The student would take outside courses, taught by departments, to make up a total of three courses each quarter. If the student chooses to major in a discipline related to the program of the college, this program should be considered as satisfying all or almost all of the prerequisites to the major. His work in the college should be considered as fulfilling a substantial fraction of his breadth requirements.

Courses within the college could include lectures, seminars, tutorials with teaching assistants and faculty, and independent study. The methods of instruction and the amount of choice in outside courses would vary from college to college. One plan is to have a core lecture course (250 students, one lecturer each quarter) and a tutorial each quarter in the freshman year, followed by supervised but fairly independent study on a topic related to the course in the sophomore year.

The numbers of staff and students allow for considerable contact in small instruction groups. It is feasible, and important, for each student to have at least one quarter of small group instruction with a faculty member each year.

In the college setting, with a common intellectual framework and considerably more continuity in personal relationships, it is reasonable to expect that this kind of instruction will be educationally satisfying. It is also reasonable to assume that students will be given genuine academic counseling based on some knowledge of their personalities and intellectual capabilities. It may be possible to make more realistic decisions about the student's total work load.

Staff. Staff for the colleges should be secured from departments. Colleges would neither admit graduate students nor hire faculty. They should be permitted to hire visitors on a small scale, subject to the availability of money. Research personnel could participate in the college program to a limited extent. Nobody should be permanently attached to a college and the number of faculty working full time in the colleges should be small. The typical tour of duty in a college might be half time for three years. Terms should be staggered, so that the staff would be a continuing body, but one that changes slowly over time. This would allow the colleges to develop corporate and distinctive styles, and prevent these styles from becoming frozen.

In devising programs, the colleges will have to find means of engaging the professional concerns of the faculty. In order to remain a permanent feature of the campus, colleges would have to attract faculty of high academic standing. Such people will not be available if the educational programs appear uninteresting to them. Recruitment looms as the most serious problem facing the colleges. The colleges offer some incentives that may overcome these difficulties: greater freedom to develop new courses, the chance to work with colleagues in related fields, the opportunity to teach in a different and probably more rewarding setting. The colleges also provide for the development of a closer relationship between faculty and the graduate students who serve as teaching fellows: a relationship in which the graduate student undertakes substantial teaching responsibility with more adequate guidance from the faculty.

More material incentives should also be offered. A few faculty in each college should be on eleven month contracts so they can develop the college organization and courses. All faculty who participate in the college program should have additional paid leave, perhaps on the ratio of one quarter for every three quarters spent in the program. This compensates for the extra demands on time that participation in the college program will entail.

Space. The success of a college will depend substantially on its physical environment. The colleges should have contiguous space for offices, meeting rooms, lounges, and a library. It seems desirable to have one of the colleges residential. Perhaps one of the existing residence halls could be converted for this purpose. It is clear that availability of space will be an important problem.

Administration. The college should be headed by a full-time faculty member, the master. The master should be appointed, say for three years, by the Chancellor on the advice of the faculty of the college. To get started, the first master and perhaps two of the first faculty should be appointed to each college by the Chancellor on the advice of an Academic Senate search committee. This cadre would proceed to design a provisional program, recruit staff, acquire space, and consult relevant departments about courses.

At least initially, the colleges should report to the Chancellor's office and to a review committee of the Academic Senate. This committee would consider the programs as they developed, and visit the colleges to observe their operations at first hand. It would not be empowered to change decisions of the college. At the end of a given period, say three years, the review committee would report to the Academic Senate on the performance of the colleges and would make recommendations for revisions of their structure. At least during the first period, the colleges should not be subject to outside controls on staffing or curriculum.

➤ THE ACADEMIC SENATE

The Academic Senate has a great deal to contribute to the direction of the university, but it has not adapted quickly enough to changing circumstances, so that its promise is often unfulfilled. The actions of the Senate sometimes appear inconsistent. Sometimes the Senate has been vulnerable to the charge of being manipulated. Partly, this is because the Senate is often not well informed on the issues before it, or even interested (frequently, this just shows good judgment). Ordinary meetings are usually poorly attended. Critical meetings are usually amorphous: large, public, and impersonal. This is particularly important because the Senate has not yet developed adequate mechanisms for formulating and debating issues, although many of the formal and informal mechanisms that do exist have proved their value.

To overcome these problems, and to make its maximum contribution to the university, we strongly believe that the Senate should reconsider the merits of a representative assembly, along the lines recently proposed by the Senate Policy Committee. We also recommend an overhaul of the Senate committee structure. (We understand the Senate Policy Committee is studying this problem.) We also recommend that more attention be paid to the relation between the Senate, the Chancellor, and the ASUC (the latter agency is discussed again below).

We are satisfied that there is no real duplication between Senate committees and administrative committees. We are less satisfied about the possibility of duplication and redundancy within the Senate's own system. We also find that Senate committees are understaffed. We think the administration should make some of its staff members available for use by the major Senate committees; there is no point in creating duplicate bureaucracy. Although Senate committees are formally advisory, they are of considerable importance. They are among the major agencies that formulate policy for Senate consideration, and their advice is very often taken by the Senate and the administration. These committees have continuing responsibilities; they develop experience and judgment. The Senate should aim to strengthen these agencies. At present, a large amount of Senate business is channeled through BASIC, an informal committee composed of the chairmen of the main Senate committees; the initials of these committees from the acronym. We do not think this arrangement is a satisfactory substitute for the overhaul under consideration by the Senate Policy Committee.

The administration should continue to consult regularly with the Senate Policy Committee and with appropriate Senate specialist committees. The administration should report regularly to the Division on major administrative actions taken or contemplated, and on policy alternatives. Individual administration specialists should report orally on the Senate floor, and receive questions. This would be particularly helpful in the areas of budget, educational policy, and student affairs. The Senate should extend membership to the appropriate members of the Chancellor's staff. We are not suggesting the administration should bare its soul continuously. We are suggesting a definite increase in the flow of information, focused on significant issues.

The probable costs of this operation are not negligible, but the probable gains have also to be considered. The administration seems at times to be out of touch with major currents in faculty opinion. Conversely, the faculty often seems unaware of the world inhabited by administrators. There is a certain amount of mutual suspicion. No series of proposals can hope to solve this problem completely. We do think substantial progress can be made. The Senate and the administration can act on the basis of fuller understanding. Mechanisms can be provided whereby the Senate can criticize individual administrative actions without attacking the entire administration. Administrators can keep in touch with a spectrum of faculty opinion through formal and informal consultation.

We turn now to the relation between the Academic Senate and the ASUC. The present arrangements seem to us to have little merit. We conclude this section by suggesting that some obsolete machinery be dismantled. More efficient alternatives are suggested below. The addresses by the ASUC president have not proved valuable, and this seems inherent in the present arrangements. He should address the Senate perhaps once a year, and whenever else he and the Senate Policy Committee think it desirable. The Student Affairs Committee has not found any clear role. It should be dissolved in favor of more specific student-faculty cooperative mechanisms. The student petition item on the agenda has proved of little value, and could be deleted without much loss.

⊰ STUDENT PARTICIPATION

We are convinced that students on this campus can be given greater responsibility. The first application of this principle, for us, is to give each individual student greater control over his own life, both academic and nonacademic. This means, for example, reducing instead of increasing the number of required courses. We are also convinced that students should be given a greater opportunity to participate, in clearly defined and limited ways, in the direction of the university. The main test for such participation is its effect on the main interest of the university: learning and understanding, of old knowledge and new.

There are certain areas in which students have experience and insight to contribute, for example: how a set of courses actually functions, what is a reasonable workload for students, how well the library serves student needs. Furthermore, it is reasonable to expect somewhat greater institutional loyalty when students have a visible stake in the university, and have nonrevolutionary methods of influencing policy. (However, we do not have high expectations about the extent to which student attitudes can be affected in this fashion, for many of the factors determining these attitudes come from outside the university.) The present distance of administrators from the students who are affected by their decisions seems to prejudice reactions. Moreover, in crisis situations, it is plainly desirable to have a continuing estimate of student opinion that is as accurate as possible, and to have an official student group with which to deal, rather than a multiplicity of ad hoc groups with no clear lines of responsibility and no fixed identity.

There are substantial arguments against markedly increasing the amount of responsibility students have for making decisions that affect others, students or faculty. These arguments derive from the test of university interest stated earlier. They are obvious to the point of triteness, but are still worth review. To begin with, the presence of students in many contexts would adversely affect the candor, and consequently the usefulness, of discussion. Candor is premised on confidentiality, and it is unclear how to assure this with students present; indeed, a common argument in favor of the presence of students is that it makes the decision-making "open." This problem is most acute in areas where the professional competence of faculty members is a major issue (appointments, allocation of resources), where competence of students or groups of students is at issue (curriculum, examination standards), and where there is a partial conflict between the campus and outside agencies (admissions). Furthermore, students lack experience. They are not in a position to make informed judgments on many questions. They are not aware of many real constraints on action, nor can they guess very well what the probable consequences of action are. Students have transitory status in the institution; they will not be held responsible later for what they do now. In fact, given the usual lag between planning and execution, students will not have to live with the consequences of their policy decisions.

The student body is enormously heterogeneous, with great variation in ability, purpose, and affiliation. The primary loyalties of many students are directed to small and impermanent groups whose values clash with each other; the values of some groups have been observed to clash with those of the university. In such a situation, it is cant to speak of a student "class" that has to be represented, or that can be "educated" about the realities of the university. Information in student groups has a half-life of two years. Rediscovering the facts of academic life with the frequency this implies is a discouraging prospect. Another discouraging phenomenon is that student representatives who do become aware of the real problems are quite vulnerable to the charge of "finking out."

In view of the size and heterogeneity of the student body, student representatives on administrative or policy agencies must be chosen by a political process in which individual views are mediated by social institutions. This is substantially true even in departments of moderate size. Existing political processes and institutions in the student body have very definite styles, and are simply irrelevant to large numbers of students. Even the burning question of participation burns only for a minority. Most students prefer to lead private lives. There is a consequent risk that student representatives will really represent only a small fraction of the student body; which fraction will vary from case to case and year to year. The risk may sometimes be worth running, but it cannot be ignored. It may be that student political processes can be substantially modified; but social engineering is not an exact science.

The sensible course is to proceed in a genuinely experimental way, considering at each step the experience of the previous steps. It is not enough to make large-scale commitments but describe them as "experimental." Criteria for success are slippery, and certain kinds of commitments can be withdrawn only with great social embarrassment.

In general terms, we would try to resolve the question along the following two lines.

1. Encourage the ASUC (Associated Students, University of California) to reorganize itself. For a trial period, give it some clearly defined and limited responsibilities, and some real autonomy. This is discussed later in more detail.

2. Improve the methods whereby students are consulted on academic policy questions, both at the campus and departmental levels.

The ASUC should create a Committee on Educational Policy (perhaps the existing SERF Board is the appropriate agency). This committee should be charged with developing student ideas and policy recommendations in this area, and informing students about the problems that exist. This committee should include students from a variety of academic backgrounds. The corresponding Academic Senate committee should be charged to consult with the student committee as appropriate. Similar arrangements on the Library and on Academic Freedom should be undertaken. Members of the administration should consult with these student committees at the appropriate times. In other areas, students should always be free to make written submissions to Academic Senate Committees. Specific arrangements such as these give substance to student-faculty cooperation, and are more desirable than the unfocused Student Affairs Committee.

Students in a department, particularly graduating seniors and second or third year graduate students, have a considerable amount of information about the mechanics of a department's operation. They know more clearly than the faculty what the actual impact of the courses and instructors has been. The responsibility for evaluating this information rests with the faculty, but the information should be available. We do not think policy should be imposed on departments here, but we do suggest they move in the direction of learning more about the effect of their programs on their students; each department should take advantage of the possibilities of its own situation. Three useful innovations would be the following. Each year, the department chairman or his representatives could interview a certain fraction of the graduating students, both graduate and undergraduate, to discover their opinions on the curriculum and the instruction. The interviews might cover, say, the top 5 per cent and 5 per cent selected at random, in the large departments. Each year, the department could hold at least one general meeting for all its faculty and undergraduate students (if there is significant turnout in large departments, natural subdivisions should be found). This meeting would be open to discussion by students and faculty on the department's policy and performance. It would not be expected to reach any decisions, but it might be quite instructive for the participants. The large departments could invite their graduate students to set up an advisory committee on such questions as curriculum and examinations. We are not impressed with the need for further formal consultative mechanisms. We feel they would be empty, without real interest for the majority of students or faculty, and in many cases would be irritants rather than constructive agencies.

They would consume time, generate frustration, and occasionally serve as platforms for the professional participators.

We would now like to make a series of recommendations concerning the ASUC. These are interconnected and related to some of our previous suggestions on student participation. In particular, (1) and (2) are necessary conditions for some of the extended student participation we suggest, for this participation is predicated on a more viable and representative student government.

1. The graduate students should reconsider the advantages of joining the ASUC, taking into account the possibility of changes in the direction we suggest.

2. The ASUC Senate should be enlarged to say 100 members, each representing 200 to 300 students. These constituencies could be of various kinds: departmental, college, ad hoc. A larger body, with more natural constituencies, could better represent the heterogeneous student body.

3. The administration, alumnus, and Academic Senate representatives should be withdrawn from the ASUC.

4. The ASUC should be given a certain sum of money per student, to spend as it pleased. This money should be collected for it, as at present, by the administration, in the form of a student fee. The ASUC could also be given a budget from university funds or other sources to administer specific activities such as the band, but this should be renegotiated every year.

5. The ASUC should have the right to increase its tax, with the agreement of the administration, and a ratification by vote of its members.

6. The ASUC should be given the responsibility for administering one section of the campus: the union, the office building, restaurants, and lower plaza. It should be clearly recognized that title to these buildings, and ultimate authority, rests elsewhere, and that delegation will be withdrawn in case of gross abuse. Some part of the student fees should be earmarked for maintenance of these facilities.

7. Fairly strict guidelines should be drawn up to prevent activity in the ASUC area from interfering with other university activities. Within these guidelines, the ASUC should make and enforce its own rules in the area. The ASUC should not have the power to

assign academic penalties. It could have the right to initiate cases in the disciplinary process (see our next set of recommendations below), perhaps through its own advocate (recommendations 3 and 4). In the event the ASUC did not take adequate steps to protect the guidelines, the administration should resume this responsibility.

8. The ASUC, with the advice of the political groups, should appoint moderators for the noon rallies, to ensure that questions are received and opposing viewpoints can be expressed.

9. The ASUC should be asked to administer the Placement Centers for student employment, and that part of the Student Housing Service which does not relate to university residences.

10. University residences should continue under the administration of the Dean of Students. He should be advised by a committee of dormitory residents. Administration here should be kept to the minimum level needed to protect university interests.

The ASUC should name student representatives with one-year terms of office to the following committees, which are advisory to the administration. The student component should report to the ASUC. The faculty component should be appointed by the Academic Senate, and should report to that body. Each committee should have one administration representative. The numbers of the student and faculty components are suggested for each committee.

1. Rules Committee (4 students, 4 faculty). Modifies an existing administrative committee.

2. Athletics (5 students, 5 faculty, 1 alumnus). Modifies an existing administrative committee. The Academic Senate Committee on Athletic Policy should be dissolved.

The remaining committees should have 3 students and 5 faculty.[7]

3. Museum. To advise on the new art museum.

4. Arts and Lectures. Modifies an existing administrative committee. mittee.

5. Visitors. It should be possible to bring visitors, in general not academics, to visit the campus for short periods of time, say up to one year. These visitors could give a few lectures, meet informally with students and faculty for discussions, and so on. Funds should

[7] We have no objection to paragraph (2) on page 144 of the majority report.

be found for six visitors, with a term of six months each. This combines an existing Regents' program and ASUC program.

⚜ DISCIPLINARY PROCEDURES

There is a strong argument for administration involvement in disciplinary procedures. Quite generally, the administration is responsible on a continuing basis for the overall welfare of the campus, and for its external relations. Specifically, the administration is held responsible for maintaining order on the campus. It is the only agency with a real stake in defending the university interest in the enforcement of rules that are locally and temporarily unpopular: it will be around to take the consequences of nonenforcement. The faculty position, by contrast, often seems to be peace this year, worry about next year when it comes. There is a correspondingly strong argument against complete discretionary authority. Pressures internal and external, for or against disciplinary action, might be unbearable at times. And for reasons real or imaginary, there is simply not enough trust around to make a discretionary system workable.

As far as we are concerned, justice does not demand that every institution should be a state in microcosm, leaving aside the interesting question of which state is the proper macrocosm. It does demand procedural safeguards against arbitrary and unfair administrative discipline, safeguards that take into account the nature of the institution, the nature of the penalties, and the nature of possible review. We are satisfied that present disciplinary procedures on the campus meet this test. They compare favorably with the procedures required of universities in relevant court cases, and equally favorably with the procedures set by law for administrative and regulatory agencies. De facto, they meet the standards set by the AAUP. They were overwhelmingly endorsed by the Academic Senate, on a motion by the Academic Freedom Committee, in the spring in 1966. By comparison with Berkeley, such universities as Chicago, Harvard, and Oxford still use the star chamber. Consequently, we have no sympathy for the argument that further elaboration of procedural safeguards will eliminate an important source of distrust on the campus. Indeed, there are relatively few people on the campus, faculty or student, who have a detailed knowledge of current procedure. Even fewer care. Attendance at Commission hearings on the topic was approximately 25, counting Commissioners, witnesses, and the press. The issue of due process has been a convenient, if artificial, rallying point. We believe the issue will be pressed so long as the disciplinary process is not controlled by the activist students.

After hearing the very lengthy and detailed arguments on the operation of the disciplinary process, we have formulated some suggestions for improvement. It is idle to pretend to derive such suggestions from general principle. However, our revision seems a desirable modification in procedure, which increases the protection of the accused without compromising the university interest.

1. The Men's and Women's Judicial Committees and the Faculty Hearing Officers should be abolished. The Committee on Student Conduct (CSC) should be altered to consist of three students and five faculty. The chairman should be a professor of law. The students should serve for one-year terms. The faculty should serve for staggered two-year terms. The students should be appointed by the ASUC and the faculty by the Academic Senate.

2. The CSC should have a minor division, consisting of one student and one faculty, and a major division, consisting of two students and four faculty. The members should rotate through the divisions, except the chairman should not serve in the minor division.

3. The administration should name an advocate to present cases before the CSC.

4. Discipline should be initiated by the administration through the advocate, who gives written notice of charges to an accused student. The notice should specify the rule violated and the acts that violate it. Notice must be sent within two weeks of the discovery of the offense, and within one year of the offense. The hearings should start no sooner than one week and no later than two weeks after notice, except by mutual consent. Notice is either minor (discipline limited to warning, censure, restitution if under $100, 15 days or less of disciplinary probation) or major.

5. With minor notice, the student may choose to be heard either by the Dean of Students or by the minor division of the CSC. Hearings are informal and decisions final, except that if the student feels substantial injustice was done, he may petition the major division of the CSC for a hearing. The burden is on him to show that a review is needed. If the student does not respond to notice within one week, this is equivalent to a plea of no contest, and the case is decided by the Dean.

6. As a matter of current policy, the Dean disposes of most disciplinary cases he hears by informal procedures such as counseling. Formal penalties, if any, are viewed as incidental to this process. To protect this process, he should have the right to refer a disciplinary case to the CSC. In any event, his preliminary discussions with the student should be confidential. If the student appears before the CSC, that committee should know only that the student and the Dean did not agree on a resolution of the case.

7. A confidential, nonpsychiatric counseling service should be available to students, separate from the disciplinary process. This should be administered by the Dean's office.

8. With major notice and the mutual consent of the advocate and the student, the case should be heard first by the minor division of the CSC, to attempt an informal resolution of the problem, including the assignment of penalties. All parties must concur in the resolution. Otherwise the case is heard by the major division. The proceedings in the minor division are confidential, and the committee members do not participate in the major hearing. In a major hearing, the body knows only that an informal resolution in the minor division was not obtained.

   According to this procedure, the overwhelming majority of the cases should be settled informally by the Dean and the minor division, through counseling and light penalties.

9. Hearings before the CSC should be private. Hearings in the major division may be informal or adversary, at the student's choice.

   It seems unwise to have public hearings conducted by a committee, especially a committee involving students. Committees would have a hard time keeping order, and students (both defendants and members of the committee) would be subject to intolerable pressure in political cases. Provision for a verbatim record in (12) below is an adequate safeguard for the interest of the student.

10. The student must respond to notice and choose the style of hearing within one week. Failure to respond is equivalent to a plea of no contest, and the case is heard by the major division.

11. Decisions by the major division are advisory to the Chancellor. If the Chancellor wishes to alter the decision, he must do so within two weeks of receiving the recommendation, and must give a written decision to the student and the CSC. To increase the penalty, he must review the record, he cannot use new evidence, and he

must provide a written explanation of reasons to the student and the CSC.

12. In adversary proceedings, the administration should provide for a verbatim record. The decisions of the CSC are written, and form part of the record. The student may see the record and make written comments, which then form part of the record. The student may have counsel, is not required to give self-incriminating evidence, will be told the evidence against him and the identity of its sources. He is entitled to present evidence and witnesses on his own behalf, and cross examine witnesses against him. The CSC will not receive private communications on matters before it. The burden of proof is on the advocate.

This does not differ substantially from present practice.

13. In a disciplinary proceeding, the validity of a rule cannot be challenged as a defense for violating it. The student can, of course, argue that the act in question does not violate the rule in question.

It should be relatively easy for students to test rules by argument; provision is made for this below. It should not be possible to "test" rules by violating them; hence the provision above. The strongest argument for allowing a student to defend a rule violation by challenging the rule is the possibility that he violated it unintentionally. This argument is most speculative. We have found no disciplinary action based on such an unintentional violation.

The university-wide "standard of conduct" rule is something of a special case. We do not see that it can be dispensed with short of writing several volumes of university law, and consequently transforming the whole nature of the institution. However, we do think the standard of conduct should be made somewhat more specific. We also think that many standard of conduct cases could be successfully defended by arguing that the standard of conduct, as defined by the relevant context, was not violated by the act in question.

14. The Academic Freedom Committee of the Academic Senate should advise the Chancellor on drawing up a set of guidelines for the validity of rules. These guidelines should be somewhat more specific than the December 8 [1964] resolutions have proved to be.

15. Students should be able to challenge specific regulations before the Academic Freedom Committee, on the grounds that they violate the guidelines. The ASUC Academic Freedom Committee could

be consulted during the deliberations. Rulings of the committee should be advisory to the Chancellor.

16. The faculty component of the Committee on Student Conduct should report periodically to the Academic Senate, and recommend such changes in procedure as are desirable.

PART SIX

APPENDICES

APPENDICES

Appendix A

ᚼᚼᚼᚼᚼᚼ

Charge to the Commission

The resolution approved by the Academic Senate and later ratified by the ASUC Senate charged the Commission as follows:

The Policy Committee and the Committee on Student Affairs propose that the Academic Senate and the ASUC jointly establish a faculty-student study Commission on University Governance. Specifically we propose that:

1. The Academic Senate authorize the Committee on Committees to designate six Senate members of the Commission, one of whom to serve as cochairman.

2. The ASUC designate, or institute appropriate means for

designating, six student members of the Commission, one of whom to serve as cochairman. The student membership should be broadly representative of the student body as a whole, undergraduate and graduate, including those students and student groups most active in expressing grievances about current conditions in the University. The Policy Committee does not believe that the kind of balanced and representative student membership that is essential to the success of the Commission would be likely to be secured by election. The time required by an election, moreover, would greatly delay the institution of the commission. Unfortunately, no alternative machinery or agency exists that represents the entire student body, including graduate students. The Committees believe that the ASUC can devise means for a prompt and fair choice of student members in whom the student body can have confidence.

3. The Commission consider, but not be limited to, the following matters:

(a) Defining those areas in which, and the institution through which, the making and administering of policies should be delegated wholly to students or wholly to faculty or administrative officers; those in which students should have primary responsibility, with participation by faculty members and administrative officers; and those in which faculty members and administrative officers should have primary responsibility, with appropriate participation by students.

(b) Assessing what steps might be taken at college and departmental levels to increase and improve the appropriate participation of students in the formulation of educational policies, including measures for the improvement of teaching and the advancement of scholarship.

(c) Strengthening and expanding the present system of student government into an effective agency or agencies through which all segments of the student body could implement their views and interests on such matters as they deem to be of concern to them; and the delegation to such agencies of substantial responsibilities.

(d) Institutional arrangements, such as a broadly representative Campus Council, student representation on faculty and administrative committees, or formal relationships between student committees and committees of the Academic Senate, for appropriate student participation in the consideration of campus-wide questions.

(e) Means for improving the quality of the free forum and

encouraging civility and a sense of commitment to an intellectual community on the part of all participants, while adhering to the principles of free speech as set forth in the Division's resolutions of December 8, 1964, and while recognizing that political advocacy cannot be separated from controversy and emotional commitment.

(f) The fairness of disciplinary procedures and methods of reviewing the content of rules, at the time both of formulation and adjudication, in the light of constitutional principles and the Division's resolution of December 8, 1964.

(g) Policies, and their enforcement, concerning the activities on campus of those not formally members of the University community.

In charging the Study Commission to consider these matters the Division makes no *a priori* assumption as to the necessity or desirability of any specific charge which is mentioned.

4. The Commission report its conclusions and recommendations for action to the Berkeley Division of the Academic Senate and to the ASUC for appropriate action. A public hearing or hearings should be held before any recommendations are reported. The Commission is urged to seek substantial agreement on its recommendations from both the faculty and student members; but in cases of disagreement on important matters, the reasoning of both majority and minority should be fully reported. The Commission should submit at least a preliminary comprehensive report during the spring quarter of 1967, and a final report at the beginning of the fall quarter of 1967.

5. The Commission be authorized to appoint subcommittees of faculty and students from outside its own membership, but which may include Commission members, to conduct studies of particular problems or areas of concern.

6. The Commission should consult with the Committee on Student Affairs in matters of mutual concern.

7. The Commission maintain full communication with the Chancellor's office and provide maximum opportunities for that office to communicate its view on matters before the Commission.

8. The Commission consult with the Chancellor's office concerning its budgetary needs and facilities for its work.

For the purpose of implementing the foregoing proposal, the Policy Committee presents the following recommendations to the Berkeley Division:

Resolved, That the Berkeley Division of the Academic Senate invites the Associated Students of the University of California to join it in establishing a student-faculty Study Commission on University Governance, as proposed by the Berkeley Division of the Academic Senate.

Resolved, That the Committee on Committees is directed to appoint six division members of the Commission, one of whom is to be cochairman.

*   *   *

As provided in the resolution, the faculty members were appointed by the Academic Senate's Committee on Committees and approved by the Senate. The ASUC appointed a subcommitee to interview candidates for student membership on the Commission, which recommended a slate of nominees to the entire student Senate. The Senate heard brief presentations from the committee's nominees and from several alternate candidates. After considerable open discussion, several changes in the nominated slate were made and the student members were then approved.

The Academic Senate Committee on Committees appointed the following members: Caleb Foote, Professor of Law and Criminology (cochairman); David Freedman, Professor of Statistics; Albert Fishlow, Professor of Economics; Beryl J. Roberts, Professor of Public Health; Sheldon S. Wolin, Professor of Political Science; and Reginald E. Zelnik, Assistant Professor of History.

The ASUC Senate appointed the following members: Richard Beahrs, John Meyers, Jill Morton, and Martin Roysher, all undergraduates; Henry Mayer and Lewis Perl, both graduate students. The ASUC Senate did not designate a cochairman. Mr. Beahrs served as student cochairman in February and March 1967, after which Mr. Mayer assumed that responsibility.

Appendix B

Recommendations of the Byrne Report[1]

(Submitted to the Special Committee of the Regents of the University of California, May 7, 1965)

PRINCIPLES

The very success of the University of California in its effort to blend quality with quantity in higher education has created many of

[1] So far as we know, the Byrne Committee Report is not available directly from the Board of Regents. However, it is reprinted in full in the *Los Angeles Times,* May 12, 1965, part IV, p. 1, and the full text was reproduced in Appellants' Opening Brief, People of the State of California, Plaintiff and Respondent vs. Mario Savio and 571 others, Defendants and Appellants, Criminal No. 235, in the Appellate Department of the Superior Court, County of Alameda, State of California, pp. 329–392. This brief has been widely distributed to libraries.

today's difficult and pressing problems. The successes of the past and
the plans for the future require that the Regents evolve a new pattern
of government and organization for the University.

Three principles should guide the Regents in shaping the Uni-
veresity's government and organization.

1. The crucial power of the Regents is the power to reinvest in
others the high faith placed in the Regents by the people. This suggests
that the Regents can and must show the same faith in the individual
members of the academic community that the people of California
have shown in the Regents, and must accord them the rights due to
responsible citizens of a free community.

2. The wise use of power requires its wide distribution. This
suggests that the Regents must be willing to delegate their enormous
powers as the people have been willing to delegate theirs.

3. The principle of autonomy, so vital to the University in securing its place in society, should also apply to each campus in the
University system. This suggests that the campus is the basic unit of
academic life and should, therefore, be the basic unit of University
organization and government.

Now is the time for the Regents to respond to changes occurring on almost all fronts: in the larger society, in the mix and character of graduate and undergraduate students, in the stabilization of the
size of the Berkeley and UCLA campuses, in the requirements for
administering an ever larger and more complex enterprise, in the ordering of values among faculty and students.

The time has passed when the University was sufficiently small
and manageable for twenty-four Regents, drawn almost entirely from
outside academic life, meeting two days a month, eleven times a year,
to act as its legislative, executive and judicial branches of government.

The time has arrived for the Regents to charter separately each
campus as an autonomous university within a commonwealth of universities under Regental jurisdiction, according to each university
maximum authority over its own affairs and maximum freedom to
shape its own profile of excellence.

⊀ *ACCORDINGLY* ⊁

1. *We recommend* that the Regents separately charter each
campus as an autonomous university within the system of higher learning under Regental jurisdiction.

a. The Regents have shown wisdom and have demonstrated great perseverance in holding to the ideal of diversity in planning for the nine campuses of the University. We believe that diversity in planning should now be extended to diversity in operations, by establishing each campus as an autonomous member of a University commonwealth and giving it maximum freedom to differ from the other campuses.

b. We urge that charters be drawn for each University of the commonwealth, establishing:

(1) That all powers and authority necessary to self-government and self-determination be placed with the Chancellors, faculty and students of the individual university, reserving to the Regents and the President only those powers and authorities essential to constitutional unity of the whole.

(2) That the Chancellors, administration, and academic community of each separately chartered university be held responsible for results achieved, not for conformity to method on a statewide basis.

(3) That to the maximum extent possible, resources be allocated on a campus-by-campus basis, rather than item-by-item.

(4) That each Chancellor be appointed by the Regents and report to the Regents through the President, with complete responsibility for leadership and management of the university under his jurisdiction.

(5) That the Chancellor have power to and be encouraged to redelegate the authority and responsibility vested in his office.

c. We recommend that the charters provide for full freedom of organization by faculty and students, so that the Chancellor may have a resource responsive to the wishes of the members of the academic community to aid him in its governance. Guided by broad legislation at the Regental level each university should have:

(1) The freedom to establish its own educational policies and standards.

(2) The responsibility for establishing its own reputation for excellence in teaching.

(3) The freedom to give shape and substance to its own conception of academic freedom and responsibility.

d. We recommend that the charters provide for and encourage the establishment of broadly-based student governments, which:

(1) Will be a vital resource to the Chancellor in meeting his responsibility as the chief executive of the university.

(2) Will serve as the primary formal channel of communication to the Chancellor of student opinions and concerns.

(3) Will respond to the interests of students, whether in academic, political, or social matters. Further, it should attract the participation of students whose interests are diverse.

(4) Will be permitted to take and announce positions on issues of importance to the membership, within or outside the University, provided that the membership wishes to commit that power to its governing board, the vote on the issue is announced, and the announcement identifies the group, disclaiming authority to speak for the University.

e. We recommend that provision be made in the charters for their change and evolution as documents of government, with full recognition given to the variations in maturity among the existing campuses.

f. We recommend that the relationship between Chancellors of the individual universities and the President and Regents be centered on:

(1) Review and approval of goals and objectives for the individual university, and appraisal of long-term performance in relation to goals.

(2) Consistency as to basic principles underlying legislation throughout the commonwealth.

(3) Allocation of funds.

g. We recommend that the charters provide for direct communication and appeal to the Regents from any component of the University system.

(1) Any formally recognized group within the University should have the opportunity to communicate in writing to the Regents through that group's constituted officers or representatives.

(2) All such communications should be forwarded to the Regents through the respective Chancellors and the President, with each accorded the opportunity to submit separate commentary to the Regents on the communication.

(3) All such communications should be officially recorded in the minutes of Regental meetings and notice of their receipt and disposition should be given to the group originating the communication.

h. We recommend that the Regents establish visiting committees, each composed of three Regents, assigned to learn about individual universities. A particular visiting committee would be assigned to each university in the commonwealth for a definite period. Assignment of Regents to committees would be such that no Regent would spend more than three years in succession on the visiting committee to any one university.

2. *We recommend* that the Regents and the President undertake complete revision of the form and substance of all existing documents of governance of the University.

a. A university community which includes 100,000 people and serves many times that number through a network of campuses, institutes, and operations in more than fifty foreign countries can no more function without a carefully drafted, systematic, comprehensive and published set of statutes than can a city or a state. In this regard the Regents and the President have before them a task of great magnitude and importance.

b. The existing By-Laws and Standing Orders of the Regents no longer fulfill their role as basic documents of governance. The term "Standing Orders" is inappropriate to a University community and is inconsistent with the delegation of executive powers to officers and offices other than the Regents.

c. We therefore propose:

(1) That the By-Laws be redrafted and limited in scope to the affairs of the Regents, i.e., wholly separated from statements of policy or enunciation of rules governing the University itself.

(2) That charters be prepared for each university within the system of higher learning under Regental jurisdiction, as outlined above. These should be constitutional rather than legislative documents.

(3) That the documents which set forth the laws of government for the system as a whole be renamed the "Policies of the University of California." In this connection, the Regents should instruct the President to make a thorough assessment and review of all existing policy; gaps should be filled and inconsistencies should be remedied.

(4) We urge that all basic documents of government—By-Laws, Charters, and Policies—be codified and made available throughout the University system, and to the public on request.

3. *We recommend* that the Office of the President be constituted to give leadership to the entire University system.

a. We recommend that the Presidency and the Chairmanship

of the Regents be merged into one, with the President serving as ex officio Chairman of the Regents and having the powers now vested in the Chairman.

(1) The Regents expect the President to give leadership to the University; correspondingly, the Regents should be willing and able to accept leadership from the President.

(2) The size and diversity of the Board make continuity in leadership desirable, and argue against a rotating Chairmanship. Only the President could be a permanent Chairman.

(3) The President now sets the agenda for Regental meetings; we believe he should also preside. He is now the spokesman for the University to the public; we believe he should also be the spokesman for the Regents. He should recommend policy for Regental approval; we believe that he should have the opportunity to lead Regental discussion and the responsibility for consensus.

(4) Under a Commonwealth system, the Chancellors would give leadership to the academic community. The President should give leadership to the whole, and speak with authority to the rest of the state.

b. We recommend that the President have the authority to suspend a Chancellor, subject to later action by the Regents.

c. We recommend that the President have primary responsibility for presenting formulations of policy to the Regents, for long range planning, and for preparation of the University budget. Submissions to the Regents in these three areas should reflect the advice and participation of the Council of Chancellors.

d. We recommend that the executive officers reporting to the President have responsibility only for those University operations which can most effectively be administered on a system-wide basis.

e. Central control of University administration has been the means through which the University's plans for expansion have been implemented. We recommend that the President and the Chancellors be charged by the Regents to plan now for the rate and manner in which administrative autonomy can be realized, especially with respect to:

(1) The prompt conversion of the primary role of state-wide administration from one of control to one of service.

(2) The minimum degree of standardization required in a commonwealth system.

f. We recommend that the Office of the President and of all other University officers who are concerned with the commonwealth as a whole, together with these activities and functions serving the entire commonwealth, be removed from Berkeley to a location of prominence in San Francisco.

g. We recommend that the Regents authorize a full reevaluation of the role of administration in University government, with particular emphasis on:

(1) Allocation of a greater portion of the operating budget to salaries which will attract and hold executives and administrators of the highest calibre.

(2) Encouragement of faculty members with administrative talent to use it.

(3) Training and further development of administrators.

4. *We recommend* that the Regents re-formulate their role in the government of the University.

a. The Regency is an institution unto itself, giving expression to many values of the highest order, accumulating through the years practices good and bad, and often holding to positions of mind and assumptions about role which run counter to the realities of today. The present moment holds a rare and pressing opportunity for the Regents to make fresh choices about the institution of Regency.

b. The Regents have been a major force in building a statewide University system; it is now time to shift from *being* the government of the University to *providing for* the governance of the University.

c. We recommend that the Regents concentrate on their legislative function and fully delegate the executive and judicial functions of government.

d. We recommend that the Regents assure that their appointees are men in whom they can vest maximum faith and then permit them to make all operational decisions other than those involving investments.

e. The Regents should clearly distinguish between matters of policy in University government and matters of operations and firmly refuse to make operational decisions on behalf of any office or official of the University.

f. We suggest that the basic roles and functions of the Regents are as follows:

(1) To provide for and sustain a system of governance for the University.

(2) To establish the fundamental policies which govern and guide the University system.

(3) To choose, appraise, and remove the principal executives of the University.

(4) To assure that sufficient funds are supplied to support the University.

(5) To provide for the management of University investments.

(6) To allocate funds among the separate universities which make up the University commonwealth.

(7) To protect the University commonwealth from unwarranted attack as it carries out its purposes.

The function of a great university is to maintain a tradition while transforming it. To do the same may well be the ultimate test of the institution of Regency.

Appendix C

※※※※※※

A Sketch of the Lower Division Colleges[1]

❧ THE STRUCTURE ❧

It is proposed to set up four new instructional units, the colleges, for lower division Letters and Science students. Each college would have 250 freshmen (all numbers tentative), 250 sophomores, 40 half-time teaching assistants, and 10 FTE faculty (3 full-time, 14 half-time). Subject to budgetary limitations, the composition of the staff should be decided by the individual colleges. By the second year of operation, two-fifths of the lower division population in Letters and

[1] See background for this proposal in Chapter Five.

Science would be in the college program, and the remaining three-fifths in the regular program.

These colleges would be administratively responsible for this fraction of lower division instruction; they would be small enough and might be competitive enough so that this responsibility could be properly discharged. They would provide structures on a human scale, to which students and faculty could relate, and also furnish a clear locus of responsibility for the education of the lower division student.

Incoming freshmen would decide whether they wished to enter the regular program or the college program, and if the latter, which college. It should be moderately easy to transfer from one college to another, or from the college program to the regular departmental program. Students would therefore have the possibility of making informed choices among competitive and relatively coherent programs.

If the colleges succeed, four more should be created, to cover all of Letters and Science lower division. Furthermore, the colleges might go into upper division instruction on a small scale. For example, they might offer individual interdisiciplinary majors under the supervision of the college faculty. However, after two years in the college, the student would normally declare a major and enter a department. Thus, departments would continue to be responsible for upper division and graduate work.

⅀ THE ACADEMIC PROGRAM ⅄

Colleges should be organized around a topic or a set of disciplines. They should be considered neither as junior departments nor as miniatures of Letters and Science. The programs should be substantially different from college to college, and should change over time within each college. Students going through one college together would, however, follow relatively similar programs. This should facilitate the process of students learning from each other.

A college might offer a grouping of related disciplines in which the assumptions, techniques, and questions in one stimulate inquiry in another. For example, an integrated program in Mathematics, Physics, and Philosophy could provide effective mathematical tools for physics; interesting physical examples, questions and intuitive background for mathematics; and a philosophical analysis of the nature of mathematical and physical knowledge. Another college might offer a program integrating Economics, Psychology, and Statistics. An effort could be made to evaluate critically the assumptions and underlying behavioral economic models in the light of current theories of human psychology and to reevaluate these theories and the experimental evidence for them. At the same time, the experimental methods of both disciplines could be compared, contrasted, and used as illustrative examples in a course on statistical inference.

A college might also be organized around a topic common to the disciplines involved, but which each discipline approaches by different methods and with different questions in mind. Some examples:
(1) The Developing Nations (Economics, Political Science, Sociology, and Anthropology)
(2) Conflict and Conflict Resolution (Political Science, Psychology, Economics, and Mathematics)
(3) Myth and Ritual (Anthropology, Classics, Comparative Literature, Near Eastern Languages)
(4) Language and Culture (Linguistics, Philosophy, and English).
This list is meant only to indicate the possibilities. The choice of actual programs and their precise formulations must be left in the hands of the individual colleges.

Although some integration of knowledge will naturally result from these combinations, the aim is not only to integrate bodies of knowledge, but also to show diverse approaches to a common concern. The combinations should engage the interest of the student and lead him to appreciate the academic skills used in dealing with these concerns. The college program should clarify the student's choice of major field, give him a better understanding of its aims and methods, and stimulate his interest in acquiring the advanced skills necessary to digging more deeply into his chosen field of concentration.

Given the student's general orientation toward, say, social science, he can acquire a surer understanding of the approach and demands characteristic of particular disciplines in that field.

The college program should be counted as two courses each quarter in the freshman year and one course each quarter in the sophomore year. The student would take outside courses, taught by departments, to make up a total of three courses per quarter. If the student chooses to major in a discipline related to the program of the college, this program should be considered as satisfying all or almost all of the prerequisites to the major. His work in the college should be considered as fulfilling a substantial fraction of his breadth requirements.

Courses within the college should include lectures, seminars, tutorials with teaching assistants and faculty, and independent study. The methods of instruction and the amount of choice in outside courses would vary from college to college. One plan is to have a core lecture course (250 students, one lecturer each quarter) and a tutorial each quarter in the freshman year, followed by supervised but fairly independent study on a topic related to the course in the sophomore year. The numbers of staff and students allow for considerable contact in small instruction groups. It is feasible, and important, for each student to have at least one quarter of small group tutorial with a faculty member each year.

In the college setting, with a common intellectual framework and considerably more continuity in personal relationships, it is reasonable to assume that students will be given genuine academic counseling based on some knowledge of their personalities and intellectual capabilities. It may be possible to make more realistic decisions about the student's total work load.

✇ STAFF ✇

Staff for the colleges should be secured from departments. Colleges would neither admit graduate students nor hire faculty. They should be permitted to hire visitors on a small scale, subject to the availability of money. Research personnel could participate in the college program to a limited extent. No one should be permanently attached to a college and the number of faculty working full time in the colleges should be small.

The typical faculty assignment in a college might be half-time for three years. Terms should be staggered so that the staff would be a continuing body, but one which changes slowly over time. This would allow the colleges to develop corporate and distinctive styles, and prevent these styles from becoming frozen.

In devising programs, the colleges will have to find means of engaging the professional concerns of the faculty. In order to remain a permanent feature on the campus, colleges would have to attract faculty of high academic standing. Such people will not be available if the educational programs appear uninteresting to them. Recruitment looms as the most serious problem facing the colleges.

The colleges would offer some incentives that may overcome these difficulties: greater freedom to develop new courses, the chance to work with people in related fields, the opportunity to teach in a different and probably more rewarding setting. The colleges may also provide for the development of a closer relationship between faculty and the advanced graduate students who would not only serve as teaching fellows, but would also participate with the faculty in planning and evaluating curriculum and instruction.

❧ SPACE ❦

The success of a college will depend substantially on its physical environment. The college should have contiguous space for offices, meeting rooms, lounges, and a library. Perhaps one of the existing residence halls could be converted for this purpose. It is clear that the availability of space will be a crucial problem.

❧ ADMINISTRATION ❦

The college should be headed by a full-time faculty member, the master. The master should be appointed, say for three or four years, by the Chancellor on the advice of the faculty of the college. The first master, and perhaps two of the first faculty, should be appointed to each college by the Chancellor on the advice of a search committee. This cadre would proceed to design the program, recruit staff, acquire space, and consult relevant departments about courses.

At least initially, the colleges should report to the Administration and to a review committee of the Academic Senate. This committee would consider the programs as they developed, and visit the colleges to observe their operations at first hand. It would not be empowered to change decisions of the college. At the end of a given period, say four years, the review committee would report to the Academic Senate on the results of the colleges and would make recommendations for revising the structure and for permanent control mechanisms. At least during the first period, the college would not be subject to outside controls on staffing or curriculum. They would be subject to standard budgetary procedures.

Appendix D

✄✄✄✄✄✄

A Proposed Departmental
Advising Plan[1]

✄ ADVISING GROUPS ✄

The core of the proposal is the creation, within each department, of several small advising groups or "sections." Ideally, the sections should consist of one professor, 10 juniors and 10 seniors, although 15 juniors and 15 seniors is probably more realistic in view of manpower problems. (For example, in a department with 600 undergraduate majors and 60 instructors, we hypothesize 20 would be major advisers at any one time.) Entering junior majors would be assigned

---

[1] See Chapter Eight for background information.

to their section at the end of the sophomore or the beginning of the junior year in the following manner. The entering student would submit a list of problem areas within the major discipline that are of particular interest to him (that is, a prospective History major might list Far Eastern History, Latin America, Economic History, and so forth). Wherever possible, the Department would assign the applicant to a section led by a professor who shares one of the students' interest areas (joint applications of small groups of students who already know that they share a common interest should be considered). Thus to the degree that it is feasible, the members of each section would be united by at least some common emphasis within the major. The fact that the correspondence of emphasis is not likely to work out very neatly (since many students are still unsure of their major interests at this stage) is not a serious drawback, since a certain amount of cross-fertilization and variety is also worthwhile.

Once formed, the section would become a semi-official unit of the department, with allowances, of course, for some fluidity and turnover. The section would meet with its adviser at least once each quarter for a joint discussion of the planning and progress of the major programs of its individual members, and at least once at the end of each year for an evaluation of the strengths and weaknesses of the departmental program of the previous three quarters in the light of the experience of the section members.

The aim of the quarterly meeting would be to assist the students in the planning and implementation of a rational and coherent major program (that is, the traditional advising function) in a setting that encourages the students to share their ideas and problems both with their colleagues and their major adviser. In many cases these sessions should obviate the necessity of individual visits to the adviser for the signing of study lists (although in some cases individual visits will also be required), thus avoiding needless repetition. In the group setting, the planning of common programs among small groups of students with common interests, under the guidance of a single faculty member, would be encouraged. Such programs could serve as a positive force against the intellectual atomization of the nonprofessional student body.

The aim of the annual meeting, in addition to the planning of the following year's programs in the case of juniors, would be the development of suggestions for the improvement of existing departmental programs. In addition, such sessions might germinate small-group 199 courses as well as interesting course proposals for the consideration of the Board of Educational Development.

An auxiliary function of the advising sections is to assist new majors in accommodating rapidly to their new departments by putting them into immediate contact with seniors who share similar interests. Finally, although we are aware that scarcity of resources will make implementation of this part of the plan difficult, it is our hope that some of the more successful sections could engage in voluntary activities of an intellectual and social nature that would prove to be a useful supplement to the students' formal program, while contributing some real intellectual content to the advising system itself. These activities might include special section meetings to hear occasional papers by the professor, one of the students, another member of the department (including, in particular, graduate students who are working on theses in areas related to the group's special interests) or outsiders. In the interest of both economy and the cross-fertilization of ideas, such meetings might be held jointly by two or more sections with different but related orientations, or even by two sections from different departments. They might also include, where appropriate and feasible, field trips, visits to cultural events, and even informal "bull sessions" in the apartments of members. Small financial subsidies from the department would of course encourage such projects.

⋊ COUNCIL OF MAJORS ⋉

To provide a rational basis for student participation in deliberations on departmental policies, departmental student organizations would be created based on these advising sections. At the end of each academic year, each section—using whatever selection procedures it agreed on—would select a high junior to be its departmental representative for the following year (his senior year). Since the members of each section would have been in close contact for at least three terms, it is likely that their choice would reflect the abilities and commitment of the student chosen. The quality of representatives should be much higher and more relevant to the department's academic needs than the quality yielded by a single department-wide election. The several students thus elected would constitute a departmental Council of Majors. Each representative would continue to be in close and frequent contact with his section throughout his tenure on the Council, thus ensuring responsiveness to the ideas and problems of his colleagues.

The primary purpose of the Council of Majors would be to serve as a mechanism, along with the department's graduate student organization, for working with the faculty in establishing the regular channels of participation suggested in Chapter Eight, and for assuring that the ideas and proposals emanating from the individual sections are adequately communicated to the department. Undergraduate student representatives for the various departmental committees would be chosen by this group. If student representation on regular departmental committees has not yet been provided for, the Council would select members for the department's Student-Faculty Relations Committee. It would also establish liaison between the students in the department and the Student Senate's Board of Student Participation in Governance (see Chapter Eight). Finally, it would coordinate activities among the various sections as desired.

Appendix E

❧❧❧❦❦❦

Student Senate Constituencies, Committee Organization, and Recruitment of Students

We have proposed that the Student Senate be composed of approximately 75 members elected from constituencies. The argument against a large Senate has generally rested on grounds of inefficiency. It is argued that a larger Senate could not deal with the range of administrative problems coming before the body and that it would be too large a group to work together efficiently. The argument is easy to refute. Anyone who has observed the present Senate in six- and eight-hour sessions knows it is not an efficient body now. The Commission's proposals for an independent Student Union Board of Directors will remove many of the time-consuming administrative details that currently preoccupy the Senate.

Despite the undoubted advantages of this approach, there remains the exacting problem of defining appropriate constituencies without arbitrarily forcing individuals into constituencies for which they feel no identification. The search for a principle of division leads to a choice among unsatisfactory alternatives. Some students feel primary identification with their academic department, others with their living unit, still others with a particular political group, and others still feel no well-defined allegiance at all. The most reasonable approach seems to be to choose a convenient unit, one that offers at least formal identification for the entire student body and one that provides some promise of developing natural groupings. The resources of the central student organization could be used to enhance the development of local groups, and substantial freedoms could be built into the system for allowing individuals to shift from a specific constituency to an ad hoc group of their own devising or a general, at-large voting unit.

Academic units (departments, schools, colleges) offer a number of virtues as formal constituency units. First, they already exist and are reasonably well defined. Second, the Commission's proposals for lower division colleges and departmental student councils drawn from advising groups offer promise of increased coherence and communication among the students in these units. Third, if students are to play an important role in shaping educational decisions, the interaction between organized local units and a central assembly will be extremely useful for discussion and evaluation of policies. Academic constituencies would thus aid the process of redirecting the focus of the Student Senate from separate extracurricular affairs to shared involvement in the major activities of the University. Although it is true that at present most departments do not have the kind of living space and easy access necessary for sound constituency-delegate relationships, the promotion of such improvements in the environment would be an important task for the Student Senate. (The Centennial Fund is planning a major project in this area.)

The Commission thus suggests that the central Student Senate be composed of 65 to 75 members, elected on an average ratio of one senator for each 400 students. Students would vote in specific constituencies (for example, College of Environmental Design, Political Science graduate students) with a minimum constituency size of 250.

Groups with 250 to 450 voters would have one senator; 450 to 850 would have two senators, although such a large group might find some means of subdividing. Students who are not registered in any specific constituency would vote in one of three general constituencies: lower division, upper division, or graduate, with the same ratio of senators to eligible voters.

Within this basic framework it might be possible to devise natural constituency groupings based on principles not now apparent. The Senate might therefore consider establishing an Electoral Commission to supervise the registration of students in constituencies and to consider proposals for new ad hoc groupings.

⇘ SENATE COMMITTEE SYSTEM ⇙

A larger Student Senate would have sufficient manpower to establish the strong committee system the ASUC Senate has sorely lacked. A strong Senate committee system is absolutely essential for effective work at the central level. The Senate might well establish two types of committees, one to guide its internal operations and a second for the discussion and preparation of legislation. The internal committees could include units on Policy (to serve as a steering group), Appropriations, and a Committee on Committees (for the crucial task of appointing students to a variety of campus-wide positions, as well as Senate committees themselves). The "legislative" committees might include units for Academic Affairs, Campus Governance (to oversee joint policy committees, receive recommendations, have jurisdiction over political matters), Student Welfare and Services, Community and State Affairs. These committees would review proposed legislation, hold hearings on such bills or investigative hearings prior to the drafting of specific proposals. They should be composed of Senators, with non-Senate research staffs.

The student body executive officers could establish Directors for supervising programs and developing new ideas in each area. Thus there would be a Senate Committee on Academic Affairs and a Director of Academic Affairs to implement policy and programs approved by the Senate. These directors would constitute the President's Cabinet. At present the ASUC Cabinet is a catch-all, infrequently used body composed of a variety of program chairmen. It includes the head of the Publicity Bureau as well as the head of the community action programs, the chairman of the Student-Education-Faculty Relations Board, and the head of Freshman Orientation (which might, logically, be a subordinate program under Academic Affairs).

⇒ *RECRUITMENT OF STUDENTS* ⇐

We also hope that the Student Senate will take particular cognizance of the onerous problem of recruiting talented, imaginative students to serve in policy-making positions (both as student representatives to joint bodies and in the student organization directly). No single device can be prescribed as the solution to this problem. In large measure, the process of attracting capable students will be aided by the expansion of the student's role in decision-making. The more opportunities that exist—at all levels of university governance—for students to take active roles, the easier it will be to attract, recognize, and utilize the services of promising students. The greater the range of significant and challenging policy questions that engage the student government, the higher the caliber of students likely to volunteer their services becomes. If the Student Senate were to finance a variety of research efforts and if it were possible to grant *ex post facto* academic credit for students who employ their academic talents in the direction of creative policy research and/or reflection and analysis on the problems of policy formulation and implementation, these devices might also help stimulate greater civic contributions among students and attract excellent students.

The identification and selection of talented students will be aided greatly by open discussion of the qualifications and range of opportunities available. Devices such as the Joint Appointments Commission, in which faculty and students make concerted and continuous serious efforts to identify capable people for the judicial system, will help create a pool of potential delegates. The Senate should make systematic requests of faculty, deans, student clubs, and political groups for the names and recommendations (for either specific or general assignments) of likely students. Departmental student associations and other decentralized groups can serve as workable channels for sending talented students from local to campus-wide positions. Open discussions and talent searches by student body leaders in the various constituencies might also be useful. For example, a hearing on problems of campus building plans in the plaza of the College of Environmental Design (organized with the cooperation of that College's Student Action Group) might lead to the development of useful proposals and the recruitment of knowledgeable individuals.

PART SEVEN

INDICES

Index to Commission Proposals

ੴੴੴੴੴ

This index summarizes the proposals advanced by the Commission in the body of this report, with page references to facilitate location of the relevant text. The proposals vary from general suggestions without specific elaboration to concrete recommendations.

The first three chapters are analytical and include supporting arguments for many of the proposals advanced later in the report. Chapters Four through Six are general in nature, and the most important recommendation that emerges from each involves changes in mood and attitude. Most of the proposals, therefore, fall into the last four chapters, with further detail provided in the appendices.

The extensive proposals in Chapter Ten that relate to rule-making and rule adjudication are not fully digested here; the Table of Contents of the Commission's proposed Basic Regulations (pp. 177–179) is a convenient means of reference to specific parts of this proposal.

Chapter Three.   Roles in Governance

3-A   Devise methods whereby academic research staff, teaching assistants, librarians, and persons in similar categories can be drawn into participation in governance (pp. 42–43, 72–73, 103)

Chapter Four.   Open Discussion

4-A   Encourage institutional self-examination through better access to pertinent information, collection of materials relevant to university governance, and incorporation of analysis of university policies and problems directly in the academic program (pp. 49–50)

4-B   Institutionalization of formal and informal forums for open discussion of problems and policy formulation (p. 51)

4-C   Devices to encourage openness such as advance publication of draft proposals, improved access to information, public hearings, circulation of minutes and agendas (p. 55)

Chapter Five.   Decentralization

5-A   Reexamination of Byrne Report recommendations (pp. 58, 60–61, Appendix B)

5-B   Preparation by Academic Senate Policy Committee of model charter for Berkeley campus autonomy (pp. 58–61)

5-C   Formation of Special Commission on Campus Decentralization under Vice-Chancellor for Academic Affairs (pp. 59, 72–74)

5-D   Campus administrative decentralization (pp. 61–63)

5-E   New procedures to facilitate consideration of proposals for creation of new and smaller programs (pp. 64–66)

5-F   Facilitate creation by local units of physical centers such as lounges for personal and intellectual contacts among students and between students and faculty (p. 66)

5-G   Simplification of administration (p. 67)

5-H   Establishment of Lower Division Colleges (pp. 68–72, Appendix C)

Chapter Six.   Student Participation

6-A   General modes for student participation in educational policy-making (pp. 82–85)

6-B   Student participation in regulation of conduct and direction of welfare services (pp. 85–90)

Chapter Seven.   Faculty and Administration

7-A   Revision of procedures for discussion of proposed administrative policies on the floor of the Academic Senate, particularly as regards budgetary policy (pp. 98–100)

7-B   Appointment of all faculty representatives on administrative committees by Committee on Committees of the Academic Senate (pp. 100–101)

7-C   Channeling of all administration requests for official faculty advice or opinion to the Academic Senate Policy Committee (p. 101)

7-D   Creation of Emergency Advisory Committee (to the Chancellor) to improve communication and focus responsibility in times of crisis (pp. 101–103)

7-E   Dual-track reform of Academic Senate which emphasizes decentralization of Senate functions while strengthening existing structure to meet immediate demands placed upon it (pp. 74, 103–106)

7-F   Reassess role of overloaded Senate Policy Committee (p. 105)

7-G   Postpone reconsideration of proposal for Representative Assembly (p. 106)

7-H   Postpone consideration of proposed Berkeley Campus Council (p. 106)

7-I   Integrate administrative committees concerned with basic policy questions into committee structure of Academic Senate (p. 106)

7-J   Approve pending proposal to broadcast meetings of Academic Senate to other members of campus community (p. 107)

7-K   Abandon proposal to appoint Academic Senate Ombudsman, substitute a Senate information office (pp. 107–108)

7-L   Reexamine role of Student Affairs Committee of Academic Senate, treating it as transitional step toward student participation rather than its final manifestation (p. 108)

7-M   Relieve faculty members of excessive administrative duties by restricting committee work to essential policy-making and providing committees with adequate staff assistance (pp. 108–109)

Chapter Eight.   Student Participation at the Departmental Level

8-A   Membership for students on regular departmental committees (pp. 112, 121)

8-B   Invitation to student representatives to attend and to participate (but not vote) in regular department meetings when proposals are under consideration from the various committees on which students sit or other matters of concern are raised (pp. 112, 121)

8-C   As an interim measure, formation of departmental student-faculty relations committees to plan a comprehensive program of student participation (pp. 116–117)

8-D   Formation of Departmental Councils of Majors to formulate student policy proposals and to nominate students for various departmental committee assignments (pp. 119–120, Appendix D)

8-E   Restructuring of departmental advising programs to provide constituent groups for advising and to serve as nuclei for Departmental Councils of Majors (pp. 119–120, Appendix D)

8-F   Variety of methods suggested for securing student participation in the evaluation of faculty candidates for tenured appointment (pp. 121–123)

8-G   Securing of supplementary funds from foundations or the Centennial Fund to undertake experiments in improving or initiating advising plans, tutorial groups, and other constituency plans (p. 124)

8-H   Board for Student Participation in Governance to be created by the Student Senate (with an initial predominance of graduate students) to evaluate departmental programs, disseminate information, and provide advice for local units in planning and assessing their programs (pp. 124–125)

Chapter Nine.   Student Participation Campus-Wide

9-A   Dissolution of the organization known as Associated Students of the University of California, Berkeley (pp. 127–128)

Index

⊱⊱⊱ ⊰⊰⊰